DOGS

MODERN GROOMING TECHNIQUES

DOGS
MODERN GROOMING TECHNIQUES

by

HILARY HARMAR

ARCO PUBLISHING COMPANY, Inc.
NEW YORK

Published by ARCO PUBLISHING COMPANY, Inc.
219 Park Avenue South, New York, N.Y. 10003

Library of Congress Catalog Card Number 73-111384
ISBN 0-668-02284-1

Printed in Great Britain

Contents

Author's Preface

This book is really a sequel to my book "Dogs and How to Breed Them". When the book was started it was to have been a general book on the care of dogs, but later my publisher decided that it should be a book on grooming only.

I had not realized at the time just how much clipping, trimming, plucking and stripping is actually done on so many breeds today; particularly in the U.S.A. where practically every breed is scissored in some way or other. In fact by the time that I had finished the book I almost felt that it should be entitled "Dogs and How to Fake Them"!

Little did I realize then, how much there is in grooming, trimming, clipping and stripping dogs. What a fascinating subject it becomes when talking to the experts! What endless tips there are to improve each breed! I had no idea until I started to write on grooming what an inexhaustible subject it is. It is also a controversial subject, since no two dog breeders probably would prepare their dogs in an identical way.

I have chosen certain methods which I have personally found to work: I like experimenting, and I change my views and ideas and ways of doing various grooming procedures to see which I find works the best. It has been an amusing occupation experimenting with the different trims on some of my own breeds. The Shih Tzus have been given Bedlington ear tassels, my Pomeranians have had to suffer the ignominy of the Poodle Lion Trim and the Continental Trim; whilst my Maltese have had to go into the Poodle Puppy Trim!

There are no set rules and regulations laid down in the breed standards regarding the correct methods of clipping, stripping or trimming the various breeds. Fashions are set by successful, strong-minded individuals, and the novices naturally tend to follow suit. (Woe betide them, if they do not!) so that eventually a particular method of preparing a dog for a show becomes an unwritten law.

In recent years excellent new gadgets and machinery have come on to the market, making the more tedious preparation of the dog far easier. These include electric clippers, fine thinning shears, powerful hair dryers, to mention but a few.

All these aids make the grooming and trimming far quicker,

A*

which is of mutual benefit both for man and dog; and surely, as time passes and fashions change, more and more dogs will probably come under the clippers and thinning shears. This will be heresy to the old-timers no doubt, but perhaps better for the dog; and, moreover, in these days time gets more and more precious.

I have had a most interesting time collecting material for this book by visiting a number of large grooming establishments both in the U.S.A. and in England. I am most grateful for all the tips which I have been given by various specialists in those breeds which I have not owned or groomed. I would particularly like to thank Mr. and Mrs. Gibbs for their help and co-operation in the series of grooming photographs taken in their Dog Parlour at Blindley Heath; Miss Marilyn Willis for her help with the excellent Standard Poodle grooming photographs; and Mr. Joe Cartledge for his help and co-operation with information concerning terriers, and assistance with the excellent photographs which were taken at his kennels.

As usual, I must thank the two brilliant animal photographers Sally Anne Thompson and Anne Cumbers, who have once again produced such outstanding and explicit photographs for my book. I hope that pet dog owners who had never previously thought much about grooming their particular breeds will have learnt some useful hints; and, perhaps most important of all, that dog owners in general will have absorbed a little knowledge about the various parasites which afflict dogs, and that this knowledge will prevent unnecessary suffering to their dogs in future.

I am eternally grateful to all my dogs past and present from whom I have learnt so much and from whom I never cease to learn; to my husband for all his help and advice; to my daughter Carolyn for her remote control help from the U.S.A.; and last but by no means least to Mrs. Hilda Brookfield for taking my dictation so efficiently, for so kindly typing the script, for offering many useful poodle suggestions and but for whom this book would have taken many more weeks to complete.

HILARY HARMAR

Brook Cottage, Tandridge Lane,
Nr. Oxted, Surrey, England

THIS BOOK IS DEDICATED TO
ALL DOGS
AND
TO "LADYE" MY
FIRST DOG WHO WAS NEVER
GROOMED—
A GENTLE, RETIRED, RACING GREYHOUND

What has a Dog to do with a Bath?
GREEK PROVERB

CHAPTER I

Grooming

GENERAL

A dog's grooming is most important, not only for the look of a well kept dog, but also for the dog's well-being and for his self respect. Unfortunately, when a great many people first buy a dog they never for one moment consider whether they are prepared to spend time or money on keeping a long-coated breed. In fact, there is also often little consideration given to the thought of the correct diet that all dogs require in order to keep them in good condition. If a dog is not given the correct feeding, housing, bedding, exercise and grooming, he will never have a good coat or look cared for and well turned out. This particularly applies to the long-coated breeds, or the breeds which require a great deal of work to be done on their coats, like the Poodle varieties, the American Cocker Spaniel and the Airedale. It must, however, be remembered that a superb coat is not produced on a dog merely by regular brushing and grooming. Good coats are hereditary and therefore have to be bred for, just as with any other show requirements. If the coat is not in the genetic make-up, no amount of brushing, oiling, conditioners or anything else can produce one.

However, a dog with a naturally excellent coat can quickly have it ruined. One of the most important requirements for producing a good coat is a healthy, well fed, well exercised dog. In other words, the dog must be in tip-top condition. Feeding, therefore, is extremely important.

FEEDING

Many dogs are not given sufficient fat in their diet, and these dogs will always have dry, uninteresting coats. In cold weather dogs may be given as much as 25% fat in their diet. That is one quarter of all they eat. Fat is cheap to buy and dogs will love it raw. During warm weather the fat content may require to be cut down quite considerably. Dogs are individuals in their food requirements, and there is no absolutely hard and fast rule. If a dog has not been having much fat in his diet, start adding a little extra each day to make certain that he tolerates it, slowly working towards the goal of 25%. It will be noticed within three weeks that the dog's skin becomes more pliable and soft, and that, when stroked gently with the palm of the hand, a glorious sheen will be produced on the coat.

Although a dog may have the breeding and the feeding to produce a superb coat, his coat requires one more thing, particularly in the long-coated breeds, and that is care. The amount of care required depends on the breed, but it consists of brushing, combing and massaging, some breeds require clipping and trimming, and others, plucking or stripping, not to mention bathing.

If a long-coated breed is chosen, remember that the coat has to be BRED for, FED for, and CARED for.

There are many delightful dogs which have extremely difficult coats to manage, and because of this they are usually only popular with show people and are therefore seldom found as pets, or, if they do go to pet homes, they generally look untidy and uncared for. There is a simple answer for this, and that is to have the coat trimmed down or clipped not too short. The little Maltese seen at the shows dripping in its long, silky, white coat looks as if butter would not melt in its mouth. You should see mine when they have been in the stream and just clambered up a muddy bank!

Except for the show dogs, I keep all my Maltese with their coats cut about one inch in length, leaving a long, flowing tail. The tips of the ear feathering and moustaches are cut square. There is then practically no work to be done on the coat, and the dogs really look most attractive. People are never quite sure whether they are elongated poodle puppies or what! But they are great little dogs in their "Aztec" trim.

There are many other breeds which can be scissored down to suit the busy pet owner, who cannot afford to patronize the dog parlours. It is quite amusing making up one's own pet trim for the Apso, the Shih Tzu, the Bearded Collie, the Old English Sheepdog or the American Cocker Spaniel. Sacrilege to some breeders this may be, but it is the height of wisdom for the busy pet owner and it is certainly more sensible from the dog's point of view. Dogs have their own self respect too, and they prefer to be clipped, trimmed and tidy, rather than to be knotty, matted, unkempt and dirty.

TYPES OF COAT

Considering the tremendous number of breeds that are to be found in various parts of the world, the variety of coat and coat texture is not very great. For convenience, breeds can be divided into long-coated, short-coated and hairless, though the latter I suppose can hardly be described as having a coat. These types can then be sub-divided according to the texture of the hair: harsh, normal and soft.

Some breeds have a dense undercoat, others a slight undercoat whilst others have none at all. Breeds like the Spitz breeds, which originated in northern climes, have harsh outer coats and profuse, thick undercoats. Labradors have coats of medium texture, whilst the Maltese and Yorkshire Terriers have the finest and silkiest coats of all. Japanese and the long-coated Chihuahua and Papillon come somewhere between the two.

Each type of coat obviously requires different treatment, to obtain the best results from grooming. Some coats are better if bathed frequently, other coats are better if they are practically never bathed at all. Whilst the hairless breeds, like the Mexican Hairless Dogs, or Xoloitzcuintlis as they are called in Mexico, and the Chinese Crested Dogs, require no brushing since they have no coat to brush. They do, however, require body massage, and to have their skin oiled regularly to keep it soft and supple.

Not only must the dog owner feed his dog well to produce a good coat, but he must also know what implements and tools are required to obtain the best results with the coat. Breeds which require an undercoat are never combed except when moulting, whilst other breeds are practically never brushed. The length of bristle on the brush is also important, as is the texture and type of bristle. Not only must the tools be correct for each breed, but also the correct shampoos, lotions, and conditioners must be used. What is meat for one breed is poison for another!

MOULTING

This is a natural process when the dog sheds his coat. Dogs kept in natural surroundings without artificial light moult twice a year, the exact time and frequency depending on the country and the climate. The seasons and sunlight both affect the shedding of the coat. In England dogs generally moult in the spring and autumn. But, since the majority of dogs are kept as house pets, and therefore live with their owners in artificial surroundings of central heating and electric light, it must be realized that this will affect the normal shedding of the coat.

What generally happens is that, instead of the coat being shed bi-annually, the dog sheds its coat all through the year. This is a great nuisance, unless the dog is groomed daily.

Breeds like the poodles are popular because, although they shed their coats like other breeds, the hair, instead of falling off, sticks to the new coat as it comes through. Many fastidious families and house-proud owners naturally prefer these breeds, because their hair is not strewn all around the house. Breeds like the Collie have so much coat to shed twice a year that, unless they are groomed regularly they can prove to be a nuisance.

In breeds where the tendency seems to be for them to moult all through the year it is even more necessary to groom them regularly. One should remove the hair with a brush, or fine comb, in order to prevent the hairs from going all over the house, furniture and clothes. Surprisingly, the short-coated breeds are often the worst offenders, their hairs being somehow more difficult to remove from clothing than the hairs from long-coated, silkier breeds. The long hair does not seem to stick into the material of clothes and chair covers but just lies on top, and comes off easily and quickly with a light brushing with an Addis Boffin brush. The best way to remove dog hair from anything is either with a fold of Sellotape or with one of the special, static, wire-haired brushes. A vacuum cleaner is also excellent.

GROOMING

This is a term which can be used for the entire toilet of any breed, but generally it refers to brushing, massaging and combing. Loosely used, it may also mean well groomed or well turned out, or well put down, incorporating everything to do with the look of the dog, and this would include how a dog was clipped, scissored and trimmed, or, in the case of terriers, how well they were plucked, stripped, scissored and in some varieties, like the Scottish Terrier, it would also include clipping.

Coats, as I have said before, must be BRED for, FED for, and CARED for. A bad coat may be caused by any number of troubles. It may be due to bad health, insufficient care, incorrect feeding, damp bedding or damp sawdust. Damp sawdust can cause ugly pink staining on the coat, which in particular applies to white-coated breeds. A common cause of dry, staring coats is an infestation of worms.

In some breeds, where the hair is long and exceptionally fine and silky, the coat may be completely ruined by harsh, rough handling and the use of too strong shampoos. Coats can often also be ruined by the use of incorrect grooming tools: harsh brushes with bristles which are incorrect for the breed, and steel combs with rough points, can all ruin a good coat, and so can careless and rough brushing and combing. Breeds which require dense undercoats should not be combed.

Dry, brittle coats may be caused by fleas and other external parasites, worms, ill-health or even insufficient fat in the diet. The latter can be rectified easily by adding ordinary fat to the diet. Linseed oil or suet added to the diet brings up a superb sheen within three weeks, and olive oil has the same effect; but it is not a good idea to prolong the use of this, because the oil coats the lining of the stomach, particularly if given on its own, and this inhibits the natural secretions of the stomach.

It is really quite astonishing how much there is that can be learnt about grooming and how to turn a dog out beautifully.

Like so much else in life, unless a person has experienced the problems of becoming an expert in any field, the results are probably never quite appreciated except by another expert. In the field of the art of grooming, there is all the knowledge of all the numerous grooming paraphernalia which should or should not be used. There are myriads of potions, lotions, sprays, shampoos, and other aids, which can all contribute to the end product being so magnificent. On the other hand, some of the expensive potions and lotions may achieve exactly nothing towards improving a dog's coat. It is a matter of experimenting, and observing other dogs and, if their coat looks something extra special, buttering up the owner by praising his lovely dog may well be rewarded with information as to how the coat was achieved.

I was given a tip in California which I have tried out and found to be excellent. It is particularly good for dogs living in hot dry climates. After a puppy coat has changed, the coat is sprayed with a preparation called Rad, which is now obtainable in England. This is done regularly once a week. Mirror-Coat is added to the diet daily in the correct dosage for the breed, and Vitamin B_{12} is given by mouth daily for one month, then left off for two weeks; and then the entire procedure is recommenced, including the rest period, and continues for the dog's entire show career. Mink oil is also used regularly but sparingly on the coat.

Breeds with long, heavy, pendulous ears, like the delightful spaniels, frequently suffer from ear troubles, but this is only because their ears are not attended to regularly, and, if they are left dirty, ear mites may invade the orifice of the ear, causing much distress and misery. There is no need for any of this, as there are some excellent preparations on the market and, if any of these are used regularly, ear troubles can be avoided with the greatest of ease.

Unfortunately, there are a number of breeds which grow unnecessary hair in the ear canal. This affliction can be particularly bad in breeds where the ear orifice is exceptionally small. Nevertheless, provided that the hair is removed weekly, dogs with this trouble can go through life unaffected. Sealyhams, Maltese and Poodles are some of the breeds which require watching for this complaint.

Not all the long-coated breeds are difficult to maintain in a perfectly groomed state. Surprisingly, breeds like the Pomeranian and the Finnish Spitz require extremely little brushing except at certain times of the year. But on the whole, the longer and silkier the coat, the more careful and regular attention is required, not only in brushing or combing, but in regular oiling, spraying and bathing to prevent the coat from splitting and breaking.

Besides all this attention, breeds like the beautiful Maltese and sweet Yorkshire Terrier require to have their coat turned up in wrappings of paper or polythene. They should be groomed carefully every day, and unhappy indeed is the owner who neglects such a breed for a week or two and then tries to groom him and get the dog back into show condition! The neglected five or ten minutes a day's grooming will end up in hours of hard, uninteresting work, trying to disentangle the long, matted, felted coat. Not only is this time consuming, but it is often painful for the dog and during the process a great deal of the coat may be destroyed. The damage caused by only a week or two's neglect may take several months or even more to repair before a dog will be in show condition again.

Breeds with slightly harsher-textured coats such as the Shih Tzu, Lhasa Apso, Pekingese, etc., require regular grooming, but not quite to the extent of the silky coats, so that a few days' neglected grooming are not quite so disastrous.

There are many breeds which are long-coated but which require very little attention to keep the dogs looking smart. Breeds like the charming Japanese, Chihuahua and Papillon could hardly be easier to look after.

Regardless of the type of coat that a dog has, or even whether it has been tampered with by scissors, clippers or plucking, all breeds really do require to be given a good finger massage all over the body or to be groomed thoroughly through to the skin regularly once a week. Long and silky-coated dogs should be done daily. Dogs unlike cats are unable to attend adequately to their own daily toilet and must, therefore be groomed by their owners. Hand massaging keeps the skin and muscles supple, increases the blood supply to the area, and helps to diminish the doggy odour which is so much stronger in some breeds than in others. Chihuahuas, for example, are a breed which practically speaking have no natural doggy odour.

The smooth-coated breeds are on the whole extremely easy to groom. The only hard work about them may be due to the size of some of them. Obviously, a Great Dane requires more work than a Miniature Pinscher or a Chihuahua, whereas breeds like the Bloodhound or the brachial-faced breeds, such as the Pug or Bull Dog, require extra attention because of their wrinkles. The folds of skin in these breeds require to be kept clean and dry, because the area hidden from the air often becomes sore and, if neglected, can even become infected. In severe cases of neglect chronic eczema may develop.

Breeds with heavy, pendulous lips must have extra attention to ensure that their lips are clean and that no old food has accumulated in them, particularly in the flews and lower folds. This often neglected area may become extremely sore, and it may turn septic and smell putrid.

Breeds with really harsh coats and with dense undercoats are not difficult to keep well turned out. They do, however, require special attention when they are moulting, or in the case of bitches after they have had a litter.

Grooming a dog can be great fun, and it can be a surprisingly relaxing therapy, provided that it is done regularly and is not done as some tedious, dreary chore. It is good for the dog, stimulates his circulation and is excellent for his self-respect and well being. Dogs, like people, like to be loved and admired, and grooming certainly makes them feel good. It is a time when owner and dog can get together for the mutual benefit of both.

TRAINING TO BE GROOMED

The best age to start grooming a dog is while he is a puppy. It is not too soon to start while he is tiny and still with his dam. The first grooming should consist of gently stroking the body with the hand. As the puppy gets larger, this can be extended to include the head. Breeds like the Pomeranian, where the hair has to be encouraged to stand up the wrong way, should be stroked from the tail upwards (but not on the head).

When the puppy is about three to five weeks old, it can be trained to lie on its back, in order to have its tummy stroked. This is a very useful lesson for all breeds as it can be extremely expedient later on, particularly in the large breeds, when dogs get very wet underneath. It makes it much easier all round if they will turn over automatically and lie on their back to be dried. It is even more essential for small breeds to be trained to lie down, particularly for those which require a great deal of grooming, like the Maltese, Shih Tzu, Pekingese, and similar breeds. It is certainly much easier to groom them when they are lying on their backs, particularly if the person grooming them prefers to do so on his or her lap, rather than on a table.

Grooming training is most important for breeds which require to have a great deal of time spent on them, particularly those like the Poodles and the American Cocker Spaniel, all of which require not only frequent bathing but a great deal of brushing, not to mention hours of clipping and trimming, during their show careers.

Such dogs must be trained to stand, to lie on their sides and on their backs, to extend their forelegs, bend their feet, and be taught to shake the water from their coat, all on the word of command. They must also learn that grooming is work, and not a time for playing around.

It would be interesting to work out the number of hours a top Standard Poodle would have had spent on his entire grooming during his lifetime. All dogs must learn from an early age to have their ears attended to, their teeth cleaned and their nails trimmed, as part of their general grooming routine.

GROOMING EQUIPMENT

There is much feeling amongst expert breeders regarding which is the best equipment to use for grooming their various breeds. The novice will be able to make a hash quite quickly with the best equipment, whilst an expert deprived of his correct brushes and combs would probably be able to produce a magnificently groomed dog. It is not so much a matter of which implement is to be used but of how it is used. Although the old adage holds, that a bad workman blames his tools, it is equally true that the best equipment undoubtedly saves time and produces the best results when in the hands of an expert.

Whatever the breed or whatever the size, a dog is all the better for a quick grooming every day. Some breeds would literally take only a minute or two at the most, whilst others would be all the better for a mere ten minutes a day, with a really down-to-the-skin grooming once a week. It is not really a lot to ask of any owner of a dog, but oh! how few will bother to do the grooming after the initial novelty has worn off.

There are certain grooming tools which every dog owner should have and there are also several items which should be included in a dog's general grooming equipment whatever his breed. There should be a special grooming box divided into compartments, or a hanging linen folder divided into compartments, to fit each piece of grooming equipment. The latter is useful in that it can be rolled up and tied with tape.

DOG GROOMING EQUIPMENT

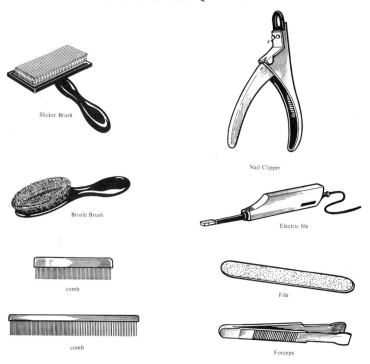

Slicker Brush

Nail Clipper

Bristle Brush

Electric file

comb

File

comb

Forceps

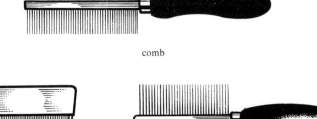

comb

Nit comb

Double sided comb

The grooming box should include:

1. A suitable brush.
2. A comb (for long-coated breeds).
3. A hand-glove (for smooth-coated breeds).
4. A velvet pad.
5. A toothbrush or flannel for cleaning the teeth.
6. Guillotine nail clippers or nail file.
7. Ear Powder.
8. Flea Powder.
9. Boracic powder.
10. Tooth scaler.
11. Eye-Brite for removing eye stains.
12. Peroxide 10 vol. for cleaning teeth and diluted 1 in 5 with milk for removing stains.
13. Cotton Wool.
14. A collar.
15. A lead.
16. A bath towel
17. Artery forceps.
18. Thinning shears.
19. Friars Balsam or Permanganate of potash.
20. Johnson's baby powder.
21. Trimming scissors.
22. Nail file
23. Mink Oil.

It is most important that both the dog and the person grooming should get pleasure out of the procedure, and that it should not be considered just another dreary chore to be got through as quickly as possible. Most people find that it is easiest to groom a dog on a table, except in the very large breeds, when the dog should stand on the floor. In many breeds dogs can be taught to jump up on to the grooming table. Until the dog is trained to stand quietly, it may be necessary for him to be tethered to something such as a ring in

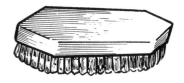

Whale bone brush

Stripping comb

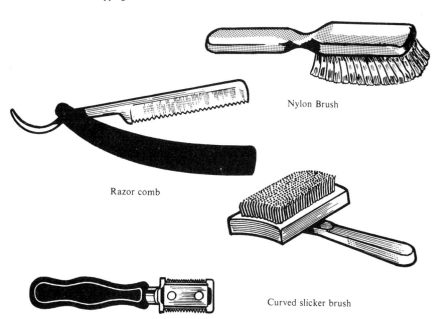

Nylon Brush

Razor comb

Curved slicker brush

Duplex dresser

Pocket stripping knife

Strapped fibre brush

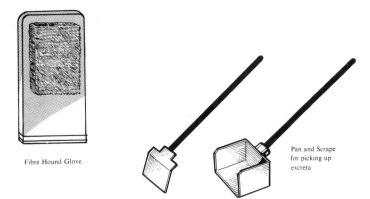

Fibre Hound Glove

Pan and Scrape
for picking up
excreta

the wall, to which he should be attached by a collar and lead. No
dog should ever be left standing on a table unattended, because
many a serious accident has occurred when a dog has suddenly
jumped off the grooming table on to a slippery floor, perhaps
breaking a limb, or being strangled by the collar.

It should go without saying that the surface of the table should
not be slippery, and that the table itself should be firm and steady.
It is an excellent idea for the dog to stand on a special rubber mat.
Professional handlers use special grooming tables, the height of
which can be adjusted according to the size of the breed. It is very
useful too to have a large looking glass behind the grooming table,
to enable the reflection of the dog to be seen whilst grooming.

It is tremendously important that the dog should enjoy his
grooming session. With breeds where grooming takes a long time,
the dog should be allowed to have frequent intervals in order to
stretch himself and to have a little exercise. This prevents him
becoming bored, and also gives the person grooming the dog a rest
too! To ensure that the dog is never frightened by any of the processes involved:

1. He must be lifted up gently on to the table and must not be
   shoved up unsuspectingly, or he must be taught to jump up.
2. He must be talked to in a soothing voice all through the
   grooming and, if he must be reprimanded, it must be done
   by the voice in a stern tone. When he has complied with the
   order, he must be praised.

3. The order and time of grooming should be the same each day, if this is possible.
4. There should be a definite routine order of work, as this is better both for the dog and the groomer.
5. There should be a titbit as a peace offering at the end of the grooming session, and, when training, at the beginning too.
6. Never break off grooming because the dog is being difficult. Rather do over again an area which he enjoys having done and then stop. Like this, he will associate grooming with something pleasurable.

Suggested order of work

1. Start with the eyes, and wipe each eye with a separate swab of cotton wool. If there are eye stains, dry the area with cotton wool, and press* boracic powder on the stained area.
2. Look at the ears for mites, wax or soreness.
3. Look at the anus and see that it is clean.
4. Start brushing very gently over the head, down the neck and vigorously over the body and down the sides. Then brush the tail and each leg in turn and finally the stomach. The brushing should be done in the direction in which the hair grows, except with Pomeranians and some similar breeds.

   Large smooth-coated breeds are better massaged with a hound brush in a circular motion. A little mink oil may be sprayed sparingly on a brush, and a final brush over the coat will give it a glorious sheen. A last rub over with the hand or a velvet pad or glove or with a silk handkerchief does also bring up a wonderful sheen.
5. Clean the teeth with a piece of lint or cotton moistened in a solution of half peroxide 10 vol. and half milk, or in a mixture of baking soda and salt sufficiently moistened.

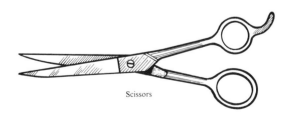

Scissors

* See Appendix Page 301.

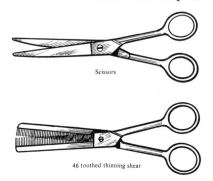

Scissors

46 toothed thinning shear

GENERAL GROOMING PROCEDURES

I. GROOMING THE SMOOTH-COATED BREEDS

THE DAILY TREATMENT

Requirements vary considerably according to the size of the breed.
A Chihuahua requires a soft-bristled brush with short bristles; a
small baby's brush is excellent, and a finish should be given with
a velvet pad or the hand. Breeds like the Bloodhound require a
good vigorous brushing, and a large Strong Bristle brush or a
curved nylon brush are both excellent. After brushing, a good hand
massage to the skin helps to keep it loose and supple. If the coat
looks dry, a weekly spray of Rad or a little human hairdressing
oil can be put on the hands and then gently rubbed over the coat. I
prefer to use mink oil sprayed on to a brush, but this oil must be
used sparingly. A final sheen can be worked up with a silk handkerchief or a velvet pad.

PRESSURE POINTS

Some of the large breeds require special care of the pressure points,
as these areas frequently become bald. These include the areas
which become affected by a hound or dog lying on hard ground, or
where the stern or tail becomes really sore from continually being
knocked, as occurs with many Great Danes. The area can be covered
with Benzyl Benzoate emulsion and in the latter case a leather tail
shield can be worn until the tail has healed.

Hounds and Retrievers require strong, vigorous brushing, and a
fibre glove is excellent for this. Hand massaging is essential too. A
handful of straw twisted and rolled round and knotted into a wisp
can produce an excellent and cheap brush, but care must be taken
lest the straw should harbour parasites.

PENDULOUS EARS

Breeds with pendulous ears require constant attention to the external ear canal and also to the inside and outside of the ear leathers, particularly at the edges, where they collect dirt, food and grease. This frequently causes the edges to split, which is extremely sore. The ears may be washed gently in warm water to remove the dirt and treated with benzyl benzoate emulsion. The ears must be kept dry and clean. A useful tip is to put the dog's head into an open-ended stocking whilst it is eating. This keeps the ears out of the food and water bowls, and prevents chaps forming which are apt to be difficult to cure.

ERECT EARS

Dogs with erect ears seldom have ear troubles, but it is another matter with dogs with the pendulous variety, and particularly with the breeds which grow hair in the ear canal, as do many of the terriers and long-coated breeds. The ears should be held erect and examined. They may be cleaned out with a swab of cotton wool held on the end of a pair of artery forceps. On no account should the ear be probed any further than the eye can see. If the ear looks dirty with accumulated wax, a little warm olive oil or ear drops may be dropped in by a dropper and the surplus oil removed with a piece of clean cotton wool. The ear can then be lightly dusted with an excellent ear powder, the recipe for which will be found on page 36. Some breeders prefer to clean the ears out with a swab of cotton wool moistened in ether or alcohol and then dusted. Only one or two hairs should be tweaked out of the ear canal at one session.

FEET

Feet should be examined for split or sore pads and the surrounding area should be included in this examination.

ANUS

The anus should be examined to make certain that the area is clean and that there is no trouble ensuing from the anal glands.

WRINKLES

These must be wiped clean with cotton wool. This can be moistened with olive oil, and the wrinkles should then be dried and finally dusted with Johnson's baby powder.

MOUTH

Lastly the teeth should be cleaned and examined for any food lodged between them. In the case of breeds with pendulous lips, such as the Bloodhound, the mucous lining should be examined, particularly the flews and fold in the lower lip. The latter often harbours food which eventually causes soreness, and, where there is neglect, the area can become septic and suppurate. This can be gently wiped with T.C.P. solution and kept free of food. A solution of half and half cold milk and peroxide vol. 10 is excellent for cleaning the teeth, as is a mixture of salt and baking soda moistened sufficiently to form a paste, or even human toothpaste. Dogs do not care for the teeth cleaning operation. It is therefore important to do it gently, quickly, yet thoroughly, and to give great praise afterwards.

Remove boracic powder from eye stain area with a soft toothbrush.

Give a final check over that all is well. Then release the dog from his grooming with a flourish and reward him with a titbit. Take him for a short walk, or give him one or two throws with a ball to retrieve, or do something which he enjoys.

THE WEEKLY TREATMENT

This is basically the same as the daily grooming. If the dog is living in an area where there are fleas, then the coat should be dusted thoroughly with anti-flea powder, and he should wear a plastic flea collar. These last for three months and certainly keep external parasites at bay.

THE MONTHLY TREATMENT

This is the same as the daily and weekly grooming procedure; but in addition at this grooming session the nails must be either cut or filed. Some breeds which are given enough road exercise may not require much attention to their nails, but the majority of dogs do require to have their nails cut. They should be cut just below the quick with guillotine nail cutters, or they may be filed with an ordinary carpenter's cross-cut file. Dogs which have not had their

DOG TREATMENTS

Hold the dog's head up.
Open side of
lip using two
hands

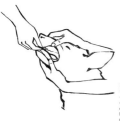

Insert
spoon
containing liquid
or pour medicine
direct from bottle,
having measured
the correct quantity
first

HOW TO ADMINISTER A LIQUID WITH HELP

HOW TO CONTROL A DOG WHILE
SCALING TEETH
Showing correct position
of the arms and hands

Open mouth
insert spoon with
lip socket

HOW TO ADMINISTER A LIQUID
WITHOUT HELP

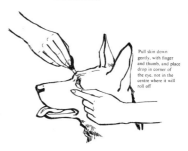

Pull skin down
gently, with finger
and thumb, and place
drop in corner of
the eye, not in the
centre where it will
roll off

HOW TO ADMINISTER EYE DROPS

dew claws removed, must have the nails of these claws dealt with.

TEETH (MONTHLY TREATMENT)

The monthly treatment is to remove any light tartar with an ordinary charcoal pencil. If the tartar is thick, then it should be removed with proper teeth scalers. Dogs dislike this, which is not surprising since it must be painful. In bad cases the dog should be given a sedative beforehand, or in some cases the veterinary surgeon must deal with the problem under a general anaesthetic. Care must be taken not to do too much scaling, as it is liable to do damage to the tooth enamel, as some enamel is inevitably removed in the process.

ANAL GLANDS (MONTHLY EXAMINATION)

These may require attention.

FAECES (MONTHLY EXAMINATION)

Faeces should be taken to the veterinary surgeon to test for the presence or not of worms.

II. GROOMING THE LONG-COATED BREEDS

Requirements vary considerably according to the size of the dog and the texture of the coat. The silky-coated breeds will be dealt with separately.

TRAINING TO LIE DOWN FOR GROOMING

It is invariably easier to groom the reasonably small, long-coated breeds on the lap or on a table. For this it is a great deal easier if the dog has been trained to lie on his back and side from the time he was a few weeks old. Older dogs can be trained, but it must be done gently and with care not to frighten them. It is only natural that a dog will struggle and try to resist to begin with, but a little patience, a soothing voice and a gentle tickle to the abdomen works wonders. In the early stages the dog must not be expected to lie still for more than a very short period, but as he learns and understands what is required of him, the time that he will remain still and quiet will lengthen. He must have plenty of praise. It is, however, tremendously important that on no account should the dog be hurt in the particular grooming process while he is being trained. It is better to leave a tangle for an hour or even a day or two rather

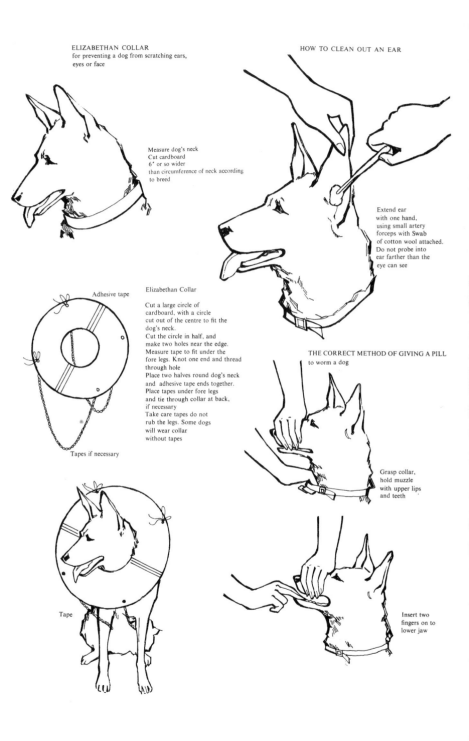

ELIZABETHAN COLLAR
for preventing a dog from scratching ears,
eyes or face

Measure dog's neck
Cut cardboard
6˝ or so wider
than circumference of neck according
to breed

Adhesive tape

Elizabethan Collar

Cut a large circle of
cardboard, with a circle
cut out of the centre to fit the
dog's neck.
Cut the circle in half, and
make two holes near the edge.
Measure tape to fit under the
fore legs. Knot one end and thread
through hole
Place two halves round dog's neck
and adhesive tape ends together.
Place tapes under fore legs
and tie through collar at back,
if necessary
Take care tapes do not
rub the legs. Some dogs
will wear collar
without tapes

Tapes if necessary

Tape

HOW TO CLEAN OUT AN EAR

Extend ear
with one hand,
using small artery
forceps with Swab
of cotton wool attached.
Do not probe into
ear farther than the
eye can see

THE CORRECT METHOD OF GIVING A PILL
to worm a dog

Grasp collar,
hold muzzle
with upper lips
and teeth

Insert two
fingers on to
lower jaw

1.   One of the author's tricolour American Cocker
Spaniels three months after her last clipping and
trimming. She was left like this on purpose for
this demonstration photograph.

Photo: Anne Cumbers

2.   The same champion bitch perfectly clipped and trimmed.

Photo: Anne Cumbers

than to hurt him trying to tease it out while he is learning to lie quietly.

When all is ready, allow the dog to relieve himself and then start the grooming routine. This should always be done in the same order and preferably at the same time each day.

1. Start with the eyes, wipe each with a separate swab of cotton wool soaked in warm water or in Eye-Brite, and dry the eyes with fresh swabs of cotton wool. Treat the eye stains with boracic powder pressed over the stained area if necessary, or this may be done with zinc oxide powder.
2. Check the ears for wax or mites and look at the tips of the leathers. Put a little ear powder in the ears if the hair requires to be plucked from the ear canals, but only pluck out one or two hairs at a time.
3. Make certain that the anal area is clean. If it is not, brush out dried soiled hair, or if necessary wash the area and dry it. If there is a parting, straighten it with a comb, slightly stretching the skin as the parting is made.
4. It is best to start grooming from the extremities, though not essential. Start with the dog lying on his back in your lap, or on his side, depending on the size of the dog. Then part his hair and pick up one side of it in the opposite hand to the one holding the brush, taking about an inch or so at a time. The brushing is started in smooth even strokes going right down to the skin. Working upwards all the time layer by layer, but brush the hair downwards. In the larger breeds it is necessary to divide the coat into three or four-inch strips, working each strip up separately until the top is reached. In most breeds it is better to start at the abdomen and to work up to the chin.
5. Turn the dog on his side and starting at the feet, go up to the top of the back in strips of three or four inches as before. Then do the same on the other side.
6. Turn the dog on his front with his head facing forwards and, unless it is a breed with a centre parting, start brushing in layers from the tail upwards to the top of the head. If a hair spray tonic is used weekly, such as *Rad*, St. Aubrey Coatasheen, or Mink Oil, it should be applied at this stage.

B

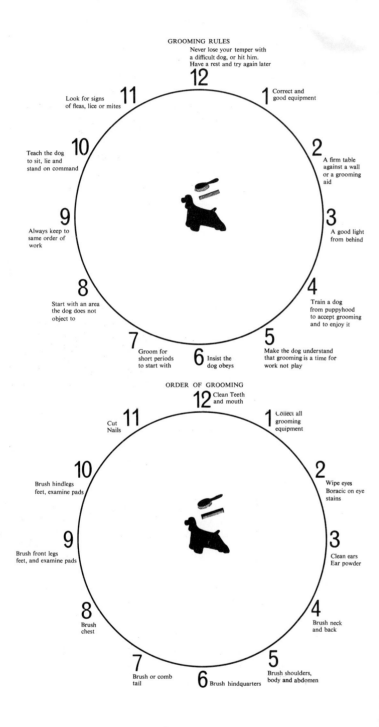

GROOMING RULES

12 Never lose your temper with a difficult dog, or hit him. Have a rest and try again later

1 Correct and good equipment

2 A firm table against a wall or a grooming aid

3 A good light from behind

4 Train a dog from puppyhood to accept grooming and to enjoy it

5 Make the dog understand that grooming is a time for work not play

6 Insist the dog obeys

7 Groom for short periods to start with

8 Start with an area the dog does not object to

9 Always keep to same order of work

10 Teach the dog to sit, lie and stand on command

11 Look for signs of fleas, lice or mites

ORDER OF GROOMING

12 Clean Teeth and mouth

1 Collect all grooming equipment

2 Wipe eyes Boracic on eye stains

3 Clean ears Ear powder

4 Brush neck and back

5 Brush shoulders, body and abdomen

6 Brush hindquarters

7 Brush or comb tail

8 Brush chest

9 Brush front legs feet, and examine pads

10 Brush hindlegs feet, examine pads

11 Cut Nails

7. Next brush the ears carefully.
8. Then brush or comb the tail.
9. Brush the face and moustaches removing any boracic powder from the eye stain area with a small tooth-brush.
10. Plait or tie back the hair according to the breed. Rubber, bands should be used with care and should always be cut off, never pulled off, as this breaks the hair.
11. Clean the teeth with half and half hydrogen peroxide 10 vol. and milk, or moistened baking powder and salt.
12. Finally stand the dog and comb or brush (according to the breed) the hair into the correct position. Mink oil used sparingly is excellent. Finish the proceedings with a flourish and a plethora of praise, and a tasty titbit and perhaps a game of ball or a walk.

WEEKLY GROOMING

This remains the same as the daily grooming unless a weekly conditioner spray tonic is used, such as Rad or Coatasheen. The ears, however, should have a dusting with the ear powder and, if there is any likelihood of fleas, ticks or lice, the coat should be liberally powdered with a suitable insecticide, or the dog should wear an anti-flea plastic collar to keep parasites away. White coated breeds can have a coat-cleaning done with a little Johnson's baby powder, or starch, and the former can be placed in the folds of the skin too if there are any wrinkles. It is not recommended to use powder too frequently in some breeds as it is apt to dry the coat.

MONTHLY GROOMING

This remains the same as the daily and weekly grooming, but the nails, ears, teeth and feet require to be attended to. Moreover, many breeds require trimming and clipping at this time.

NAILS

These must be cut with guillotine nail cutters just below the quick. If the quick is cut, dab with finely or powdered Permanganate of Potash. In breeds where the nails are required to be kept really short they should be cut frequently so that the quick recedes up the nail, a small carpenter's file may be used to smooth the rough edges of the nail. If the dew-claws have not been removed, it is necessary to cut the nails on these.

Arrows indicate
the direction in
which the glands
should be pressed

There are two glands
situated on either side of
the anus

With index finger
and thumb
press together
with an
upward
movement
using firm
steady pressure
while squeezing
the glands empty

The anus
should be
covered with a
piece of
cotton wool
or lint as
the contents
are foul

HOW TO EXPAND ANAL GLANDS

TEETH

Any light tartar which may have formed on the teeth can be rubbed off with a charcoal pencil. If the sediment is thick—and since this is always teeming with germs—a tooth scaling is required. Dogs detest this and it may be necessary to administer a sedative before attempting to scale. In severe cases, it is better to get the veterinary surgeon to do this, probably under anaesthetic, but too much scaling certainly damages the enamel.

FOOT TRIMMING

The hair between the pads requires to be cut away and the foot trimmed neatly.

WORM TESTS

In countries or areas where there are fleas, the faeces should be taken to the veterinary surgeon for testing in case there are worms. If the result of the test is positive, the dog must be dosed twice after the last worms were seen in the stools.

HAIRBALLS

Many long-coated breeds suffer from this complaint, particularly if they are inclined to lick their coats. Hair accumulates inside the dog and becomes a ball in the intestines. A monthly dose of Olive Oil will rid the dog of this foreign body.

TONICS

There are many conditioners, treatments and so called aids to help the growth of luxuriant coats. Each breeder has his own pet aid, shampoo and treatment.

ANAL GLANDS

These must be evacuated if necessary.

FAECES

These should be tested monthly for worms and worm eggs.

III. GROOMING THE SILKY- AND SOFT-COATED BREEDS

These breeds require a great deal of care in the management and maintenance of their coat. It is absolutely essential to use combs

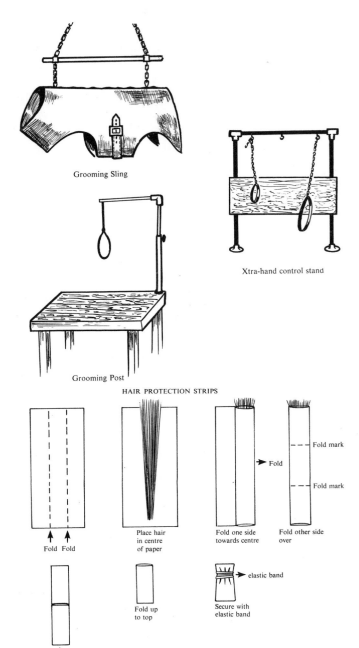

Grooming Sling

Xtra-hand control stand

Grooming Post

HAIR PROTECTION STRIPS

Fold Fold

Place hair
in centre
of paper

Fold one side
towards centre

→ Fold

Fold mark

Fold mark

Fold other side
over

Fold up
to top

elastic band

Secure with
elastic band

Fold end
upward

Hair protector may be made of tissue paper, toilet paper
or fine polythene. The top is secured by an elastic band
twined round several times. Hair protectors must be removed
on alternate days to prevent the hair from felting.

with extremely smooth teeth and soft bristle brushes, and great care is needed when grooming so that hardly a hair is lost in the process! However, it is most important to groom right down to the skin.

The dogs should be trained to lie on their backs and on their sides.

BRUSHES

The best brushes for the long-coated dogs are brushes which have long bristles (particularly if the bristles are of uneven length) so that the bristles can reach down through the coat to the skin. Some breeders prefer bristles with unevenly bunched bristles. The bristles may be made of a number of materials. The best are probably real bristle or whale bone. Nylon does not seem to affect the coat of some breeds, but it is too harsh for others. Hindes make a good wire brush with long pins, and there are various brushes made by Warner, which are excellent. A natural Bristle brush is a really efficient implement and popular with many breeders.

The St. Aubrey brush is made of plastic and is another good brush of great value for the long-coated breeds. The wire curry comb can be useful for working on any large matting that may have accumulated. It is, however, too severe on the normal coat.

Many of the brushes have the pins or bristles rather far apart. This is quite good for the initial part of the grooming, but for a really good finish, the bristles should be close together, because this naturally divides the hair evenly. This is particularly noticeable if dogs are photographed with very good cameras, where every hair is shown to perfection or otherwise.

COMBS

Many of the long-coated breeds are better combed than brushed, particularly if an undercoat is not desired. There is nothing better than a good steel comb with smooth teeth for removing an unwanted undercoat. These combs come in many sizes and shapes, with or without handles, and it is really a matter of personal preference as to which is best. Most breeders recommend the solid brass combs with chromium-plated, tapered teeth.

A nit comb is useful for removing nits and for the finer hair on ears and face. It must, however, only be used on a well groomed dog, because it is extremely apt to remove too much hair unless used with great caution. A nit comb is useful in some breeds for removing the undercoat, but this is a slow method, though effective when a dog is moulting.

For dogs like those in the Spitz breeds, and for Old English Sheep-Dogs and the Standard Poodles, all of which have very thick coats, a large aluminium comb with wide set teeth is required. These are generally about seven inches long, and are wide-backed and light to use.

As with most things, it is wise to buy the very best grooming equipment. It may entail a slightly more expensive outlay, but the best really does pay dividends. It is most important, too to use the correct tools with the respective breeds. The variety is, of course, enormous, but with careful selection, and observation of the old hands in any particular breed, it is reasonably easy to buy what is required. Naturally breeders sometimes differ in their opinions as to which grooming tool is best, but in these cases, it probably does not matter too much which one is chosen. Nevertheless a careful study of the best turned-out dogs will often pay dividends. Combs with a strong end tooth are excellent for teasing out knots or matting which will have appeared generally from neglect. Matted hair is best soaked in Almond Oil and then divided into four and teased cut with the fingers, a Curry Comb, or the end tooth of a comb, according to the texture of the coat. Cutting through the centre of matting with a pair of scissors may help in large difficult mats.

IV.   GROOMING THE SMALL LONG-COATED BREEDS

Most breeders of the long-coated small breeds prefer to groom their dogs on their laps, but the principles are the same whether the dogs are groomed on the floor, a table, or on one's lap. Breeds like the Pomeranian are best groomed with brushes that have bristles which are hard and of uneven length. A comb is required not for the dog but for cleaning the bristles of the brush, although a comb may be useful for teasing out tangles too.

The dog is first laid on its back, lying between the knees of the person grooming it. Some breeds require the coat dressed with oil or Linatone, the dog then looks an exceedingly bedraggled specimen. The hair, however, absorbs the oil quite rapidly, and after two or three days the oil disappears. The more a dog is bathed, the quicker the coat picks up the dirt, until with brushing, the natural oil covers the hair and it then becomes dirt resistant. Breeds like the Maltese should be bathed monthly and, provided that they are brushed regularly, they keep their coats surprisingly white. If they are bathed more frequently, they should have their coats oiled for twenty-four hours before bathing. Pet Maltese, Shih Tzus and other similar breeds whose owners cannot be bothered with the grooming of the long hair, can look quite smart if the coat is cut to about one inch all over, and just the tail and ear fringes are left long, with a slightly longer beard and moustache, which may be cut either square or rounded.

The majority of long-coated breeds require to have their feet trimmed and the hair which grows between them cut away. Maltese, Shih Tzus, Fox Terriers, Sealyhams and a number of other breeds grow unwanted hair in the ear canal. It is most important that this should be plucked out regularly, a few hairs at a time only, otherwise plucking out a lot of hair at a time is cruel.

PLUCKING HAIR FROM THE EAR CANAL

The unfortunate breeds which grow hair in the ear canal must undergo the torture of having this hair removed regularly. The hair should be plucked out every few days from the time the dog is a tiny puppy all through his life. It does not really hurt the dog very much if only a few hairs are pulled out at a time. It is a different matter if a whole bunch of hairs are plucked out all at once. If there is a profuse growth of hair, then the ear canal should be lightly powdered with Ryotin or some other similar ear powder. This should be left in the ear for a short time and the hair can then be plucked out either by the finger and thumb or with eyebrow tweezers or with small artery forceps, rather depending upon the size of the dog, but I much prefer to use artery forceps as they prevent the hair falling into the ear canal. Only a few hairs should be plucked out each day until the growth is under control. Then perhaps a weekly session might be sufficient, but this depends on each individual dog.

SPECIAL CARE OF THE EYES WHEN GROOMING

It is obvious with some breeds of dog, particularly those with large or rather prominent eyes, that in the course of grooming that the eye could get damaged. It is therefore, wise when grooming these breeds, and also the Yorkshire Terrier, that the eyes should be shielded when grooming the face and head. The eyes

B*

should be shielded with the hand by extending a thumb and index finger across the eyes and stop. The hair is then groomed carefully on either side. Puppies are extremely likely to jump about when being groomed, or to turn their head rapidly to look at something that has attracted their attention. The result could be serious if the eye were damaged by the bristles of the brush.

V. GROOMING THE HARSH LONG-COATED BREEDS

These include such breeds as the Collie, Samoyed and Pomeranian. These breeds seldom require bathing, because this most certainly softens the coat. Most of them do require regular brushing, but probably twice a week is sufficient except during the periods of moulting, when they require extensive hard brushing and combing to get rid of the old dead hair. Many of the harsh-coated breeds have a dense undercoat and this should never be combed except when the coat is being shed. There is no better way of removing an undercoat than by combing. Some breeders are against excessive grooming and consider that a hard grooming once a month is adequate. The operative word here is 'hard', but much depends on how the dog is kept and whether once a month is in fact sufficient.

If the dogs get dirty, it is probably better to clean the coat with a form of dry cleaning. Fuller's earth is good, and for white dogs ordinary starch is excellent. Another first class method for these breeds is St. Aubreys Coatasheen, which is, in fact, made for Poodles and is an excellent preparation.

Chalk can be used on the white harsh-coated breeds for shows, but it *must* be brushed out thoroughly. Some breeds like the Fox Terrier should be washed or bathed immediately after a show if chalk has been used on the coat, as the chalk rots the coat in a slow insidious manner. Chalk however does not seem to harm the really harsh-coated breeds like the Sealyham, etc.

VI. GROOMING THE LARGE BREEDS

This differs very little from grooming the other breeds except that the dogs stand on the ground. They must be trained to stand still and to extend their front legs to have the feathers brushed or combed out. They must also learn to stand on three legs while the feet and paws are being attended to. The easiest way to examine the feet is to lift them up like those of a horse, making the dog bend all his feet backwards in turn. In this position the hair below the pads can be trimmed easily.

Large breeds are often likely to damage their tails by knocking them constantly. This is particularly likely in the smooth-coated breeds, and the tail should therefore be closely examined and treated if necessary. Large breeds often suffer too at their pressure points. Not only does the hair get worn away at these places, but the actual skin area gets sore and red. Benzyl helps to keep the skin soft, which encourages the hair to grow through again easily. It helps if the dog is only permitted to lie on something soft. A sack filled with soft wood-wool shavings, or with a number of other sacks, makes a useful soft bed to lie on. Large breeds can be quite hard work to groom and require a tremendous amount of elbow grease to produce a shining coat. It might be an idea in some breeds to use a vacuum cleaner over the coat, using one of the small attachment brushes, as is now used on horses. This certainly takes the hard work out of grooming and is excellent for removing the scurf. I must admit that I have not as yet heard of anyone doing it. But why not? The grooming routine is the same for all varieties of coat.

GROOMING TERRIERS

Surprisingly this is one of the most complicated variety of dog to be groomed, perhaps because it includes stripping and plucking. Some of the Terriers require hours of time and energy to get them up to show standard, and many months of continual hard work. There are, however, a few terriers which are not nearly so complicated to keep in good trim and which, in fact, hardly need anything to be done to them. In spite of this, they are still able to look like a neatly trimmed dog; and this is more than can be said for some of the more complicated varieties which are hardly recognizable as the same breed as their brothers in the show ring, when they are not plucked and trimmed.

Undoubtedly terrier breeders gain much pleasure from the work that they put into their dogs, preparing them months in advance for a show. But like everything else, once the dog is groomed and plucked into shape, it is not difficult to keep him up to standard, by regular topping. The difficulty arises when a dog is let go for months and months, so that his coat is completely out of hand. Getting such a dog back into show trim entails hours and hours of hard work in order to get him right again. Pet owners who buy a terrier at a show and think that their dog will resemble the ones in the ring without doing anything to them will be sadly disillusioned all too soon. The coat will probably grow and mat beyond control until the dog is taken to some dog parlour for treatment. Naturally the dog parlour cannot spend more than a few hours on the dog, and so they resort to the easiest and quickest method of dealing with the dog to make him look better. The result is that the dog is nearly always clipped instead of being plucked. Nevertheless, provided that the clipping is done to conform to the stripped manner of the breed, the dog can be made to look a well groomed and well cared for dog for a moderate sum of money.

The pet owner of a terrier must decide whether to take up stripping as a new hobby and learn how to master the technique and strip his own dog, or he must resort to the dog parlour for keeping his dog well groomed. If the worst comes to the worst he can invest in a pair of scissors or even some clippers, and keep his dog smartly cut or clipped, but anything is better than allowing the coat to become completely out of hand. Perhaps it might be easier and better to choose an easily maintained terrier or perhaps to own another breed altogether.

The harsher the coat, the harder and stiffer should be the bristles of the brush. The comb too requires to be coarser. Most terriers are brushed with bristle brushes or hound gloves, and the length of the bristle is determined by the length and density of the coat. Most terriers require plucking or stripping two or probably three times a year. Some of the terriers, unfortunately, have hair growing in the ear canal, and it is essential that these hairs should be plucked out weekly. The Fox Terrier has an exceptionally small ear orifice and this sometimes causes trouble. Most terriers are groomed on the table, and the white dogs are chalked.

ORDER OF GROOMING TERRIERS

This is the same as for most breeds. Weekly grooming requires the hair to be removed from the ears. In monthly or six-weekly grooming the dog will need some stripping, plucking and trimming to keep him tidy. The main stripping and plucking should be done when the dog is moulting, because otherwise it is cruel. It should be done when the hair becomes clumped together and it begins to look dead and lifeless.

GENERAL COAT TREATMENTS

There is undoubtedly a plethora of coat aids. It can be quite an expensive hobby trying them all out and sifting the corn from the chaff, and there is a great deal of chaff. The shampoos, coat dressings, rinses, tonics, sprays and other applications are legion. As always, breeders have their own pet aids and, once having found what they consider best for their particular breed, quite naturally they continue to use the same products.

A beautiful coat is inherited, but this in itself is not always sufficient and much depends on the climate in which the dog lives. The coat has also to be maintained in perfect condition. The maintenance of a perfect coat begins internally. A dog must be in the pink of condition. He must have correct and adequate feeding and this means that he must be given all the essentials and also sufficient fat in his diet. He must have sufficient and correct exercise to keep him healthy. His coat must be brushed and combed, and his skin kept supple and free from all parasites, particularly fleas. Fleas are the cause of worms and there is perhaps nothing so detrimental to a coat as worm infestation.

INTERNAL AIDS

Perhaps the best internal therapy for a good coat is the administration of Linseed Oil. This can be put in the food once a day, the dosage being according to size. A half gallon can of this can be obtained from most drug stores. The directions on the label should be followed. The result of a wonderful shiny coat will be seen in a matter of three weeks after taking the oil regularly. It may be better to discontinue the oil from time to time, especially in particularly hot weather.

Olive oil is often recommended, but it should not be given by mouth alone for long periods, because it coats the lining of the stomach and prevents the flow of digestive juices and the absorption of certain foods. If olive oil is used, the Toy breeds require about a quarter of a teaspoonful daily, working up to a teaspoonful after a month. Large breeds can be given larger quantities, starting with a teaspoonful and working up to a tablespoonful. Suet is another form of fat which is extremely good for coats. Do not give all three at the same time, however, as this will upset even the strongest dog's digestion! Dogs which are given 25% fat in their daily diet will not require other oils to help their coats.

So much for internal aids for a good coat. Shampoos must not be harsh and detergents should never, never be used. There are many excellent shampoos for dogs, so buy a good one.

Once again these are legion in number. The question is to find the right one for the right coat. It is difficult to recommend particular makes unless they have been personally tried out. Many of the old home-made recipes have been handed down for generations of dog breeders, and some of these are excellent but sometimes rather messy to prepare. Whatever the recipe is, it must never be too thick or heavy for the coat to which it is to be applied. I remember once a Poodle breeder giving me a recipe which was meant to grow five inches of coat in two months. I thought that this would be simply wonderful for my Maltese, so off I went with all haste to the chemist and had the brew made up, but instead of being a liquid preparation it turned out to be a strong paste. The Poodle breeder proceeded to apply the heavy ointment to the lovely silky coat. I was becoming more alarmed every minute as the sticky honey-like substance was applied, as it would be to a Poodle's coat rather roughly. When it came to shampooing it out two days later, nothing would make the grease dissolve, and, after bathing and drying, my beautiful Maltese looked a wreck. The moral is that in some ways it may be better to buy the correct coat conditioner from a firm which is expert in the business rather than to experiment on a silky-haired breed.

There is really nothing better for silky coats than almond oil, which is gentle and fine for the coat. Many Yorkshire Terriers spend most of their lives coated in this ready for shows.

St Aubrey Royal Coatlin is always a popular conditioner and it prevents the coat from matting. It is easily applied and it is not of too heavy a consistency even for the most delicate of coats. Mr. Groom, Inc. New York have produced a useful coat-growing preparation known as Mr. Groom Coat Conditioner, which helps to grow the coat and tends to prevent matting. Some firms produce an emulsifying wax sold in blocks which can be used as a base for making up ones own conditioners. This method is obviously very much cheaper and probably more economical than buying one of the well known ready-made-up products, particularly if there are a number of dogs which require coat treatment. The time factor in preparation may, however, be a disadvantage. Rad Groom is a useful product and an excellent conditioner and should be sprayed on to the coat weekly. Any light oil can be used to get the coat unmatted. Something like Almond Oil, soaked into the mat until it is well saturated is then worked on gently with a stiff brush or the end tooth of a comb, in conjunction with a trunk hair dryer. The hair can be gradually worked apart with the fingers. It is best to work from the bottom of the knot teasing out a few hairs at a time so as not to break them, gradually working through the mat teasing carefully to the top. The strong blowing of the hair dryer (which should be set at warm or cold) helps to separate the hairs.

Breeds with coarse coats can have a really stiff brush used on the matted area, provided that it is used sensibly. The hair on the matted area can be literally scrubbed in some breeds without damaging the hair. Where the knot is large it may be necessary to cut right through the centre with a sharp-pointed pair of scissors, or a special mat blade can be used. Then work from the bottom of the knot outwards. If the knot is between the fore or hind legs or under the body, it may be possible to cut it out altogether as the missing hair may not be noticed. Another favourite place for mats to occur is behind the ears and on the neck and elbows. Sometimes it is necessary to cut these away if the coat has been neglected.

DRY CLEANING

There are various dry cleaning agents which are very useful on certain breeds and at certain times.

White terriers are usually cleaned with chalk for shows which is good for keeping the coat harsh, but it must be brushed out thoroughly after use, as chalk actually rots the hair if left on the coat. For the softer-coated breeds starch is cheap to use and produces excellent results. Johnson's baby powder is excellent, especially on the white toy breeds. It cleans the coat well and leaves the dog smelling sweet and clean. It is better than some of the more scented human talcum powders. Corn meal bran is a good old-fashioned cleaning agent. Any of these dry cleaners are sprinkled liberally all over the coat and allowed to sink right down to the skin. This should then be rubbed in all over and allowed to remain on for some time before being brushed out. The cleaning agent absorbs the dirt and dust. It should be brushed out so that none remains in the hair, otherwise it merely dries the coat and this loses its natural lustre.

Dry cleaning agents are extremely useful, particularly on young puppies before they are permitted to be bathed, and on ageing dogs where there is a fear of their catching a chill. They are useful too if only part of the dog requires cleaning. Moreover, they are excellent for cleaning a dog up quickly for an unexpected sale. The coat, however, should always be quite dry before they are used, because otherwise a fearful pudding will be made!

RECIPE FOR EAR POWDER

4 parts Zinc Oxide Powder; 4 parts Boracic Acid Powder; 1 part Iodoform Powder.

Mix the powders together thoroughly and keep in an air tight jar.

Dust the ear canal weekly.

The powder may also be used before removing the hair from the ears.

NAIL CLIPPING

Most dogs have eighteen nails altogether, four on each foot, and two dew-claws, one on each foreleg. Some dogs, and particularly some breeds, have a rudimentary claw on each hind leg, which is caused by a recessive gene. In most breeds these appendages are removed on the fifth day after birth, except in the Pyrenean Mountain Dog, where they have a set on the hind legs, which are never removed.

The nail itself is composed of a modified skin substance which has become horny. Inside the nail there is a blood and nerve supply. During the dog's life the nail continues to grow, the rate of growth depending on the breed and the circumstances. Dogs that have correct conformation of the feet and are given sufficient hard road exercise, wear their nails down by the constant friction of the horny nail on the hard surface of the road; but dogs with incorrectly formed feet and which get very little hard exercise, particularly pampered Toy breeds, grow very long toe nails. If these nails are not clipped short at least once a month, they will continue to grow and they will in some cases curve right round until they become imbedded in the pads. This is not an infrequent occurrence with the dew-claws, particularly in the long-coated breeds where they may grow unobserved by the dog's owner.

Nails were originally weapons of offence or defence and are particularly useful for holding bones and for burying them. They are also used for scratching the skin. When the nail is not being used, it remains contracted by ligaments in an upward direction, but when the dog is tense or frightened it will be observed that the nails are extended. This is particularly noticeable when the nails are being clipped, and great care should be exercised not to cut off too much nail, because in doing so the nerve and capillaries in the nail may be severed, causing pain and bloodshed. A dog, cannot manipulate his nails to anything like the extent that a cat can.

If the nails are allowed to become too long, it causes extreme discomfort to the dog and he cannot walk properly and may even go lame. In time the dog will lose the power of traction in the pads, so that it will be difficult for him to walk on slippery surfaces. These dogs will also find it difficult to go up and downstairs. Nails should be clipped or filed regularly in most breeds, and it is quite a good plan to make a routine of clipping the nails on the first day of each month or the first Sunday of each month. If the nails are trimmed too short it causes intense pain and often profuse bleeding, depending on how far the capillary blood vessel has been severed. Bleeding can be stopped by the use of Monsel's powder or powdered permanganate of potash. The dog should be prevented from walking on hard surfaces for a short while. Surprisingly, a nail cut too short never turns septic, although other nail infections are not uncommon.

It is important that puppies should have their nails clipped at five days, and thereafter once a week or once a fortnight according to the breed. After the age of three months the nails should be dealt with regularly once a month.

Tools Required

Guillotine nail clippers	Powdered permanganate of
Nail file	potash
Monsel's powder	

Electric nail files are made for dogs but most dogs dislike them. They work rapidly and must therefore be used with care.

Method

1. Sit the dog facing you on a steady table, or get someone to hold the dog in his arms if the breed is small enough.
2. If possible, prevent the dog from seeing his nails being clipped by shielding his eyes.
3. Hold the foot in one hand.
4. If possible, ascertain exactly where the quick in the nail ends.

5. Place the guillotine over the nail and clip rapidly and in one cut.
6. Start with the hind dew-claws, if there are any.
7. Clip the nails on the hind legs first.
8. Clip the foreleg dew-claws, if there are any.
9. Clip the nails on the forefeet.
10. In the event of accidentally clipping the quick, apply Friar's balsam or powdered permanganate of potash immediately. Comfort the dog, because he has been hurt and will probably resent the other nails being dealt with.
11. Keep the dog off the ground until the haemorrhage has stopped.
12. Nails may be smoothed over by using an emery board or nail file, depending on the breed. A cross-cut carpenter's file is excellent for large breeds.

If an electric cautery is used to stop a nail haemorrhage, care must be taken only to touch the bleeding point for a fraction of a second, because the heat will otherwise damage and destroy the live tissue in the nail for a considerable distance.

It should be remembered that the more frequently that the nails are cut, the shorter they may be kept, because each time that a nail is cut or filed the quick tends to recede up the nail.

Breeds which are required to have exceptionally short nails should have the nails trimmed weekly from early puppyhood either by filing or cutting.

CHAPTER II

Bathing the Dog

BATHING

How often should a dog be bathed is the often repeated question? This of course entirely depends on the breed, where the dog is kept, and the sort of climate and environment he comes from.

On the whole I am not a great advocator of bathing dogs except in some breeds where it is desirable for shows. The more dogs are bathed the dirtier they become. This is because the natural oils are removed from the hair, and until these are replaced, the hair accumulates dust and dirt.

The average dog probably only requires a bath once or twice a year provided that he is groomed adequately and regularly. Dogs which are shown frequently nearly always have to have a good bath the day before a show and this may mean a bath once a week for breeds like the Poodle or Maltese, or the American Cocker Spaniel.

Dogs do not normally enjoy being bathed, although perhaps the Gun Dogs dislike it least. But, fortunately, dogs quickly get used to any routine, and if bathing is part of their weekly routine they accept it and perhaps even enjoy the procedure and all the grooming and paraphernalia which accompanies it.

Bathing a dog should be done with the minimum of fuss, and it must be done gently and reasonably swiftly. It is important that everything concerned with the bathing should be got ready in advance. This includes the basin or bath, shampoo, towels, dryers and grooming equipment, etc.

Bathing should not be done if the dog is off colour. Puppies are better not bathed until after they are six months old. No dog should be bathed until at least two hours after it has had a meal. No bitch in whelp should be bathed until four weeks after she has been mated. Also no dog which has had an operation should be bathed for at least a month after the operation. It is not wise to bath dogs with skin complaints. There is, however, a time when dogs should be bathed and very seldom are, and that is after they have been swimming in the sea. Salt water is not good for the skin and can be most irritating.

SHAMPOOS

There are a plethora of shampoos, rinses, conditioners, insecticides, repellents and so on. Breeders have their own fads and fancies and naturally some shampoos are more suitable for some breeds than for others. St. Aubrey make a large selection, and there are some excellent egg yolk shampoos. I am rather in favour of shampoos which contain pest repellent, and for soft-coated breeds Johnson's baby shampoo is excellent. Mr. Groom, and JDS is extremely popular with many breeders. Coat conditioners are wonderful for matted coats when used in conjunction with a strong, powerful blow dryer. The Spirit shampoos can also be used as a semi-shampoo without having to wet the coat right through. I have at various times used a great many shampoos. I have tried those made specifically for black dogs on white dogs and vice versa and would not really know which was which. It is very much a matter of experimenting and, when a shampoo is found that suits the breed, it is probably best to continue to use the same one. On the other hand new formulae are always coming on the market, and it is quite interesting to experiment with these.

There are all sorts of rinses which can be used to make grey dogs look bluer, apricot dogs look more apricot, white dogs whiter, etc. What it really boils down to is that the rinses are really dyes! The blue preparations for white dogs are well worth using, since the coat certainly looks whiter than white afterwards!

Dyes are not permitted by the Kennel Club for show purposes. Application of rinses would often be difficult to detect, particularly on solid colours. Judges generally look carefully at the Yorkshire Terriers. Any form of dyeing here is easy to see as the coat is naturally of two colours. By lifting up the coat casually in the ring it will be reasonably evident if the coat has had some extra help as the hair instead of being shaded becomes all one colour! The honest judge does not care to be hoodwinked and the dog is merely not placed. It would be difficult to prove and would not be worth the candle to make a complaint.

PREPARATION FOR BATHING

This entails not only the actual requirements for the bathing but should also include the extra careful cleaning of the kennel, bed and sleeping quarters in general. Blankets and bedding should be washed, dried and aired and then liberally sprinkled with some insecticide. The corners of the kennel and the surrounding area should also be powdered.

As soon as all this is accomplished, then everything necessary for the bath must be prepared well in advance. Doors and windows must be shut to exclude all draughts. The grooming box should be checked to make certain everything is there. This should include:

Cotton wool for the ear plugs	Eye swabs
Vaseline	Boracic powder
Eye ointment	Diamondeye or Eye-Brite
Clean brush and comb	Ear dusting powder or Ear-Rite
Guillotine nail cutter	Tooth cleaner (Peroxide 10 V.)

Nail file
Trimming scissors
Thinning shears
Tooth scaler
Forceps
Tweezers
Plastic apron
Gum boots
Chamois leather

Zinc oxide cream (eye stains)
Electric clippers
Oil for lubricating clippers
Two heads for clippers
Friars balsam or Monsel's
    powder
Benzyl benzoate emulsion
Castor oil
Common salt

The following items should be prepared in advance:

The chosen shampoo, conditioner, two rubber mats, two polythene bottles, two jugs, a basin, a spray fixed on the taps and a dryer. Towels should be put to warm. A large clean chamois leather is excellent for drying the coat.

DRYERS

There are a number of dryers on the market, some very expensive and some less expensive. Which type is the most suitable entirely depends on how many dogs there are to be bathed, how frequently they have to be bathed, and the size of the dogs. For one average-sized dog, an ordinary home hair dryer will suffice. If there are a number of dogs, then one of the excellent dryers on the market for drying poodles would be splendid. I particularly like the trunk dryers with cold, warm and hot settings, and find them most effective for matted areas of the coat. Where there is only one dog, however, and he only requires to be bathed on high days and holidays, then some makeshift arrangements can be made, or the dog can be dried rather slowly in front of a fire, or better still in front of an ordinary household electric blower. One excellent way of drying a short-coated dog, provided that he is small enough, is to place him in a box, such as a tea chest, which is covered with a frame of chicken wire to prevent him jumping out. Over this can be suspended an infra-red, dull-emitter, electric lamp. This means he does not have to be under complete supervision for the entire drying process. It would, however, be necessary to make certain that the lamp was fixed at an adequate distance away, to prevent the dog from getting too hot. One advantage of this method is that it is certain that the dog will not be in any draught, which would be extremely dangerous after a bath.

There are specially made drying boxes where the dog's body is

Trunk dryer

Hand dryer

Dryer

Infra Red Heater

Hand dryer

inside a box, but his head remains outside. The dryer is worked electrically. Some people have endeavoured to make this type of box themselves, but this is extremely dangerous as the amateur probably does not understand the electric part, and many a "do it yourself" affair has caused the death or serious burns to a dog. I personally do not care for these methods of drying and would never recommend them.

THE BATH

If the breed is reasonably small then the kitchen sink is probably as good a place as any to bath the dog. Very large breeds may have to be bathed in the family bath, or, if this is objected to, some large receptacle like an old sitz bath or something similar should be used. However, whatever is decided upon, the bottom of it should be covered with a non-slip, rubber mat. If the sink is used then the draining board should also be covered with a mat. As soon as everything is completely ready and organized, the dryer should be switched on to warm up. The dog should be taken out to relieve himself, because after the bath he should not be let out again for some time after he has been dried and cooled off. In cold climates it would be better to keep him in until the following day.

PRE-BATH GROOMING

Grooming a dog right through to the skin removing all knots, mats and tangles is essential before a bath, and it is especially important for breeds with long coats, particularly the soft- and silky-coated dogs. If this is not done, the coat mats and tangles in the most terrible manner which really needs to be seen to be believed. I have seen this happen in a Maltese with a magnificent long silky coat, the mats and tangles being made worse by rubbing the coat with soap, instead of gently massaging the shampoo in a downward motion, hardly ruffling the hair at all.

BATHING ARRANGEMENTS

Just before the bath the shampoo should be mixed and put into a pint-sized polythene bottle with a special screw top with a hole in it. An old Squeezy bottle is excellent. Another similar bottle can contain the conditioner or the rinse, whichever is being used. It is essential to wear a plastic overall or a large rubber apron, and in

some cases gum boots are not a bad idea. Shoes full of water are
not the most comfortable things to wear!

If it is the dog's first bath, take things quietly, talk to him re-
assuringly and bath him swiftly but gently. It is an excellent idea
for someone to lend an extra pair of hands to steady him in case
he decides to take a flying leap on to the floor. Everything that the
dog could knock over must be removed.

Before lifting him up into the bath, plug each of his ears with a
twisted swab of cotton wool. This should have a little Vaseline
on the end, as this helps to keep the plug in the ear and is also water-
repellent at the same time. The eye lids can be wiped over with a
little eye ointment, and a drop of castor oil can be dropped into
each eye. This helps to prevent any soap getting into the eyes.
If the shampoo happens to be an insecticide, or a wash is being
used, the anus, vulva, nose and penis should be lightly wiped over
with Vaseline as well as the scrotum. If the ends of the ear leathers
are hard or greasy, these should be softened by oiling them or
putting Vaseline on them some hours or in bad cases even the day
before bathing. Benzyl benzoate emulsion is also good.

There is some controversy as to the correct temperature that
the water should be for bathing a dog. Many veterinary surgeons
say that the temperature should be 80° F or blood temperature . . .
but whose blood's temperature? If it is the dog's temperature,
then the water should be about 100° F. This always seems to me to
be on the cold side, and I generally bath my dogs in water about
120° F. and they all seem to have survived!

Few people would probably be bothered to test the temperature
of the water that they bath their dogs in, and so a warm bath as
opposed to a hot bath would be a safe enough guide, or in other
words a little warmer than the temperature of water that a baby
would be bathed in followed by a fairly cool rinse.

BATHING PROCEDURES

There is of course no absolute hard and fast rule as to the order in
which a dog should be bathed. However, it is always better to
adopt one particular routine and method. Some people prefer to
work forwards by shampooing first the tail, the back legs and the
body, then to work from the front legs, shoulders and chest and
then the back, finally ending with the head and ears. If this method
is adopted rinsing is then done starting with the head and ears,
going down the body, tail and abdomen ending with the legs. Other

ORDER OF BATHING

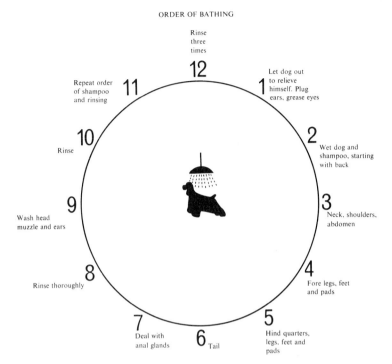

Rinse
three
times

12

Repeat order
of shampoo
and rinsing **11**

Let dog out
1 to relieve
himself. Plug
ears, grease eyes

10

Rinse

2

Wet dog and
shampoo, starting
with back

9

Wash head
muzzle and ears

3

Neck, shoulders,
abdomen

8

Rinse thoroughly

4

Fore legs, feet
and pads

7

Deal with
anal glands

6 Tail

5

Hind quarters,
legs, feet and
pads

people prefer to start with the back and work from there. Whichever method is adopted, it is always better to do the head last as
once the head becomes wet the dog will undoubtedly shake himself,
and this is best avoided until the bathing is finished.

SUGGESTED BATHING PROCEDURE

1. Let the dog out to relieve himself.
2. Wet the dog all over, except his head, with the spray hose or
   jug making sure that the water wets the skin and all the hair.
3. Pour the shampoo on to the sponge, starting with the back,
   work over a small area at a time, massaging well.
4. Lather up the neck, down the shoulders, the brisket and the
   abdomen. Massage and work lather well all over the hair.
   Work briskly but gently and talk soothingly to the dog all the
   time encouraging him not to jump about. Remember to keep
   one hand on the dog throughout the whole bathing procedure.
   If contact with the dog is lost, he will jump out of the bath,
   perhaps with disastrous results.

5. Shampoo the forelegs with the sponge and pay special attention to the feet particularly the pads, between the toes, and the toe nails.

6. Next deal with the hind legs and hind quarters, pads, toes and toe nails.

7. Wash the tail carefully, and in long-coated breeds, take care not to tangle or mat the hair.

8. Extra care must be taken over the anus area, vulva, penis and scrotum.

9. If necessary deal with the anal glands. See page 24.

10. Rinse the area carefully.

11. Lather head, muzzle, ears, paying particular attention to the ear leathers, tips and crevices. Dogs hate this part of the bath, and when the head is wet they like to shake. So be warned!

12. Take care of the edges of the mouth and round the eyes. Do not get soap in the eyes as this smarts. The best way to avoid this is to cover the dog's eyes with the thumb and first finger, at the same time tilting the head upwards, so that the water runs backwards away from the eyes.

13. Massage all over the body quickly, to warm up the dog and to stimulate the circulation.

14. Rinse well with spray or sponge or jug allowing the water to run away as the rinsing proceeds. Protect eyes again between thumb and first finger, tipping the head back to rinse.

15. Re-shampoo the dog all over. This time there will be a richer lather. Work swiftly so that the dog does not catch cold.

16. Rinse well with a spray. Three good rinses are required.

17. Put on conditioning rinse.

18. Rinse twice again or as directed.

19. Start drying head and ear leathers with a small towel or flannel.

20. Squeeze as much water out as possible from ear leathers, neck, body, tail and each leg.

21. Make dog shake on command.

22. Cover with a warm dry towel and rub. Then use a chamois leather over the coat. This is wonderful for drying a dog. The leather should be dipped in very hot water and rung out as dry as possible, and then rubbed down the coat. Keep repeating the process.

23. Remove the ear-plugs, if not previously removed by the dog

shaking, and dry the ears out with swabs of dry cotton wool.

24. Put the dog under the dryer, or beside a heater or fire, or in a specially prepared box with wire lid and under infra-red lamp. Allow the dog to lie on a thick dry warm towel, preferably with his legs tucked under him so that they will absorb the moisture.

25. Brush coat gently immediately by lifting the coat rather than flattening, or comb gently according to the breed, starting with the head.

26. Breeds requiring eye stain to be removed should have boracic powder pressed into the area, or one of the special stain removing preparations should be applied; or hydrogen peroxide Vol. 10 diluted to 1 in 5 of water may be tried.

27. When the coat is quite dry, use the cool air dryer to cool the dog down.

28. Breeds which require chalking should be chalked while the coat is still damp, the body coat should be covered over with a warm towel.

OUT-DOOR BATHING

Breeds such as the Bloodhound, which rarely if ever require bathing, can be cleaned on a warm sunny day with an anti-parasitic wash. This is mixed with water and sponged over the coat, and then allowed to dry without towelling, preferably in the sun.

When large breeds require to be bathed, breeders often find that the easiest way is to fix a spray with a mixer attachment to the taps over the kitchen sink and bath the dog outside the kitchen window. A warm, fine day must be chosen, so that the dog does not catch a chill. He should be dried with towels to get the surplus water off his coat. A large, real, chamois leather can be dipped into a pail of very hot water, wrung out tightly, and rubbed over the coat constantly, squeezing out the water from the leather frequently, and dipping the chamois leather into the hot water. It is surprising how quickly this dries the coat. When the coat is reasonably dry, take the dog for a brisk walk, preferably on a lead to start with, because otherwise he will undoubtedly make for the smelliest thing in the vicinity and have a superb roll, undoing in a matter of seconds all the good that the bathing did.

He can later be allowed to run free. He should then be taken back to the house or kennel, where he should stay out of a draught until the following day or until it is certain that he is really completely dry.

CUP AND JUG BATHING

This is really similar to the human blanket bath. It rather depends on the size of the dog as to whether a large cup or bowl is used. The dog is bathed piecemeal, washing only the areas that are in need of cleaning. It may be just the ears after a meal; or the anal regions when they have become dirty; or where small areas are required to be washed for a show, when for some reason it is not considered either advisable or necessary to bath the whole dog. Without wetting the dog's body, his feathering and ears can be shampooed in a small bowl, squeezed out and rinsed thoroughly, and dried with an electric blower. Legs can easily be washed in a tall, narrow old fashioned enamel jug and rinsed in the same receptacle.

FOOT BATHING

Breeds like the Afghan with large hairy legs get exceedingly muddy when they have been out on a wet day. If their legs are allowed to dry without doing anything to them, the mud dries off on its own and all that is required when dry is a quick brush through. If the hound is a house dog, then it is better to remove the mud simply by placing the dog's legs in a bucket of cold water. Squeeze out the surplus water and dry by an electric blower.

RAIN BATHING

Brush and massage the dog well, and then take him for a good long country walk on a tarmac road in heavy rain. Rub him down well on returning home, and dry him thoroughly using the chamois leather rung out in hot water method.

SUGGESTED AFTER-BATH PROCEDURE

1. Wipe eyes clean with separate swabs of cotton wool.
2. Get rid of stain removing powder with a small, soft toothbrush.
3. Check that cotton-wool ear plugs have been removed. Pluck out few hairs in the ears.
4. Dry ears thoroughly with cotton-wool swabs, and dust with ear powder. For recipe see page 36.

5. Clean teeth with peroxide and milk, or moistened baking soda and salt, or charcoal pencil, and scale if necessary. If tartar is bad, give sedation before bath, so that the effect will have been attained by the time that the scaling is to be performed.

6. Clip nails with guillotine cutters, or file.

7. Breeds with folds and wrinkles on head and face can have the creases swabbed down with Witch-Hazel and dusted with boracic powder or Johnson's baby powder.

8. Check the pads of the feet for cracks, sores, tar, etc. Tar can be removed with Eucalyptus Oil. If the pads are soft, soak them in a solution of one of the Gammaisomer preparations for about five minutes.

9. Do not let the dog out after his bath or allow him to sit in draughts.

10. Breeds which have to be trimmed and/or clipped should have this performed at this stage.

11. Breeds with moustaches, particularly white moustaches, such as Maltese, Shih Tzus, etc., may require treatment for staining. Fanci-full rinse or one of the human rinses for white hair are excellent, as is Eye-Brite, or a boracic powder paste can be applied and the moustache then wrapped up in paper and secured with an elastic band. Hydrogen peroxide Vol. 10 diluted with water 1 to 5 is also excellent. These breeds have to be fed before and at a show by syringe, in order to avoid wetting and spoiling their beautiful moustaches.

BREEDS WHICH ARE NOT BATHED

There are a number of breeds which are seldom if ever bathed. These are breeds which require a harsh coat, such as some of the terrier, and most of the Spitz breeds. These dogs can be kept wonderfully clean by just brushing and an occasional dry clean, or by a Spirit Shampoo, or Charbon Shampoo.

After the dog has had all his toilet requisites attended to, do remember to reward him and to tell him how good he has been. Praise him for his beautiful looks; he just loves all the admiration which he richly deserves after all the patience he has endured for the sake of his curious master or mistress, who has spent such hours on this dog cult. If it gives pleasure, the dog will endure it, because he loves to please, but he would obviously much rather rush out and find a putrid old rabbit or bone to roll on, which are so much nicer smells than those funny shampoos which Missis is so fond of. Given half the chance, he will do just this. So take care he does not escape after all the time and care which has been spent on making him beautiful. Dogs really do like to feel fresh clean and groomed, just as do humans, and they wallow in love and admiration too.

CHAPTER III

Clipping, Trimming, Stripping and Plucking

GENERAL

Clipping, trimming, stripping and plucking can be considered the advanced grooming of a dog. Some breeds are lucky, and require none of these attentions. Whilst others need only tidying up with trimming scissors round the mouth, the feet and the ears. Breeds like the Pomeranian, require quite an amount of time spent on scissoring, whilst breeds like the Show Poodle and the American Cocker Spaniel spend hours of their lives being bathed, clipped, and trimmed. Most of the Terriers, however, spend hours of their lives having their coats plucked, stripped, trimmed and even clipped.

INSTRUMENTS REQUIRED FOR TRIMMING AND CLIPPING

A bad carpenter blames his tools, but there is no doubt at all that if a dog has to be clipped and trimmed, then it is far pleasanter and better in every way to work with good tools. These are not necessarily always the most expensive, though this is often the case. Such tools include clippers, scissors, thinning shears, etc.

CLIPPERS

There are quite a variety of clippers to choose from, both foreign and British makes. There are hand clippers and electric clippers, but if a dog requires much clipping, then it is well worth investing in the best available. Naturally every poodle parlour has its own preferences for certain clippers. It is a matter of discussing with the experts which they find the best, then to have a look at them all, and finally to decide which is the best for the purpose for which they are required. I personally prefer the new Oster A5 and the Aesculap. Both are excellent machines as are many other well-known makes. The selection of a particular machine depends largely on the availability of servicing and also the price.

HAND CLIPPERS

These are perfectly adequate for a small amount of clipping and for use on dogs which will not tolerate the noise of an electric clipper. These clippers are a little difficult to use until the knack is mastered. The blade requires to be made to work as fast as possible, but at the same time, the area covered must be done very slowly. There are several companies which make a good hand model, the blades coming in various sizes. Before buying a pair make certain that a good demonstration is given, because there is quite a knack in handling them. Like all implements, clippers require careful maintenance and frequent oiling and cleaning. The blades should be kept packed away in brown paper which has been well oiled as they are inclined to rust. It is quite a good idea to keep the blades so wrapped in a plastic bag. I keep mine in small perspex containers. The clippers should be kept in the grooming box, either in plastic bags or their own special box.

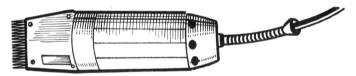

Clippers

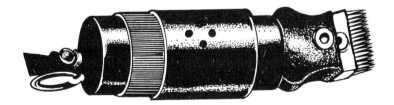

Clippers

ELECTRIC CLIPPERS

After using electric clippers there must be few people indeed who would wish to revert to hand clippers. It would be something like reverting to sweeping a carpet by hand instead of vacuum cleaning it.

Once again different people prefer different machines and so, before investing in a pair of clippers, it is worth while talking to the experts before finally deciding to invest in a particular make. There are always new makes and models coming on to the market, and some are more suitable for certain breeds than others. They vary in the number of heads and sizes which can be obtained, and they vary too in balance, weight and noise, and in the way in which the blades can be changed, all of which should be considered before purchasing. Most electric clippers are under guarantee, generally one year. Like all machinery, they do however require care and maintenance. They should not be permitted to be used if they get hot, and the blades require to be sharpened and oiled frequently. Whatever make is finally chosen, it is important to read the instructions and to carry out the maintenance implicitly to ensure the long life of the machine.

Up to date the most popular makes have been the German Aesculap and the new American Oster A5 clipper. The Oster A2 Model is also popular and there is a wide selection of fitted blades to suit all coats and clips. In fact, the choice of clipper is really quite large, and needs going into thoroughly. Most clippers have interchangeable heads, which are required for Poodles and American Cocker Spaniels. It is important when buying a pair of clippers to choose a make which runs quietly, is well balanced and steady, and is not too heavy, and that has heads which are quickly and easily attached and detached. In poodle parlours where several clipper heads are necessary, instead of changing the clipper head, there are several electric clippers with different sized blades left on permanently and the dog is moved from clipper to clipper.

CLIPPING WITH ELECTRIC CLIPPERS

This is not at all difficult to master; just a little patience is required and if possible, a lesson or two from an expert and a well experienced good, quiet dog to practise on. It is an excellent idea to watch an expert clip and trim one side of a dog, and then to try and copy the procedure on the other side, under supervision. It is surprising how much one does not take in by just watching someone clip.

Actually to clip and trim whilst being watched is definitely better, since one learns by one's mistakes!

It is better to clip a dog after he has been bathed, because clean hair does not clog the clipper with dirt, and it is therefore easier to clip. If dogs are not bathed before being clipped, they are particularly susceptible to getting a skin rash from dirty blades. This is more likely to occur in a dog parlour. Care must be taken to use the right blade to obtain any particular effect. When using a fine blade, great care must be taken that it is not cutting the hair too close to the skin. If this occurs, it can cause a nasty, septic, skin rash. If this should happen, a dusting with a special antibiotic skin powder should prevent the area from going septic. The edge of the ears is another place which is liable to become nicked unless great care is taken. Special care must also be taken when clipping near the eyes, the corners of the lips, round the anus, the teats and the genital organs, and of course in between the toes.

The clippers should be held well balanced in the down-turned palm of the hand. The teeth and the blade should be slightly tilted, when working, so that the hair is picked up between the teeth; and, as the teeth become clogged up with hair, this should be removed by gently brushing out with a small toothbrush or a specially provided brush to go with the clippers. There should be a definite order of work when clipping, and the same routine should always be adhered to.

ACCIDENTS

Unfortunately accidents are not uncommon whilst a dog is being clipped and trimmed. Nicking the skin, particularly the lips, the edge of the ears, the eyes, the tongue, the genitals, the teats the anus and the toes are probably the most vulnerable areas. More serious accidents occur if actual contact with the dog is lost during his barbering, the most common one being if the dog is left alone.

When clipping or trimming a dog, it is tremendously important that actual contact with the dog would never be lost. One hand must always be in constant contact with him, in order to prevent him from jumping off the table. If the dog feels the loss of constraint, he will immediately try to get away, and, if he happens to be on a grooming aid, it is quite possible for the dog to hang himself.

Accidents are liable to occur when a clipper head is being changed, since two hands are required for this. The only way to accomplish

C

this safely is to hold the dog's tail with the last two fingers of the left hand, and then, holding the clipper with the remaining fingers and thumb insert the new clipper head with the other hand. In this way direct contact is never lost with the dog.

GENERAL RULES WHEN CLIPPING A DOG

Twenty-four Golden Rules when Clipping
1. Preferably always clip the dog after he has been bathed.
2. Clip with a good light.
3. A steady table is essential with a non-slippery surface.
4. If the dog is attached to a grooming aid NEVER leave him alone for one second. Many a dog has hanged itself by jumping off the table. If the dog is unattached, he can easily jump off the table and break a limb, so always keep contact with the dog.
5. Run the clippers for a few minutes to warm them up before starting on the dog.
6. Make certain that the grooming box and all blades are at hand.
7. Clip puppies between four and six weeks to get them used to the clippers. They are best done after exercise and a good meal as they will be quieter.
8. Allow young puppies to watch their parents being clipped and get them used to the noise and bustle of a clipping room.
9. Start with the complicated clipping which the dog objects to *least*. Some dogs dislike the face being clipped, others particularly dislike the feet.
10. Brush dog all through thoroughly before commencing to clip.
11. Clip feet, face, tummy and tail. Do the main coat roughly and then if the dog has not been bathed previously, bath him as there is not so much to dry in these cases.
12. Clip slowly, steadily and carefully. If the coat is dense it may require to be clipped several times over the same area.
13. Talk to the dog quietly and encourage and praise him.
14. Never smack a dog for fidgeting.
15. Never use too fine a blade as this can cause a clipper rash.
16. Treat clipper rash with a good antibiotic powder immediately it appears.
17. Stretch the skin over the mouth for doing the edges of the lips and use only the edge of the blade.

18. Stretch skin gently over the eyes with the thumb, making the eye close by stretching upwards and backwards, or cover eyes with the top of the hand.
19. Never clip against the skin of the hair on the penis.
20. Protect the genitals with the free hand when clipping near the area.
21. Protect teats with a comb.
22. Clip with the growth of the hair on the edge of the ears using the edge of the clipper.
23. When changing blades never lose contact with the dog, hold his tail in the crook of the little finger in the same hand holding the clipper, with the opposite hand change the blade. The well-trained dog will not try to jump off a table if he still feels the human contact.
24. Frequently oil and clean and sharpen blades according to instructions.

SCISSORS

There is a great variety of types and many makes of scissors to choose from. Once again, it is well worth investing in the best. The best, of course, means the best for the requirement. Different breeds require different types of scissoring. Most breeds which require much scissoring can be done adequately with two or perhaps three pairs. I personally prefer the French scissors with seven-inch blades and a finger rest. These are beautifully balanced and extremely pleasant to use. German makes are always good but are inclined to be on the heavy side. Curved scissors are useful for Poodles and Bedlington Terriers. Scissors which have curved shanks are especially useful for getting into the more tricky and difficult places. Short scissors with points are useful for foot work, and blunt-ended surgical scissors are useful for removing stitches and for taking the hook ends off the claws in tiny puppies. Scissors with one blade finely serrated are also good because they hold the hair.

There are various kinds of thinning scissors, and they also come in various sizes and blades. There is a useful one which has both blades serrated. Another model has one side with an ordinary serrated edge whilst the other side is a cutting blade. There are also some extra fine thinning scissors, which are excellent for removing uneven edges after clipping.

The best scissors are always made of steel and are never stainless, so that they require to be kept wrapped up in oiled brown paper, in order not to rust. Stainless steel scissors are never so sharp as non-stainless.

To test the balance of a pair of scissors, place them on a finger so that the screw is in the centre. If the scissors are well balanced, they will remain in the horizontal position. If they are not perfectly balanced, the finger end will go over to one side, whilst if the scissors are badly balanced, they will topple off the finger altogether. It is well worth choosing a perfectly balanced pair of scissors, because they are much pleasanter to use and they will last for years.

THE CORRECT METHOD OF HOLDING SCISSORS

As with most tools, there is a right way and a wrong way to hold them, and obviously if scissors are held correctly the best results will be obtained. Perhaps even more important it will be found to be far less tiring if they are held correctly.

1. Place the thumb through the thumb hole, which in most scissors is slightly larger.
2. Place the third finger through the finger hole.
3. Place the little finger underneath the open shank at the end of the finger hole.
4. The index finger and the middle finger are placed underneath the shank which gives greater control while scissoring.
5. When scissoring keep the lower shears still, using the thumb to control the actual scissoring.

If this method of holding the shears is observed it will be found that the hand becomes less tired, particularly if there is to be a lot of scissoring required at one time. If the hand or fingers become tired the hold can be changed so that the middle finger goes through the finger hole, instead of the third finger, but it will be found that the correct method of working with scissors is better.

MAINTENANCE OF CLIPPERS AND SCISSORS

As with all dog grooming tools and equipment, it is important that clippers and scissors should be kept clean and, if necessary, disinfected. Brushes and combs and even the tooth brush used for cleaning the clipper blades should be washed regularly and dipped in disinfectant.

Clipper blades must have the teeth brushed clean. It is an excellent idea to run the blade occasionally in petrol, methylated spirits or lighter fuel. There are also special preparations made for the purpose. They should then be wiped clean with absorbent paper or an old cotton rag, dismantled carefully, and wiped over with a fine sewing machine oil.

Paraffin causes skin rashes and so should not be used. Aesculap blades have tiny squares on which to run. These and the thin felting require oiling frequently, but the oil must not get on to the blades.

After cleaning and oiling, the heads should be wrapped up carefully in brown paper which has been well oiled and they should then be stored in a dry place. If the clipping heads and scissors are not oiled and kept wrapped up, they tend to rust extremely easily. All these special clippers and scissors can be obtained from leading pet stores, or they can be bought at stalls at the leading Dog Shows. The big firms advertize in the dog papers, and their products can be ordered by mail. It is certainly worth selecting the best tools required, and it is more than worth while taking care of these tools after buying them, as they are by no means cheap. I would most certainly always recommend electric clippers as opposed to the hand manipulated ones, however small the area the dog requires to have clipped.

THINNING SHEARS

There are a variety of sizes and blades to choose from. The double-serrated blade and the single-serrated blade are used for different purposes. The extra fine-bladed shears are made in the U.S.A., Germany, France and Finland. They are available with 22, 30 or 46 teeth. These thinning shears are extremely useful for removing the ridges, where a fine clip has been used next to a longer clip. The best shears are undoubtedly the ones with 46 teeth. They are excellent for removing the undercoat, and save time and energy in comparison with the shears with less teeth. When thinning the coat on the back, the thinning shears should always be used in the opposite direction of the coat growth and almost never across it. Cutting the hair across generally causes unsightly ridges, which are extremely ugly, and show up a novice's work as opposed to that of a professional. After the undercoat has been removed, the top guard hairs can be shortened. This is done by slowly pulling the scissors upwards through the coat while cutting, and finally cutting with the growth on top of the coat as opposed to underneath. So useful are the fine thinning shears that I feel that no dog owner should be without a pair of the 46 toothed variety.

RAZOR COMBS

These are useful for getting rid of ridges left after clipping, but they are not so effective as good fine thinning shears. They contain a razor blade, which needs to be really sharp to obtain the best results. Razor combs are more usually used for stripping.

PLUCKING AND STRIPPING

This method of grooming a dog is generally employed for Terriers and the English spaniels, although breeds like the Irish Wolfhound do have the coat tidied up with a stripping comb twice a year when moulting. Neither plucking or stripping a dog should be employed unless he is moulting, but unfortunately many breeds are both plucked and stripped in preparation for shows when they are not moulting, and to my mind this is exceedingly cruel. I think it is definitely kinder to clip the coat and to remove the undercoat with fine thinning shears, but the experts shudder at such a thought. Breeds which live in the house, or under much artificial light and heat, however, probably moult all the year round, so that if these dogs are stripped and plucked regularly it probably does not hurt them.

PLUCKING

This is performed with the thumb and first finger and should only be done when the dog is definitely moulting. The "blown" dead hair is removed by picking up a small amount of hair at a time between the thumb and the first finger. This is tweaked out by a sharp downward movement, and should be accompanied by a slight twist, as with plucking birds. Only a very small area should be worked at a time, in order to avoid a moth-eaten appearance. The object is to remove the old hair evenly, leaving the soft new under-coat which is probably about half an inch long. Sometimes it is even less. Plucking is quite hard work on the fingers and, if done correctly, takes quite a long time to perform. The fingers may become sore and can be rubbed with chalk or a little resin, in order to obtain a better grip on the hair. Plucking should be done in a definite routine, starting at the back of the neck and gradually going over the whole dog. The face and head are done last. The final touches are finished with scissoring and trimming. Examples of breeds which undergo this method of plucking are the Fox Terrier, West Highland White and Sealyham Terrier.

STRIPPING

This is another method of dealing with the coat and is not so cruel or hard on the dog if he is not moulting. The hair is stripped off to the desired length by the implements used. (For implements available see paragraph on "Stripping Tools" below). The length is about a quarter of an inch when finished. Working a small area at a time, starting at the top of the neck and finishing with the head as with plucking. Once again, stripping the coat correctly takes many hours of time and probably years of experience into the bargain. Many pet owners resort to the clippers, using a coarse blade. This is reasonably effective and quick to do. The hair, however, is only cut so that it all remains the same length, and the old, dead hair still remains in the coat. Vigorous brushing with a hooked curry comb will help to get the dead hair out, but care must be taken not to damage or irritate the skin in the process. The final tidying up is done with scissoring.

THE HEAD AND FACE

I, personally, think it is extremely cruel to try to pluck or strip the head and face. Most experts agree with this, and this area is generally gone over with electric clippers, which produces an extremely good, neat result.

STRIPPING TOOLS

These consist of a stripping comb which is made of metal, one edge having a serrated blade. The handle can be of either bone or metal. A stripping knife is somewhat similar, with one serrated edge and a handle in which the knife can be enclosed, rather similar to a pen-knife or an old-fashioned cut-throat-razor. A pocket stripping knife again resembles a double-bladed pen-knife, except that both the blades have serrated edges, though these are of different thicknesses. A very useful implement is the Duplex dresser. This has a handle with a razor blade attached by two screws, and it cuts the hair as it is drawn between the serrated edges. As with most grooming implements, breeders have their own individual choice. None of them is expensive, and so it is not a bad idea to have them all, trying each one out on a different breed.

HOW TO HOLD A STRIPPING COMB

The comb is held by the handle grasped solely with the four fingers, whilst the thumb is extended so that it rests against the back of the blade. A small tuft of hair is then grasped between the blade and the thumb. It is given a sharp twist and a pull, as in plucking birds, and out the hair comes. As with all grooming, it is entirely a matter of knack and practice. But one lesson from an expert is worth a hundred books on the subject.

CLIPPER RASH

This sometimes occur after clipping with a blunt blade, which pulls the hair instead of clipping it, or from using a blade which is too fine and which therefore scrapes the skin instead of actually clipping. Some breeds and some dogs within a breed are more susceptible than others to this trouble. It should, however, be taken seriously, as any secondary infection is very apt to spread. A large area of skin affected can injure the dog's general health besides being extremely painful. It is best to dry the area with an antibiotic powder. This can be sprayed on the area carefully for several days until a scab forms. Care must be taken when grooming that the scab is not knocked off before the skin has healed and the scab is ready to drop off on its own. The next grooming or clipping session must be done with extra care, and in the case of clipping, a coarser blade must be used.

Vitacoat make a preparation which is soothing for clipping rash. However, prevention is always better than cure, make certain that the blade is not blunt, and when using a fine blade, first make certain that it is clean; and then test that the blade is not too fine by examining carefully a small area that has been clipped by it, in order to make quite sure that all is well. If in any doubt, change to a coarser blade immediately. Always remember that some dogs have extra sensitive skins.

LEARN TO DEAL WITH YOUR OWN DOG

If a prospective owner has fallen for a beautiful long-coated breed or one which has a complicated grooming procedure, it is much more fun to learn to cope with the dog and to make time for regular grooming sessions than to take the dog to a beauty parlour. Even the most unintelligent person can learn to wield a pair of electric clippers. It is surprising what fun it is moulding and snipping away until the desired effect is obtained. Even if a fearful boob is made, the hair grows again extremely quickly and most mistakes are soon lost, and in a couple of weeks have disappeared.

I would never even have considered clipping a dog until my daughter bought four adult American Cocker Spaniels (after which she promptly waltzed off to the United States, leaving me to cope!) Three of them presented us with large litters, so that in just no time at all one had to become an expert! Previously, I had always gone for the breeds which were simple to groom, like my beloved Chihuahuas, but once again my daughter landed me with three Maltese bitches, and so there was nothing for it but to learn to cope.

Much as I grumble sometimes about the work of these breeds, I do find it extraordinarily relaxing to go and do a session of grooming and clipping. The end result is so well worthwhile, particularly too, if a friend can come and admire the work afterwards.

Beautifying a small breed and keeping it bathed and groomed is an excellent pastime for old people. It keeps their hands and wits supple, and it brings out the mother instincts in women . . . or perhaps they are childish instincts, like playing with dolls and babies! Whatever they are, it is great fun, and probably brings out latent artistic instincts too.

However, if the owner of one of these "hardwork" breeds is not inclined to spare the time titivating her dog, then it is absolutely essential that the dog should pay a regular visit to a dog parlour every six weeks; or it should be completely clipped or stripped. A breed like the Maltese or Shih Tzu must be brushed and combed daily, or certainly alternate days, if the coat is to be kept in reasonable-looking trim. Failing this, it is better to cut its coat all over to one length, leaving the ears, tail and beard long. People will perhaps wonder what breed you have. Perhaps it ought to be called a Clipmalt or a Cliptzu! as it bears little resemblance to the beautiful Maltese or Shih Tzu breeds seen at the shows; but nevertheless, the dog can look most attractive.

THE USE OF SCISSORS IN TRIMMING AND SCISSORING

Some breeds require the use only of scissors on their coat, like the Pomeranian. Other breeds, like Setters, Spaniels and Retrievers

c*

only require a little plucking or clipping and the use of the thinning shears to tidy them up, except in the U.S.A. where they are clipped up the neck two months before a show. The shears are generally only used on the skull, throat and leg feathering, underneath the chest, and on the tail. The best type of thinning scissors for these purposes is undoubtedly the forty-six toothed shears. The normal pair of shears with double serrated blades will work reasonably well, but thinning takes longer.

American Cockers require to have their ears and feet trimmed with the long, seven-inch, trimming scissors. They also require their coat to be thinned with the serrated thinning scissors, and the extra finely serrated scissors with forty-six teeth are really excellent, and are a great help for removing clipping edges and generally thinning out the undercoat. A razor comb is quite useful too.

Disinfect blades after use, and between dogs

12

Lubricate and oil clippers frequently. Keep blades wrapped in oiled brown paper

11

1 Use good clippers and sharp blades

10

2 A firm, non-slippery table and a good light

Take care clipping the tail and near the anus

9

3 Start clipping a puppy as early as possible

Use only the edge of blade on lips

8

4 Do not clip a dirty, ungroomed dog

Stretch skin on eye and mouth when clipping

7

5 Guard against clipper rash and recognize, signs and symptons

Always clip down the edge of the ears to avoid nicking

6 Never clip against the growth on the penis

CLIPPING RULES

TIPPING THE COAT

Most long-coated breeds at sometime during the year get rather untidy, straggly coats. The ends become thin and brittle, giving the coat an 'out of coat' appearance. The look of the coat can be very much improved if the ends are cut evenly and clubbed. If the ruff becomes straggly in breeds like the Pomeranian where a large round ruff is required, the effect will be tremendously improved if the ends are tipped. It may be necessary to take off an inch or more, but the effect is to make the coat look much thicker. The dog should be placed on the table against the light. The coat should then be brushed downwards. The trimming should then start from the bottom upwards all the way, snipping in layers of not more than one inch at a time, taking care to keep all the hair cut in a circle. Brush the coat in many directions and re-tip for the final finish.

Breeds which have their hair cut off to one inch for the hot weather, or Poodle puppies from twelve to sixteen weeks, or pet Maltese, can all have their coat cut in a similar manner. It is apt to make the coat grow in thicker later on, which, in some breeds, is a decided advantage. In some breeds, where the coat is long, several inches may be trimmed off to advantage, the exact place being seen against the light as the hair is flipped up layer by layer.

TRIMMING AND SCISSORING

This is best done in most breeds using a comb. The hair is combed up almost to its extremity and the end of the hair is cut off just above the comb. This certainly helps to prevent ridging, which is unsightly and takes quite a time to grow out.

Great care must be taken when using scissors anywhere near the eyes, mouth, teats or genital parts, because quite serious accidents have occurred when a dog has moved suddenly and unexpectedly. The hair lifted up with the comb and then cut to the desired length gives added protection.

TRIMMING THE PADS

Trimming the pads requires care because dogs usually do not like this as it tickles. The pads must be spread apart sufficiently by pressing the first finger between the depression above the large pad. This pressure spreads out the webbed toes and then automatically makes it possible to snip the hair away from between the pads without nicking the skin. Most of the long-coated breeds have their feet trimmed to the edge of the toes in a semi-circle. The hair round the feet of the Afghan, however and some other breeds are left untrimmed. Breeders believe that hair left between the pads prevents these hounds from slipping when going over hard rocks and protecting the pads.

CHAPTER IV

External Parasites

EXTERNAL PARASITES

However well it is groomed, and however beautifully looked after, even the most fastidiously kept dog is unfortunately quite capable of catching and harbouring fleas, ticks, lice, harvest bugs, mites and other parasites. Country dogs are naturally more prone to parasites than the town dogs. They can readily be caught off the ground or from animals such as hedgehogs, which are often teeming with them, as also are rats, rabbits, field mice, etc. To prevent the invasion of parasites dogs require regular, careful and thorough grooming. Not only must the body coat be searched for the invaders, but also the insides of the ears, the ear flaps and the joints of the legs. Parasites cause enormous discomfort to a dog, and the irritation and scratching must nearly drive him to distraction. Parasites both external and internal are the cause of many troubles, one category damaging the outside of the body, the other the inside, both directly and indirectly. One of the most difficult to contend with are fleas. If a serious infestation of them gets out of hand, the many troubles which they cause may be almost impossible to eradicate.

In these days it is reasonably easy to rid a dog of an infestation of parasites, provided that the infestation is noticed immediately. All that is required is constant vigilance in order not to miss the first signs of irritation or scratching, and to act promptly to get rid of the trouble immediately. In some countries it is virtually impossible to keep dogs absolutely free of parasites for long. Most external parasites can, however, be destroyed by special insecticides, but re-infestation is often difficult to prevent. Rotenone is an ingredient used in the best dressings basically designed for use on dogs and all have a residual effect. The rate at which a dog becomes reinfested varies according to the amount of challenge from fleas and other external parasites in the dog's environment, and also varies according to the time of year.

INSECTICIDES

There are insecticide powders which are made particularly for dogs. These should be sprinkled on the skin and coat as directed. Chlordane is a particularly potent insecticide. Some of the powders which contain D.D.T. are *not* suitable for cats because cats lick their coats. If a dog is unfortunate enough to become infested with any of the external parasites, any cat or cats in the household should also be treated with a correct cat insecticide powder. The cats should be wormed too as well as the dogs, since each can pass on fleas to the other. All the areas where the dogs sleep or play must likewise be treated against infestations.

PARASITES WHICH CAUSE TROUBLES TO THE DOG

It may be considered a little out of place to describe dog parasites in detail in a grooming book, because there must be few dog owners indeed who would bother to read a chapter on dog ailments if their dogs were healthy and well.

But, in the case of parasite infestation, prevention is better than cure. It is therefore, really rather important that a dog owner should arm himself with information about parasite prevention and cure. In actual fact, the life cycle of the various parasites described is tremendously fascinating.

It is during the grooming procedures that parasitic troubles are most likely to be noticed, and this is the reason that the life cycle of parasites is included. If the dog owner can be made aware of how serious parasites can be, and can also be made to understand a little concerning how the various parasites breed and live, it will help considerably with the treatment and extermination procedures that are necessary. Unfortunately, many of the treatments take time, and they must all be carried out with meticulous accuracy. Not only must they be done correctly, but many of the treatments require to be followed up at regular intervals in accordance with the life-cycle of the parasite involved. The prevention of re-infestation too is tremendously important and often not easy to control once started.

The dog owner, however, need not panic if he finds a scab or a

EXTERNAL PARASITES

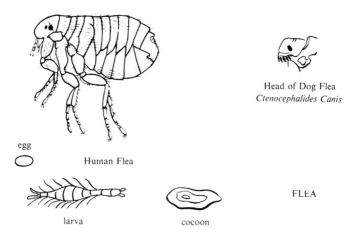

Head of Dog Flea
Ctenocephalides Canis

egg

Human Flea

larva

cocoon

FLEA

Hair with
nit cemented
at base

Sucking Louse

Biting Louse

LICE

Adult Female Tick
before feeding

Adult Male Tick
before feeding

DOG TICKS

flea upon his dog, though on the other hand he should not ignore them either, because both could be serious unless something is done about them immediately. The life cycle of the various parasites described is extraordinarily interesting. When it is realized how quickly they breed and what a short interval there is between one generation and the next, and when one learns that some of the external parasites lay five or six thousand eggs, whilst some of the internal parasites lay eighty million eggs, one wonders how it is that the entire earth is not infested with parasites. Nature is certainly very generous!

One shudders to imagine too, what it must have been like to live only a few centuries ago, when the cause of the plague was unknown, and when people who were infested with the itch mite had no idea what caused the intense irritation. It was often believed to be caused by 'improper living', bad blood, immorality or something else unconnected, and hence the expression "the seven year itch". There was no known way of getting rid of the irritation, since the cause was not known to be due to mites, and there was, therefore, no way of killing them. So the mites just went on breeding, and they bred and multiplied in the unfortunate host. Men, dogs, rabbits and ferrets are all attacked by this particular mite.

To keep a dog happy and healthy, it is obvious that he must be kept free of both internal and external parasites. Many dog owners, however, do not take this seriously enough. It is not difficult in these days, with all the powders, sprays and medicaments that are provided to destroy these pests. It is sometimes, however, more difficult to prevent a re-infestation when there has once been an infestation.

Regular grooming, regular use of flea powder, and regular worming once a year, will help to defeat the invasion of fleas and worm parasites, provided that all excreta is removed and burnt immediately. It should go without saying that immediate treatment is essential the moment any form of parasite is suspected. In areas where parasites are known to exist in prodigious numbers, as they do in many parts of the world, dogs should have frequent and regular dips to prevent infestations. The dog's faeces should be examined regularly for worm eggs, and if these are present, the dog must naturally be wormed accordingly.

FLEAS

It comes as a somewhat sobering thought that there are nearly

2,000 species of flea, and that their major evolutionary phases were passed over forty million years ago. The order is known as siphonaptera, because they have a siphon-and-tube-like mouth piece, and they are wingless, 'aptera' meaning 'without wings'. The flea is rather flat from side to side and has a tough, leathery body, from which protrude stiff hairs and spines projecting backwards, and it has extremely powerful hind legs for jumping. A flea travels rapidly by jumping when off its host.

Included amongst the 2,000 species of fleas there are 40 varieties found in Britain and there are four basic varieties which affect dogs. They are all external parasites, and include the dog flea, the human flea, the cat flea and the sticktight flea. Adult fleas will bite any host, but they are grouped according to the habits of their larvae, which feed on the debris found in the nests or dens of their preferred host, resulting in the adults only breeding in association with their own host.

STICKTIGHT FLEAS

These are sedentary fleas and sometimes known as Stickfast Fleas. They do not jump or move about, but they cling to the skin, often in quite large numbers. The female only burrows into the skin to lay her eggs, the area chosen being the soft skin of the feet, where the flea swells to the size of a pea. As soon as the eggs have been laid, they fall to the ground provided that conditions are just right, the larvae take about four weeks to hatch and they then develop in the same ways as all the other species of flea.

THE DOG FLEA

The male flea is black and the female is generally brown and is larger, being almost twice the size of the male. The dog flea can be distinguished by the two rows of dark bristles which it has on its head. The chief characteristic of the flea is its capability of rapidly crawling through the hair and then its sudden long hop, which it can make from one area to another or for that matter from one host to another, which may equally be some unsuspecting human standing close by. The dog flea, however, is more of a runner than a hopper. It is astonishing to realize that the human flea is capable of jumping a distance of thirteen inches in length and seven and threequarter inches in height. It is interesting that a similar jump for a man would be a jump of four hundred and fifty feet in length and two hundred and seventy-five feet in height. Fleas are often difficult to find on a dog, particularly on the long and heavily coated breeds. The presence of fleas may easily be recognized on dogs however by the tiny grey marks which they leave behind in patches. These patches could be said to resemble cigarette ash which sticks to the hair and skin and is in fact the flea excreta.

THE LIFE CYCLE OF THE FLEA

The complete life-cycle of the flea has four stages: egg, larva, pupa and flea. This period varies from seven to ten weeks, for thirty days of which it is adult (although this too can vary from eight to thirty-five days). During its life the flea is a blood sucker. Any one female flea can produce as many as three hundred to five hundred eggs in its life span. It is important to realize that the time can vary from between two and three weeks to between two and three months and occasionally up to two years from one generation of fleas to the next, the time factor depending on a number of circumstances and situations. Imagine the number of generations that can be pro-created in a few months under perfect conditions, when the time factor is only two weeks between generations.

The female generally lays her eggs in the host's den or nest. The eggs are smooth, small, oval and pearly white and they may be laid in the coat of the host in small batches. The eggs or the larvae then fall off when the animal moves or shakes, and some will naturally fall into cracks or crevices. Here the eggs will lie dormant until the conditions are right for them. Moisture and heat are essential for the flea eggs to hatch. The first warm, humid days will start the process, 70° F (21.1° C) being ideal. In ultra dry climates, fleas are almost unheard of and development is often impossible in hot, dry or cold climates. Within a few days of being laid (generally between two and fourteen days during the warm summer months or longer during the cold winter months) tiny eyeless, and footless larvae are born. The larva emerges from the egg by splitting the covering with a spine on its head. The larvae are creamy white, slender, hairy worm-like creatures. They have a head, biting and chewing mouth parts, thirteen body segments, and are somewhat hairy in appearance, but they are not at this stage of their existence para-sitic. These larvae scavenge round and feed on loose hair and skin scales and faeces of adult fleas and dog faeces and also dust and dirt. Fleas are wonderful feeders, as their food supply of blood is readily available. Their faeces contain much undigested blood and this is an essential element in the food of the larvae. The iron content in the blood helps to develop their hard shell-like covering. They continue to grow and live this part of their lives in cracks and crevices in the floor, but they do not live on hosts. This period generally lasts between one and five weeks and occasionally longer. They spend their time scavenging unless disturbed, when they roll up into a spiral. If two larvae are kept without food in an enclosed space, they attack each other in a death grip, tail in mouth, and eat each other until both die. When the larvae becomes fully grown, they salivate a silky thread, bend up into a U shape and spin a flat, thin, silky cocoon, the outer surface of which is covered with grains of sand or fragments of the surrounding debris. In the interior of this lies the pupa, and the cocoon remains hidden in the debris. This stage may last anything from five days to five weeks before a typical flea finally emerges. It is possible, however, if conditions are not correct, for the pupa to pass an entire winter in the cocoon before becoming a flea. When it finally emerges as a flea, the adult is immediately attracted by the first passing host. It is then ready to start its blood sucking activities immediately. Although most fleas

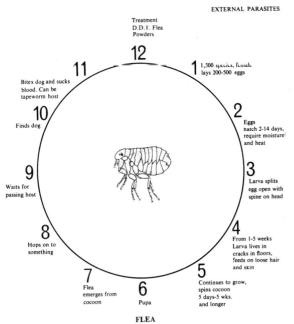

EXTERNAL PARASITES

Treatment
D.D.T. Flea
Powders

12

11
Bites dog and sucks
blood. Can be
tapeworm host

1 1,500 species, female
lays 200-500 eggs

10
Finds dog

2
Eggs
hatch 2-14 days,
require moisture
and heat

9
Waits for
passing host

3
Larva splits
egg open with
spine on head

8
Hops on to
something

4
From 1-5 weeks
Larva lives in
cracks in floors,
feeds on loose hair
and skin

7
Flea
emerges from
cocoon

6
Pupa

5
Continues to grow,
spins cocoon
5 days-5 wks.
and longer

FLEA

will change their hosts—the exceptions being the swallow flea and the rabbit flea—they do not set up a breeding population unless they are with their specific host or one similar to it. Fleas require hosts which have nests or lairs, and they will not infest nomadic animals like horses or cattle except as strays. They do, however, travel great distances, for example on migrant birds, rats, foxes, wasps, or humans, or even carried by the wind.

It is interesting that an adult flea can live for long periods without food. It is remarkable indeed that it is possible to keep a flea alive after a good feed of blood between fifty and one hundred days, but what really is astonishing is that unfed fleas have been kept alive between one and two years. Such is the versatility of the flea.

HOW THE FLEA BITES

Fleas first lubricate the area near the site to be punctured with regurgitated saliva and partly digested blood. They may pass their excreta here too, and they may contain harmful or dangerous micro-organisms, these will quickly spread into the bite, and these can then be transmitted from one host to another. This was how bubonic plague was passed and carried from infected rats to fleas. The plague originated in the Nile valley and rapidly spread throughout the world. The fleas caught the infection from the rats and passed it on to their hosts. The cause of bubonic plague was not discovered until 1894, although it was known as early as the sixteenth century that insects could carry disease. Rats also act as reservoirs for endemic typhus which can be transmitted to man by two types of flea.

After the flea has had its meal of blood, the punctured area does not generally become sore for several days and sometimes not for a week afterwards. There are generally two or three bites in a row, and these can set up quite a nasty irritation in a small area. Some people and some animals are more sensitive to the bites than others. Unfortunately, cat fleas, human fleas and dog fleas will exchange host quite readily, but they each prefer their own particular host if available.

It is quite horrifying to think that even one stray dog or cat could easily shed sufficient flea eggs and larvae on the premises of a kennel to start quite a serious infestation. If larvae are found in the house, they have probably come from eggs which have been shaken off by a dog or a cat. If the correct host is not available, the flea will make do with the nearest human, or some other animal. In a survey of two thousand fleas collected at random off humans in England half of them were found to be dog fleas.

CATCHING FLEAS

Trying to catch live fleas can be quite difficult, because they are capable of moving extremely rapidly through a dog's coat. If caught, they are not easy to kill as they have a remarkable protection against pressure. Squeezing one between the finger and thumb will have no effect on the flea and it will just hop off as though nothing had happened. If, however, one is quick enough and clever enough to catch a flea, the only way to kill it successfully is to squash it between the two thumb nails, until it pops. Only when the 'pop' is heard will it be quite certain that the flea is dead, otherwise it will just hop off and get on with laying its five hundred eggs.

It has been known for several centuries how some foxes have been clever enough to rid themselves of fleas. Thomas Moffett (Moufet) reported in 1634 that he had watched a fox gathering wool and feathers off briar hedges and various bushes until he had accumulated a large ball. The fox then held the ball in his mouth and waded into the water nearby, entering slowly until his nose was left above water. The fox then dropped the ball and waded back to dry land as fast as possible. The ball of wool and feathers was full of fleas which had escaped onto the ball instead of remaining on the fox where they would have drowned. A ball of moss may be substituted for the wool. A similar story was reported in 1944 in the U.S.A., and there are probably many similar accounts, as there are with other animals.

THE DANGER OF FLEAS

The real danger of fleas is not so much the misery and irritation that they cause by their biting and their constant running up and down the skin, but because they can carry and spread micro-organisms. They are also the intermediate hosts of the tape worm and they are known to spread certain summer skin diseases as well as the deadly bubonic plague, and myxomatosis in rabbits, and they can cause loss of weight and poor coats. Fleas breed rapidly and unless they are brought under control, a serious infestation can arise. Once having moved into a premises so to speak, they are extremely difficult to dislodge, even with the constant use of insecticides.

Few dog owners realize how serious it can be for a dog to have fleas, since fleas are the indirect cause of so many troubles. Consequently, even one flea should be regarded with concern. What happens is that a flea that has eaten a worm egg bites a dog. The dog will promptly try and scratch the place where he has been bitten. If he cannot reach the area he will scratch the nearest place that he can reach to where the flea has bitten him. If the irritation is severe, the constant scratching may even break the skin and a bald or septic spot may result. The dog will naturally try if possible to catch the flea, and he will often be seen nibbling away in a particular spot in his coat until he catches the flea between his front teeth. He then swallows the flea and trouble then occurs if the flea itself has already swallowed an embryonated tape worm egg. In this way the flea is the intermediate host of the tape worm, and the tape worm cycle commences.

LICE

Lice are also external parasites. There are several thousand known species and they are mostly red, grey or blue in colour, and they all have a similar life history. There are two distinct species of lice which afflict the dog. The biting louse and the sucking louse.

(a) The Biting Lice

There are 250 species of these. They feed on the skin scales and organic matter, but they do not suck blood for their main nourishment. The eggs hatch in five to eight days and the biting lice are mature in two to three weeks after hatching. They may be found on any part of the body.

(b) The Sucking Lice

There are at least 230 known species of sucking lice, and there are probably many more yet to be discovered. Sucking lice feed on blood and serum from the host, and their eggs take ten or twelve days to hatch. They mature in eight to sixteen days. They infest a large range of mammals including elephants and seals, but not birds.

Like the flea the louse is a wingless insect, it has a compressed head and strong claws which are developed for clinging. The louse lives out its entire life under normal circumstances on an animal or bird. As soon as it is hatched, the louse burrows into the coat with its tongue, teeth and feet and fastens its mouth piece into the skin. The female louse, however, lets go of the skin of the host after she has been mated, and she then crawls through the hair laying her eggs as she goes. These eggs are called nits, and she cements each egg carefully to one hair where they remain in situ even after the larvae have been hatched. The female lays ten eggs a day for twenty to thirty days, that is, between two hundred and three hundred eggs during her life span. These nits are tiny and greyish yellow in colour and are just visible to the naked eye. From the egg stage to death the lice remain in the same place unless they are knocked off or forcibly removed. A fully grown louse is smaller than a pin head so that it may be difficult to see especially on a heavily coated dog. From the moment that they are hatched they are identical with the adult except in size.

A large infestation of lice sucks so much blood from their host, and at the same time they give of such a tremendous amount of toxin, that the host frequently dies from poison as well as from acute anaemia. The louse which infests dogs will not stay or live on man.

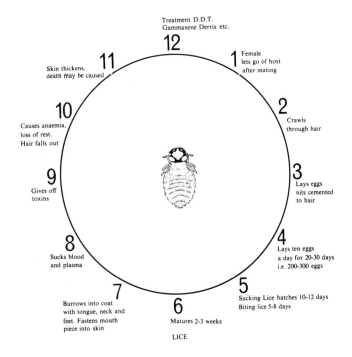

Treatment D.D.T.
Gammaxene Derris etc.

12

11 Skin thickens, death may be caused

1 Female lets go of host after mating

10 Causes anaemia, loss of rest. Hair falls out

2 Crawls through hair

9 Gives off toxins

3 Lays eggs nits cemented to hair

8 Sucks blood and plasma

4 Lays ten eggs a day for 20-30 days i.e. 200-300 eggs

7 Burrows into coat with tongue, neck and feet. Fastens mouth piece into skin

5 Sucking Lice hatches 10-12 days Biting lice 5-8 days

6 Matures 2-3 weeks

LICE

During the winter and cold months lice tend to hibernate, so that the best time to disinfest them is in the spring. Lice cause a great deal of irritation to the skin and they can not only wear away the hair, but they can damage the hair follicles as well. The constant irritation causes the dog loss of sleep and any form of rest, and not only does he lose his coat, but his general health suffers too from loss of blood and also from toxic effects. When the hair falls out, if it is examined carefully, the tiny eggs or nits can quite readily be seen glued to the side of the hairs.

Lice can be extremely dangerous to young puppies, because, if the dam is infested, they will naturally migrate to the young tender puppies in preference. If the louse infestation is large, the puppies may die of acute anaemia, so that all litters should be watched and guarded against lice. The bites frequently cause a thickening of the skin and balding which can sometimes be confused with mange. Lice can spread serious diseases such as typhus, louse-borne relapsing fever and trench fever.

SPREADING OF LICE

Although lice prefer to remain on one host, they may, in fact, change hosts. Lice move on to a new animal if the host dies, or if they become too numerous or as a result of close contact. Probably the chief way that they become transferred from a dog is when a dog scratches himself. The dog may not be able to dislodge a mature louse, but he may easily dislodge a young louse, and it will then probably attach itself to another dog within three days. When the dog scratches he also dislodges some of his coat hair and, if these hairs have nits cemented on them, they will lie on the ground until the time is propitious for them to hatch.

TREATMENT FOR LICE

The best treatment against lice is bathing with a Gammisomer Lindane wash or a shampoo which contains D.D.T., but the latter should not be used for cats. The dog is generally soaked in a wash for ten minutes and, if this is done, it will not only kill the lice but of more importance still it should destroy the eggs. The treatment should be repeated three times at eight or ten day intervals to make quite certain that everything has been destroyed. Sixide powder seems to be most effective as it apparently penetrates the leathery shells of the eggs. It is extremely important to bear in mind that, besides treating the dog it is also necessary to disinfect all bedding, beds, carpets and ground with which the dog has come into close contact. This may be carried out by liberal sprinkling of one of the new potent insecticide powders. This also should be repeated three times at the same time as the dog is treated, at weekly intervals.

To prevent reinfestation, the dog and his sleeping quarters and bed should be dusted regularly once a month but, after an infestation, treatment takes three weeks. Many dog owners do not realize this, and are extremely surprised to find that one or two applications of powder do not seem to bring lasting results. This is why it is so important to understand the life cycle of the various parasites.

Although lice can be found on any part of a dog's body, the favourite place is around the ears and particularly in the ear flap. They also favour the area at the base of the tail.

TICKS

These are considered one of the worst enemies of domestic animals, and there are a number of varieties. They transmit viral diseases, tick-born fever and other ailments. They also cause illness due to toxin. They are extremely annoying and are also difficult to get rid of. The tick has three stages of hosts. It first embeds itself in the skin of the host by its mouth piece, and while there it gorges itself with blood. To begin with it looks rather like a flat brown seed with a wart like appearance and seems to be standing on its head. It gorges the blood serum from its host and gradually swells until sometimes it becomer as large as a bean. As it fills up with blood it changes colour to a dark reddish blue.

The female stays in one spot from five to thirteen days. Between the fourth and sixth day she is visited by a male. The tiny male crawls under her and mates her while she is filling with blood. She then fills with more blood, releases her mouth parts and then drops off the host to the ground, she is by this time enormously engorged and almost helpless. Here she spends the next two to four weeks laying 4,000 to 6,500 eggs. These eggs are laid in the ground and are a brownish colour. After her enormous efforts she dies within a few days, so that she never sees the result of her labours, she may survive for several weeks. The eggs take one to two months to hatch, depending on the weather, and the six-legged larvae then crawl up any long grassy stems that may be near them.

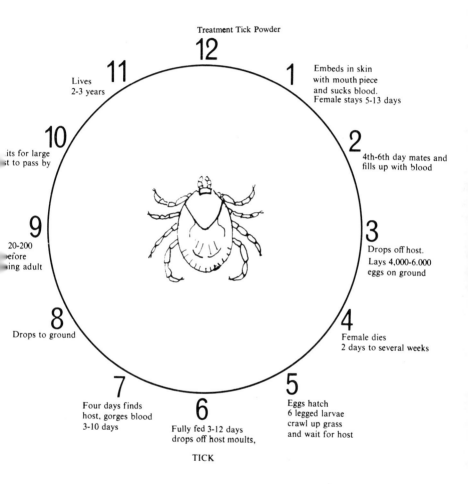

Treatment Tick Powder

12

11 — Lives 2-3 years

1 — Embeds in skin with mouth piece and sucks blood. Female stays 5-13 days

10 — its for large st to pass by

2 — 4th-6th day mates and fills up with blood

9 — 20-200 before ing adult

3 — Drops off host. Lays 4,000-6.000 eggs on ground

8 — Drops to ground

4 — Female dies 2 days to several weeks

7 — Four days finds host, gorges blood 3-10 days

6 — Fully fed 3-12 days drops off host moults,

5 — Eggs hatch 6 legged larvae crawl up grass and wait for host

TICK

Here they wait until a host passes by. This may be a rodent or some other animal. In suitable moist places they can survive alone for a year, but they are generally lucky to find a host within a few days of hatching. Not until they have actually sucked blood from a host can they carry diseases in their blood. They can become fully fed within three to twelve days.

Having accomplished their mission they drop off the obliging host and between one and thirty weeks later they shed their skins and after this become eight-legged nymphs. Before feeding, they are about 1/16 inch across. They may then have to wait between four days and a year before finding yet another host, generally another rodent. They then gorge themselves for another three to ten days and once again drop to the ground where they go through a final moult. This may take anything from twenty days to two hundred days before they eventually become adult. If they are unlucky and no large animal host passes by, they can live by themselves for a whole year. Ticks which actually reach adulthood probably have a two-to-three-year life cycle. Ticks gravitate towards paths where animals are likely to pass. It is interesting that there are not nearly so many ticks found in pathless woods as in woods where there are many tracks.

Dogs usually pick up ticks from long grasses and the ticks attach themselves to the stomach area and the pads of the feet. There are some varieties of tick which prefer the ears, but in general, they make for crevices rather than wide open spaces. Some brown dog ticks pass their early lives in houses and furniture, and occasionally adult ticks may be found in those places too.

TREATMENT AND EXTERMINATION

Care must be taken when removing ticks from the skin, because if the body is pulled off, the mouth pieces will remain in the dog's skin and these will turn septic causing nasty sores. An easy way to remove them is to paint them with petrol or some spirit like whisky (rather a waste of whisky at its present day price) and about 20 minutes after painting the body, it should be removed carefully with tweezers. The end of a lighted cigarette is a quick way of removing them as they soon release their mouth pieces when their rear end is burnt. This saves looking for the whisky and the tweezers.

Whichever method is adopted take care that neither touches the dog's skin. Ticks are particularly common in many areas of the U.S. owing to the climate and the prevalence of live stock. Ticks nevertheless cause great discomfort to the poor dog and, if there are a number of ticks sucking away, they cause a general debility and eventual anaemia.

Eradication is by the same method as for lice. Grass should be kept short and the area can be sprayed with insecticides. Tick bites should have iodine forced into them to prevent sepsis. Great care should be taken not to get any blood from the tick in the eyes or into any abrasions on the skin.

MANGE MITES WHICH AFFECT DOGS

There are numerous varieties of mite, and these, as well as ticks, are more closely related to spiders than to insects. Mites normally remain on one host, unless there is close enough contact to another which they can crawl to. Mites are all so tiny that many species are hardly visible to the naked eye. The only way that they can be correctly identified is under a microscope, so that if correct diagnosis is to be ascertained then a skin scraping is essential. As the mites multiply, their feedimg ground on the animal grows and scabs are then formed and the hair falls out. All varieties of mite secrete a poison, and it is this which causes the intense irritation. The females burrow and make tunnels to lay their eggs and they then die.

Demodectic
or Follicular Mange Mite

Sarcoptic Mange Mite

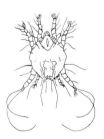

Otodectic Mange Mite
(Ear Mite)

EAR MITES

There is only one species of ear mite, called the *otodectes cynotis*, which causes otodectic or auricular mange. This mite lives and breeds in the soft skin lining the ear near the ear drum, and is also found on the external part of the ear.

It is interesting that the eggs are either hatched in the body of the female or two to four days after she has passed them. These larvae are six-legged. They turn into nymphs in two or three days and at this stage have eight legs, and they reach adulthood in three or four days. The breeding is so rapid that fertilization takes place between two and four days later, and the female soon starts laying her eggs. So rapid is the life story that it takes only from seven to eleven days from the egg stage to an adult mite. It is extremely important that dog owners should realize that a new batch of eggs is being laid about every ten to fourteen days.

These ear mites cause great irritation and distress to a dog. The discharge from the ear is a peculiar, dark, chocolate-brown, crumbly wax. It consists mostly of scabs, normal wax, plasma and lymph. The mite bites into the skin to suck the lymph and plasma.

It is quite easy to tell whether there are ear mites in the ear.

If a little of the ear wax is removed and spread in a little mineral oil on a piece of glass, an ordinary magnifying glass will show up sufficiently well whether there are mites present or not. They will resemble minute moving particles of dust. A veterinary surgeon using a strong lense can see the mites so well that they resemble crabs, and, if by any chance none is seen, eggs may be visible, so that diagnosis can be confirmed and treatment started.

SYMPTOMS OF EAR MANGE

The chief symptom is the intense irritation caused by the mites, which nearly drive the dog to distraction and, if not treated, the symptoms go from bad to worse. They may become so bad that the dog can become deaf and often has an inability to control his movements. A dog may be noticed to be walking along with its head on one side, and may be continually shaking its head sharply. When a dog does this, the mites are frequently shaken out and are liable to reach other animals nearby. This is particularly so just after treatment. The irritation is sometimes so intense that the continual scratching causes blood tumours which form between the layers of the ear flaps.

Canker is a loose term used for all ear trouble. The methods used to eradicate ear mites from the ear canal require a series of treatments. First the wax must be dissolved using alcohol, followed by a sulpha drug or something like Otodex or Ear-Rite is excellent since it dissolves the wax, and kills the mites. It is also antiseptic and contains a local anaesthetic which relieves the intense irritation and helps to prevent the dog scratching his ear.

Mites are generally killed in one application, but the eggs are seldom destroyed. Moreover, some mites will return later to their normal preferred habitat, so that treatments should be continued weekly for at least three weeks. Where there are a number of dogs, they should all be treated on the same day and each should be isolated from the others. The reason for this as stated previously is that the oil dissolves the wax and when a dog shakes his head some of the mites and wax fly out and could contaminate another dog.

Drops should be used for two or three days. Regular weekly treatments will prevent re-infestation, which is likely to occur in large kennels or where dogs are kept in close proximity to each other.

DEMODECTIC MANGE MITES

This is a mite of which there are a number of recognized species. The one which affects dogs is the demode canis.

This mite lives in the follicles of the skin. It is sometimes known as the red mange mite or the follicular mange mite. It can infest dogs and also cattle, sheep and even humans. The demodectic mite is a microscopic, slender, worm-like mite, which resembles a small cigar in shape. It has eight legs which are very short, and it lives its life deep in the hair follicles. The mites multiply so exceedingly rapidly that ten females could increase to more than 150,000 in one month.

So prodigious are these mites that one hundred females could produce two million offspring in a month, which is a most horrifying thought for any dog owner. The hair drops out in the infected areas causing bald spots. There are two forms of demodectic mange, one is pustular and the other squamous. There are often side complications of staphylococcus infections. These cause pimples which discharge a yellow cheese-like pus. The skin becomes red and the

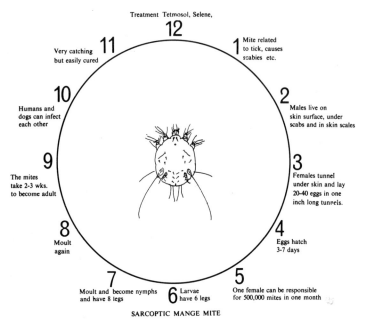

Treatment Tetmosol, Selene,
12

11 Very catching
but easily cured

1 Mite related
to tick, causes
scabies etc.

10 Humans and
dogs can infect
each other

2 Males live on
skin surface, under
scabs and in skin scales

9 The mites
take 2-3 wks.
to become adult

3 Females tunnel
under skin and lay
20-40 eggs in one
inch long tunnels.

8 Moult
again

4 Eggs hatch
3-7 days

7 Moult and become nymphs
and have 8 legs

6 Larvae
have 6 legs

5 One female can be responsible
for 500,000 mites in one month

SARCOPTIC MANGE MITE

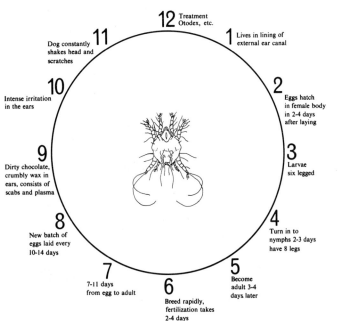

12 Treatment
Otodex, etc.

11 Dog constantly
shakes head and
scratches

1 Lives in lining of
external ear canal

10 Intense irritation
in the ears

2 Eggs hatch
in female body
in 2-4 days
after laying

9 Dirty chocolate,
crumbly wax in
ears, consists of
scabs and plasma

3 Larvae
six legged

8 New batch of
eggs laid every
10-14 days

4 Turn in to
nymphs 2-3 days
have 8 legs

7 7-11 days
from egg to adult

6 Breed rapidly,
fertilization takes
2-4 days

5 Become
adult 3-4
days later

OTODECTIC MANGE MITE

irritation is severe causing the dog to scratch incessantly, the hair comes out in tufts, pustules appear and often toxaemia sets in.

Unless the disease is treated early, the dog becomes thin and emaciated, and eventually dies. There is sometimes little pus, but this follicilar mange is characterized by a peculiar mousy smell. The squamous form causes pigmentation in the skin, and the hair falls out in rounded patches. This form of manage is often chronic.

The mange is first generally found on the muzzle, round the eyes, on the top of the head and the base of the tail, and also on the inside or front of the legs. The disease starts unobtrusively, and the unobservant dog owner may not notice the first few balding patches which appear on the dog. The balding areas are often irregular in shape and may in some cases join up to become one large bald patch. At this stage the irritation becomes intense, caused by the poison from the mites, and this is aggravated by the dog's constant scratching. The skin thickens and becomes red and, if left untreated, becomes raw and extremely sore.

Demodectic mange is a peculiar disease as a dog may have no signs of it whilst well, but odd bald spots may appear from time to time. When a dog is run down, coming into season, or after a litter. Puppies can produce it around teething time, even when the dam shows no sign of it. Some smooth-coated breeds like the Dachshund and the Miniature Pinscher are extremely prone to it, and black dogs in general often are. The mites do not seem to survive for more than three days if they are dislodged from the dog, so that it is safe to bring a new dog on the premises where a dog has previously suffered from demodectic mange. Humans can get infected and this is generally round the cheeks and nose, but luckily it is reasonably rare.

TREATMENTS

Veterinary surgeons all have their own pet cures, and nowadays mange is reasonably easy to cure, although dogs that have had it or are prone to it are liable to have relapses from time to time. Dog owners should therefore, be on the lookout for these signs when grooming their dogs.

There are many excellent drugs on the market, which are made up in penetrating oil or cream and these are gently massaged into the affected areas. The drugs penetrate the hair follicles, killing the mites. The rest of the dog should at the same time be liberally dusted with flea powder. This helps to prevent new areas from becoming infected.

There are numerous effective treatments. One of the best is a suspension shampoo, which has to be used about every five or six days. The solution must be massaged carefully into the skin and the lather must be left on for at least five or six minutes. GREAT CARE MUST BE TAKEN TO ENSURE THAT ALL THE SOLUTION IS THOROUGHLY RINSED OR SPRAYED OFF, It is a strong pesticide, and great care must be taken to see that it does not go anywhere near the eyes, nose, lips, genitals or anus, these areas should all be smeared with vaseline to protect them. Unfortunately, some dogs are allergic to it and may even develop a slight fever, and this may continue for as long as a week. Any sign and symptoms of allergy should be watched for when using such a strong solution.

Only a skin scraping can verify which particular mange is causing the disease, but demodectic mange is the more difficult to cure permanently.

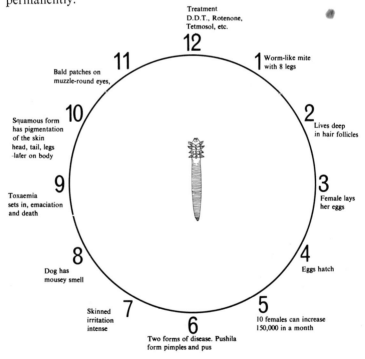

DEMODECTIC MANGE MITE

SARCOPTIC MANGE MITES

This is *sarcopters scabeii* of which there are numerous varieties. It is the same mite which causes scabies in humans. It is very catching, but luckily easy to cure. They cause a tremendous amount of damage to animals and birds, and they are just visible to the naked eye. The male has suckers on all its eight legs except the third pair, whilst the female has suckers on only the first two pairs. The other legs end in a long bristle. This mite is round and is related to the tick, and has eight legs when adult. It burrows beneath the skin in the less hairy areas of the body making tiny tunnels one inch long. It discharges a serum at the entrance to its burrow, which forms a dry pupule or scab.

The female lays between twenty and forty eggs and the eggs hatch in three to seven days. One female can be responsible for something like 500,000 mites in a month. The young new-born larvae have three pairs of legs, but they moult and become nymphs, and these moult in turn and take two to three weeks to become adult. Only the female mites burrow into the skin to lay their eggs. The other sarcoptic mites live on the surface of the skin, under the scabs and in the skin scales. For this reason they are easy to eradicate. This skin disease is, unfortunately, transmitted from dog to man or vice versa. It is often confused with dry eczema, and a definite diagnosis cannot be made until a skin scraping has been taken and examined under a microscope. Unfortunately, finding these mites in the skin is not particularly easy. It is much easier to find the follicular mange mite.

TREATMENT

There are numerous most effective drugs for curing sarcoptic mange. The disease reaches its peak in spring, and it declines at the end of the summer and during the autumn. Once again, veterinary surgeons have their own favourite prescriptions. Gammaisomer preparations are more effective than sulphur dressings. One prescription is used frequently and is generally diluted to one in nine with water, one third of the dog being covered daily for nine days. Since the disease is extremely catching, dogs must be isolated from each other. Provided that there are not very many scabs, they should be carefully removed with a little of the preparation as they appear. This is because the prescription is highly poisonous. An unsightly bald patch is left and it takes about six or seven weeks before the hair starts to grow again. All bedding should be destroyed daily and the scabs and hair from the dog should be burnt. The hands should be thoroughly washed after touching the dog, and the area where he has been standing should be disinfected and powdered with an insecticide.

HARVEST MITES

The harvest mite is sometimes called a chigger. It is of the species of *trombidium*. Under the microscope it resembles red pepper and it is blood red in colour. Its shape is similar to that of a tick. This mite burrows under the skin of various animals, including the dog and the cat, and unhappily man is not immune to it either. The mite causes an inflamed area on the skin and this can be seen with a red dot in the centre. It takes about two or three days before the spot becomes a blister, and eventually a scab is formed and, when this becomes completely dry, it finally falls off. The spots cause intense irritation.

TREATMENT

The best cure seems to be the application of strong ammonia on to the actual spot and then dusting with sulphur powder as prevention. Other useful preparations which seem quite effective are the Gammaisomers and 'Kurmange' sold under various names. These take longer to apply, but they are perhaps more lasting in their effect.

If a dog is noticed scratching suspect some form of parasite. The best way to look for fleas is to run a finger crosswise along the dog's back, turning the hair up slowly all the way from the tail to the head. Sometimes a flea will be seen making its way rapidly through the hair, but if there are no fleas to be seen their presence is reasonably easy to detect from their excreta, which resembles cigarette ash. If the trouble is lice, their little off-white eggs can generally be seen glued to the hairs. The best areas for finding lice on the dog are round the ears, the ear flaps, and around the tail area, particularly at the root of the tail.

TREATMENT AGAINST EXTERNAL PARASITES

A good general insecticidal powder should be used all over the dog, and special tablets may be given which work internally and which certainly help to keep fleas away. Some people prefer to use sprays, but if these are used, great care must be taken not to let any spray go near the eyes and nose. It is important too, that the preparation should be a non-toxic one. There are various baths and dips which are efficacious, most of these contain the same effective drugs in powder form and are made up to one gallon of water. They are reasonably long-lasting and are extremely effective, and these are strongly recommended if the infestation is more than extremely slight. Impregnated plastic collars are also wonderful parasite deterrents, and they last for three months. Fleas can be astonishingly difficult to get rid of, once they have moved into a premises, so that, as always, prevention is better than cure.

After a dog has been treated with powder or spray, it is extremely important to stand the dog on a sheet of newspaper and comb his coat very thoroughly with a fine comb. All the dead fleas will be combed out and the half dead will or stunned ones will drop out too. Just in case there are a few fleas, which might revive if given sufficient time, it is important to wrap up the newspaper and burn it immediately.

De-fleaing a dog alone is not sufficient, it is extremely important to deal with all the bedding, the bedding base or board and the kennel run, particularly powdering all the crevices and corners, and it is better to put down clean bedding every few days. This should be continued for a number of weeks until it is certain that there are no more fleas. I have found that fleas seem to disappear after the first frosts, but, unfortunately, it is only that their eggs are hibernating until the warmer weather returns. In any case, all dog bedding and sleeping quarters should be dusted with flea powder regularly once a month as a routine; and all dogs should be wormed annually, preferably in the early spring as well as at any time when the presence of worms is suspected.

Fleas cause worms in dogs, and this is the most important reason why so many precautions should be taken in keeping all dogs free from fleas.

INSECTICIDES

There are a great many insecticides on the market and these are by no means all suitable for all animals. It is therefore extremely important that the correct chemical should be used on any particular animal. Some insecticides can even lead to fatal poisoning. This may occur from absorption through the skin particularly from unsuitable sprays, or from inhalation of the droplets.

It is important when buying an insecticide to be quite certain that it is safe to use. The label should be read carefully and the instructions followed implicitly. Many flea powders, which are usually suitable against both lice and fleas, name an antidote. This is usually atropine, but it is worth while noting what it is, in case there should be trouble.

D.D.T. is one of the compounds used in many insecticides and these must on no account be used on cats. As an example as to how dangerous some chemicals can be to one set of animals, though harmless to another, some time ago a spray containing thiophosphate was used on fifty chickens and was found to be completely safe, but when used on 7,000 ducklings the whole lot died.

Insecticides should not be used on young puppies, and care must be taken with older dogs that they do not inhale the powder. The powder should be sprinkled on the coat, making quite certain that it goes on to the skin and does not just lie on top of the coat. The fleas run along the dog's skin and it is here that they must come in contact with the lethal powder.

Since even the best dogs can catch fleas, it is quite a wise precaution to dust all dogs monthly, unless they are a breed which is bathed frequently. These can probably be bathed in an anti insecticide shampoo which is long lasting and these shampoos are excellent pest destroyers.

If insecticide collars are used, insecticide powders must not be used at the same time.

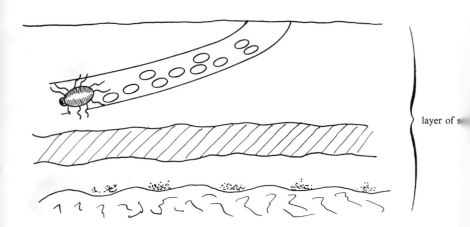

layer of s

ITCH MITE

Tunnelling into the skin where she lays 24 eggs and then dies

CHAPTER V

Internal Parasites

WORMS

Unfortunately internal parasites affect many animals, and are not uncommon in the dog. Parasites require to be dealt with both directly and indirectly so that they can be exterminated. Unfortunately there are some for which there is no drug as yet that is capable of destroying them without also destroying the host. Internal parasites not only damage the dog's body internally, but they cause a general loss of health and condition and in severe cases, can even be killers. The most common internal parasite which affects dogs are worms.

VARIETIES OF WORMS

There are many varieties of worms which infest dogs, these are round worms, tape worms, heart worms, hook worms, oesophagael worms, whip worms and fluke worms. Unfortunately there is no single drug as yet which will kill all varieties. Each type of worm requires its own special drug for its destruction. It is, therefore, essential that the veterinary surgeon should establish which variety is to be exterminated. This can easily be ascertained from the faeces of the dog, because if worms are present in the intestines, the stools will be teeming with eggs. These can be seen under a microscope quite easily. If actual worms or segments of worms are seen in the stools, tests are not usually necessary. As a general rule however, round worms are found in puppies and tape worms in the older dog, but there is actually no hard and fast rule about this.

ROUND WORMS

There are several different species of round worms which affect dogs, these include heart worms, lung worms, oesophageal worms, hook worms, whip worms and kidney worms. To dog owners, however, the term round worm generally refers to small yellowish white worms which are about five inches long. When they mature, these worms inhabit the intestines and stomach of the dog. These worms are smooth, round and pointed at both ends, and when

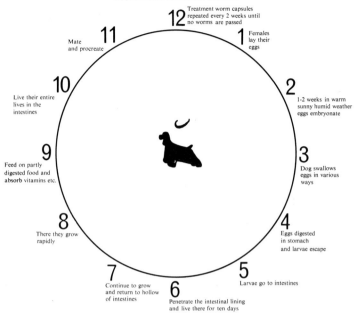

ROUND WORM TOXASCARIS LEONINA

12 Treatment worm capsules repeated every 2 weeks until no worms are passed

1 Females lay their eggs

11 Mate and procreate

2 1-2 weeks in warm sunny humid weather eggs embryonate

10 Live their entire lives in the intestines

3 Dog swallows eggs in various ways

9 Feed on partly digested food and absorb vitamins etc.

4 Eggs digested in stomach and larvae escape

8 There they grow rapidly

5 Larvae go to intestines

7 Continue to grow and return to hollow of intestines

6 Penetrate the intestinal lining and live there for ten days

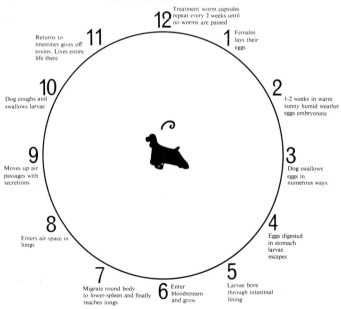

ROUND WORM TOXASCARIS CANIS

12 Treatment worm capsules repeat every 2 weeks until no worms are passed

1 Females lays their eggs

11 Returns to intestines gives off toxins. Lives entire life there

2 1-2 weeks in warm sunny humid weather eggs embryonate

10 Dog coughs and swallows larvae

3 Dog swallows eggs in numerous ways

9 Moves up air passages with secretions

4 Eggs digested in stomach larvae escapes

8 Enters air space in lungs

5 Larvae bore through intestinal lining

7 Migrate round body to lower-spleen and finally reaches lungs

6 Enter bloodstream and grow

alive are generally curled up. However, most dog owners see them when they are dead, and then they are stretched out rather like an open letter 'C'.

Most of the round worms have a similar life history, and it is important that all dog owners should take the trouble to understand what happens during this life cycle. If the life cycle of the round worm is properly understood, then the precautions necessary for their prevention and treatment for their extermination would be an undoubted blessing to the dog.

It is rather like the question, "Which came first, the chicken or the egg?" or "Where does the circle begin?" The diagrams of worm cycles on page 90 should give a quick idea as to the process of the interesting worm cycle. Within a week or two, an infected dog passes worm eggs every time it evacuates a stool. Provided that conditions of temperature and humidity are right, a tiny microscopic embryo develops in the worm egg. If, however, the worm eggs reach the ground and conditions are not perfect, it may take several weeks before the embryo develops. The dog owner should realize that the eggs in the embryonic stage are a potential source of infection for a future host. This is why it is so tremendously important that all dog excreta should be removed immediately.

Worm eggs are astonishingly tough, and they can survive in the ground long after the faeces have disintegrated and completely disappeared or have been hosed down or washed away from the dog runs. The eggs can remain alive anything up to five years before hatching. This gives some indication how terribly difficult it may be to eliminate the source of possible contamination.

Dogs and cats, and, for that matter, humans and animals can become infested in a variety of ways. Perhaps one of the most interesting facts about the worm cycle is that an embryonated worm egg cannot hatch until it has been swallowed by some creature, so that there has to be some intermediary host to incubate the egg and so start the worm cycle off.

CAUSES OF INFESTATION OF THE ROUND WORM

Domestic animals and humans can become infested in many ways. A puppy can suck a worm egg off its dam's teats, a kitten may play over an infected area and some tiny worm eggs could possibly stick to its paws. The kitten perhaps then licks her paws when washing herself and in the process she may swallow some worm eggs. An infested young puppy may perhaps defaecate in its food bowl, this often occurs when a puppy is kept in too small quarters, a dog may bury his bone in an infested area. A child may suck his thumb after playing in a contaminated sand-pit. A common source of tape worm infestation is caused by fleas, particularly the cat flea and the dog flea. These fleas feed on worm eggs which have reached the ground or they may even feed on the eggs as they are passed by the dog. The embryo incubates in the worm egg which is then inside the flea.

After the egg is swallowed by some animal or creature, it reaches the stomach quite quickly, the outer covering of the egg is immediately digested by the gastric juices in the stomach, this allows the embryo to escape, if the larvae is a toxascaris leonina it gravitates or works its way to the intestines. Here it burrows into the intestinal wall and remains there for about ten days, continuing its steady growth and development. It then re-enters the centre of the intestine until it becomes fully mature, here it continues to exist its entire life.

The *toxascaris canis* or *T. cati* are much more dangerous to their hosts. The larvae, when hatched, are about 1/100th of an inch long, it proceeds to bore its way through the dog's intestinal wall. From there it usually gets into the blood stream where it continues to grow. It is then carried to various parts of the body, through the liver, the heart, and eventually it reaches the lung. Here it moves from the blood stream into the air spaces of the lungs. It remains in the lungs for only a few days and then proceeds to climb up the trachea. This is the wind-pipe, where it is helped along by mucus secretions. When the larva reaches the top of the trachea, the irritation causes the dog to cough and clear its throat, and in so doing, coughs it up and swallows it.

By this time, the larva has grown to about one tenth of an inch in length, and once again it quickly reaches the intestines. Here it continues to develop, taking about ten weeks to mature and become an adult worm. When it is adult, it too lays its eggs, about eighty million of them—nature is always generous—and these again are passed in the excreta of the dog. This worm cycle continues ad infinitum until the host is killed or the worms are destroyed. The worms receive most of their nourishment from the tissues of their hosts (not, as many people think, from the food found in the intestine). This soon causes anaemia with a general loss of condition followed by a poor, dry staring coat. This is due to the loss of the valuable protein and minerals which are being absorbed by the worms. All this deprives the dog of vitamin B, particularly the most important B_{12} vitamin. The absorption by the worms of this vitamin may be so rapid that the dog can be quickly completely deprived of this essential vitamin altogether.

In young puppies the anaemia caused by a worm infestation can be extremely serious, and in severe cases it can cause stunted growth. Worms also produce toxins which are not as yet fully understood.

A front view of a Yorkshire Terrier who has grown a tremendous fore lock. This ust almost be a record for length.

Photo: Anne Cumbers

The migrations of larvae round the body are an additional hazard and can also be extremely dangerous, and can cause death by what is known as verminous pneumonia.

TROUBLES FROM WORM INFESTATIONS

Puppies can be infected prenatally, so that the signs and symptoms may be noticed at a very early age. The most dangerous period of worm infestation in a puppy is when it is two or three months old. A large infestation of worms can be a killer.

The infestation causes pale gums, irregular ravenous appetite or a depraved appetite, loss of weight, diarrhoea, sometimes with blood, or unformed bowel movements and/or constipation. There is generally colic, vomiting, a bloated stomach, bad breath, itching skin, irritability, a general listlessness and a dry, staring, out of condition coat.

There is often in addition, dehydration, and in severe cases, pneumonia, peritonitis occurs if the intestinal wall is perforated and if this occurs, death will ensue.

It is quite fantastic to think that over two thousand worms have been recovered from the excreta of one single dog. This alone shows how exceedingly important the control of worm infestations in dogs and cats must be and how important the elimination of the cause.

TAPE WORMS

The tape worm generally has two and sometimes three hosts to complete its life cycle. There are two types of tape worms, one has hooks and suckers and is known as the armed tape worm, and this clings to the intestines and is sometimes difficult to dislodge. The tiny head is so strong that it is able to keep the whole length of the tape worm in the intestine. The unarmed tape worm is easier to dislodge as it keeps its hold on the intestine by a pair of minute grooves. The tape worm has a number of varieties which affect different animals and man. The broad tape worm is often extremely long, and this can be as much as sixty feet in length, but in dogs it is somewhat less and is normally only about sixteen feet long. Imagine such a worm in a tiny Chihuahua. The rabbit host tape worm is sometimes five to six feet long. The unarmed tape worms which infest dogs are the fish host tape worm and often occur in dogs which are fed on fresh water fish, in certain areas of the world. A fully grown female is about eight to ten metres long in man and is capable of laying one million eggs per day.

All these worms are, unfortunately, extremely prolific in their egg production, the female whip worm, for instance, lays between 1,340 and 4,800 eggs per day. The segments of tape worms, which resemble rice, may be seen in the stools of an infested dog. These segments are teeming with eggs. When eggs become dried by the wind and sun, as they frequently do, they can be carried in dust by winds for miles from the area where they were first deposited.

DANGER OF WORM INFESTATION TO THE HUMAN

Worm infestation can be passed from dogs to humans. It is particularly liable to occur in the case of children. Should a child touch the faeces of an infested dog and then put its hands to its mouth, worm eggs which will be in the faeces, may be swallowed by the child and the eggs then quickly reach the stomach where the larvae escape and gravitate to the child's intestines and the worm cycle commences.

Tape worm infestations are particularly dangerous and they are of public health importance. Some years ago there was a national scare aroused by the dangers of the tape worm to humans. The press got hold of various stories and magnified them as they frequently do. It appeared that blindness had occurred in some children, and this, unfortunately, is quite possible. If worm eggs enter a human mouth, they are immediately swallowed and the eggs are hatched generally in the stomach and the larvae escape into the intestines. The larvae start on their normal migration round the body, but, finding themselves in the wrong host, they cannot complete their normal life cycle and they die. In the place where they die a small cyst forms. Should the cyst occur in the eye, blindness could result. If, however, the cyst occurs in some other unimportant part of the body, little damage is usually done. So, although blindness can occur, it is, luckily, exceedingly rare.

The importance of keeping dogs free from tape worms cannot be too strongly emphasized, and young children should not be permitted to play near dog excreta. Sand pits are often a source of infection from both dogs and cats. Dogs and puppies should not be permitted to lick the mouth or face as this is another time when infestation could be transmitted.

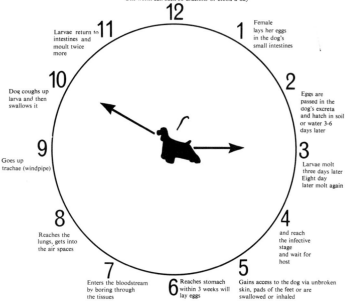

HOOK WORM CYCLE

Develop into Hookworms, cling
to small intestine and breed can cause death.
One worm can suck 30 drachms of blood a day

12

11 Larvae return to intestines and moult twice more

1 Female lays her eggs in the dog's small intestines

10 Dog coughs up larva and then swallows it

2 Eggs are passed in the dog's excreta and hatch in soil or water 3-6 days later

9 Goes up trachae (windpipe)

3 Larvae molt three days later Eight day later molt again

8 Reaches the lungs, gets into the air spaces

4 and reach the infective stage and wait for host

7 Enters the bloodstream by boring through the tissues

6 Reaches stomach within 3 weeks will lay eggs

5 Gains access to the dog via unbroken skin, pads of the feet or are swallowed or inhaled

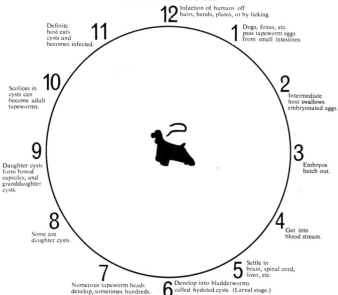

HYDATID TAPEWORM CYCLE

12 Infection of humans off hairs, hands, plates, or by licking.

11 Definite host eats cysts and becomes infected.

1 Dogs, foxes, etc. pass tapeworm eggs from small intestines.

10 Scolices in cysts can become adult tapeworms.

2 Intermediate host swallows embryonated eggs.

9 Daughter cysts form brood capsules, and granddaughter cysts.

3 Embryos hatch out.

8 Some are daughter cysts.

4 Get into blood stream.

7 Numerous tapeworm heads develop, sometimes hundreds.

5 Settle in brain, spinal cord, liver, etc.

6 Develop into bladderworms called hydated cysts. (Larval stage.)

HEART WORM CYCLE

12 The dog dies

1 Females are 10-12 inches long

2 Females do not lay eggs but produce filaria

3 The filaria exist in the blood and can be seen amongst the red cells

4 Mosquitoes suck blood from an infected animal

5 The filaria moult inside the mosquito and are at the infective stage

6 The mosquito bites another dog and passes on the infective larvae

7 The larvae can live for years in the blood stream

8 The adult worms live only in the right ventrical of the heart and in the pulmonary artery which goes to the lungs

9 Enormous numbers of heart worms can live in the heart

10 They cause cough hindleg weakness anaemia and emaciation

11 Congestion increases, the flow of blood is restricted

THE SIGNS AND SYMPTOMS OF WORMS

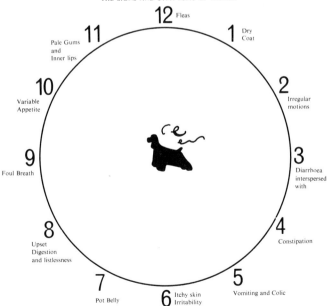

12 Fleas

1 Dry Coat

2 Irregular motions

3 Diarrhoea interspersed with

4 Constipation

5 Vomiting and Colic

6 Itchy skin Irritability

7 Pot Belly

8 Upset Digestion and listlessness

9 Foul Breath

10 Variable Appetite

11 Pale Gums and Inner lips

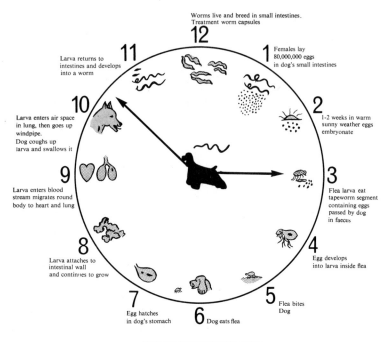

THE FLEA-HOST TAPEWORM CYCLE

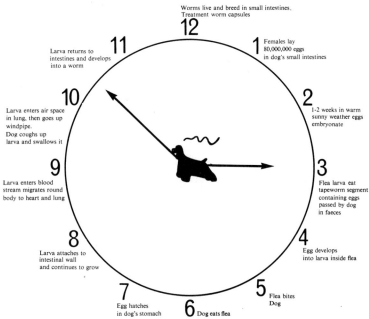

Worms live and breed in small intestines.
Treatment worm capsules

12

1 Females lay
80,000,000 eggs
in dog's small intestines

11 Larva returns to
intestines and develops
into a worm

10 Larva enters air space
in lung, then goes up
windpipe.
Dog coughs up
larva and swallows it

9 Larva enters blood
stream migrates round
body to heart and lung

8 Larva attaches to
intestinal wall
and continues to grow

7 Egg hatches
in dog's stomach

6 Dog eats flea

5 Flea bites
Dog

4 Egg develops
into larva inside flea

3 Flea larva eat
tapeworm segment
containing eggs
passed by dog
in faeces

2 1-2 weeks in warm
sunny weather eggs
embryonate

INFESTATION OF SHEEPDOGS

Sheepdogs can be a serious source of infestation, unless they are carefully looked after and are always kept free from tape worms. Sheepdogs should be wormed automatically at least four times a year, and, while the drug is taking effect, the dog should be kept shut up in order that the worms and the excreta can be wrapped up carefully and burnt.

The reason for this is important, as an infested dog will pass his excreta out in the countryside. The eggs will stick on the grass or other vegetation, and there they will remain until some sheep pass by or occasionally cattle. If a sheep eats the grass and swallows the eggs, the eggs then develop in the sheep's stomach and there they hatch into tiny embryos. These then burrow their way through various tissues and eventually find their way to those which cover the brain, called meninges. Here each one develops and a tiny cyst is formed which is full of fluid. Each cyst contains, at this stage, one tape worm head. After a time other heads are budded from the cyst lining, and in time, one cyst may have as many as fifty or so heads. The sheep generally dies about four months after the infestation. The great and real danger lies in the next stage should it take place. If a dog is allowed to eat an infested sheep's head, each worm head fastens itself on to the intestinal wall lining in the dog, and each head then becomes a tape worm, and so the worm cycle continues ad infinitum, unless controlled.

Dog owners will now perhaps realize how serious a tape worm infestation can be and how tremendously important it is to keep dogs free from worms; and, having cured an infestation, how necessary it is to dispose of all excreta immediately, so that re-infestation does not occur again. But this, unfortunately, may not be so easily prevented, especially if the ground and kennels remain contaminated.

CHAPTER VI

Grooming the Individual Breeds

AFGHAN HOUND

This is a hound which requires a great deal of constant grooming. The standard requires that the coat should be long and very fine-textured on the ribs, forehand, hind quarters and flanks. On mature dogs the coat should be short and close from the shoulders, back and on the saddle. The hair on the topknot is required to be long and silky, whilst the hair on the face is short. The legs must be well coated but the pasterns may be bare. The coat must be allowed to develop naturally.

This is interpreted in some countries to mean that there should be no trimming, scissoring or clipping anywhere. This is not so in the U.S.A., where judicious trimming is normally performed on all show dogs. This includes stripping or plucking the saddle on mature dogs, scissoring the tail feathering, cutting off the whiskers, and removing any fuzz on the cheeks. The long hair is removed between the pads and the feet are slightly trimmed to tidy off the uneven ends.

SUGGESTED METHOD OF GROOMING

Tools and Equipment required

Brush with long bristles, made of whalebone, bristle or smooth pin	Nail clippers
	Mink oil
Wide-tooth comb	Water spray
Blunt-ended scissors for mats	Trunk electric dryer

Method
1. The coat is brushed from the extremities working upwards.
2. The hair is held up with one hand whilst a thin layer of it is brushed downwards.
3. Knots and mats are dealt with as they appear.
4. Grooming is greatly facilitated by the use of the strong trunk dryer set at 'cold'. Blowing cold air on to the coat divides the

4. An Afghan arriving for his regular visit to the dog parlour.

Photo: Anne Cumbers

5. In the raised bath, having his coat thoroughly soaked down to the skin before the shampoo is applied.

Photo: Anne Cumbers

6. Great care must be taken when working the shampoo into the coat, in order not to mat or tangle the coat.

Photo: Anne Cumbers

hair and shows up any mats near the skin which might otherwise go unnoticed.

5. Bathing is required the day before a show, after first grooming
the coat thoroughly.

6. Grooming should be done every day but a good coat can be
maintained by working extra hard at it twice a week.

7. Skimming over the coat with the brush slightly sprayed with
mink oil gives a glorious sheen.

The Afghan must be taught to accept the long arduous grooming
procedures from earliest puppyhood. He must be taught to stand,
lie down, turn over, extend his legs and have his feet manipulated.
The hair between the pads is never cut, because breeders believe
that the long hair protects the pads in their native country when
galloping over the rough, rocky terrain. Since very few Afghans
can be allowed off a lead in the country, if there are sheep, cattle or
pigs about, they would be unlikely to damage their feet even if
the hair were removed from between the pads. I, personally, feel
that excessive hair between the pads is better removed in all breeds,
particularly if the feet become wet frequently, and where in England
would this not occur? Wet hair can cause soft pads and, if the dogs
walk in urine, then the feet are likely to smell too.

Afghans enjoy a good walk in the rain and when racing round a
field they are apt to come home with really muddy legs. Luckily
the texture of the coat, which is so like that of the American Cocker,
does not allow the mud to adhere to it for long and, as soon as the
coat dries, the mud generally brushes off on its own. However, if
the dog lives in the house, it is an excellent idea to dip each leg into
a tall jug or deep bucket of cold water. The leg hair can then be
squeezed dry and the legs can be rubbed downwards with a Chamois
leather dipped in very hot water. Or the legs can be dried quickly
with one of the many excellent blow heaters. Afghans should be
brushed right down to the skin on alternate days. This should be
performed every day when the dogs are moulting, to prevent unnecessary matting, and bitches should also be dealt with daily, if
they are losing their coats after whelping. The time when perhaps
most difficulties arise is when the dog is losing its puppy coat and
the new coat is coming in fast. Unless the puppy coat is removed
carefully at this time, felting will result.

As with any breed with a long coat, it is reasonably easy to keep
the coat in excellent condition provided that at least ten minutes
are spent on the daily grooming. If this is neglected for even a few

7. The coat is best dried with a powerful blower hair dryer, and is brushed out carefully during the drying operation. This dryer is also useful for separating the coat whilst grooming.

Photo: Anne Cumbers

8. The coat of an Afghan puppy.

Photo: Anne Cumbers

days, let alone a week or two, it will require hours and hours of dreary work trying to get the coat into order again. There are many good conditioners on the market, such as Simpson of Langley's coat conditioner, which are a tremendous help for dealing with matted, felted coats. They are best used after bathing and a little can be diluted and soaked into the mats. The coat should be blown dry with a strong dryer, brushing the knotted area in different directions, holding the centre of the mat in one hand while working a little of the hair free at a time. Only in very exceptional circumstances should the coat felting be cut. To prepare an Afghan for a show probably takes between two and three hours, depending on the strength of the dryer used and also on the condition of the coat. Linseed oil in the diet and 25% fat in winter and about 20% in the warmer weather helps to produce wonderfully lustrous, glossy coats. This breed is not recommended for lazy or faint hearted groomers. The coat really does require a great deal of time and effort to be spent on it, and nothing looks worse than a large, unkempt dog.

AIREDALE TERRIER

The Airedale is one of the long-legged terriers and is prepared in a similar manner to the Wire-Haired Fox Terrier. Details of preparing the Fox Terrier will be found on page 162. The Airedale and the Fox Terrier are probably the two most difficult terriers to prepare correctly for shows.

The preparation of the head however is unlike that of the Fox Terrier. The head is similar in proportions lengthwise, but the Airedale requires a stronger muzzle, giving strength of foreface. The Airedale Terrier is not chalked but the coat is polished with a hound glove.

SUGGESTED PREPARATION

Eyebrows. These are scissored closely from the outside corner to the inner corner of the eye where they are wide. The eyebrows are divided between the eyes, where there is very little stop. The hair should never be scooped out at the stop or beneath the eyes. The eyebrows should lie rather flat but at the same time they should not obscure the eyes.

Muzzle. The hair is combed forward and becomes longer until it mingles with the beard, where it is scissored to conform with the beard on the under jaw. The beard starts at the corner of the mouth and should continue in one straight line when the dog is viewed from the side, the end being squared off. Tne hair requires to be trimmed off closely between the arch of the throat and the corner of the mouth.

Head. This is required to be long and flat, but it should not be too broad between the ears and narrows gently towards the eyes. The length of the skull and the foreface should be almost equal. There is hardly any stop and the cheeks should not be full. A little chiselling is required below the eyes, to prevent the appearance of wedginess.

When preparing the head it is important to understand the proportions and shape which are desired. Clever stripping, thinning and scissoring will achieve the desired effect, although they will not deceive an expert judge when covering up a fault. All signs of being down-faced must be avoided. This is often due to too much hair being left at the stop or to taking out too much hair below the eyes. When viewed from above the head should be oblong in shape.

GERMAN SHEPHERD
or
ALSATIAN

The German Shepherd or Alsatian, as it is frequently called, is one of the most popular breeds throughout the world. The coat is not difficult to maintain in good order, but since the breed is quite a large one, there is a considerable area of coat to cover.

The standard requires that there should be two coats, but the coat is considered smooth-coated. The undercoat is dense and is thick and close and woolly in texture. The outer coat is close and of a hard texture and each hair is straight and should lie absolutely flat. The coat is therefore rain-resisting. The coat under the body and behind the legs is longer than the main body coat, and there should be a medium length of breechings. The hair is required to be short on the inside of the ears and on the head and the front of the legs. When the dog is in full coat there should be a good ruff. A coat that is too long or one which is too short is a fault.

The German Shepherd seldom requires bathing, but a bath when necessary does the coat no harm. A walk in heavy rain on a tarmac country road will clean the coat as well as any bathing.

SUGGESTED METHOD OF GROOMING

Tools and Equipment required

Short-bristle dandy brush	Nail clippers
Wide-tooth comb for cleaning brush	Ear powder
Artery forceps for ear cleaning	Spirit dressing
Tooth scaler	Mink oil

Method

As with all large breeds the German Shepherd too requires good finger massage all over the body at least once a week. Daily grooming covering the entire coat is essential to keep the coat in good order. Spirit dressing rubbed well into the coat helps to keep it clean, and a light grooming with a brush sprayed with mink oil, followed by a good hand strapping, produces an excellent bloom. A comb should only be used on the coat when the dog is moulting, because otherwise the precious undercoat will be pulled out during combing.

AMERICAN COCKER SPANIEL

Clipping and Trimming

The American Cocker Spaniel (a comparatively new breed in Britain) has been exceedingly popular in the United States for a great number of years. The breed is one of the varieties of spaniel originating from an English Cocker Spaniel, Obo I, whose son Obo II went to America in 1800. The breed has been developed on completely different lines and with a different conformation from the English Cocker Spaniel. It is also completely dissimilar in coat, this being extremely profuse, particularly on the body and legs. The profuse coat requires a great deal of attention for show purposes, and the clipping, trimming and thinning is an art which must be learnt, although with a little practice this is not difficult; whereas the English Cocker Spaniel is plucked and requires very little scissoring to produce a dog in perfect show shape. The English Cocker Spaniel and the American Cocker Spaniel should never be compared with each other. They are as different as the Cavalier King Charles Spaniel from the Clumber Spaniel and, provided that this is understood from every point of view, then there will be no confusion in the grooming and trimming of the two breeds.

SUGGESTED GROOMING PROCEDURES

Tools and Equipment required

Electric clippers Oster A5, with
    blades nos. 10 and 15
7-inch French scissors with
    shank
46-toothed thinning shears
Wide-toothed comb
Nit comb
Rake
Johnson's baby powder
Artery forceps
Tooth scaler

Hindes pin brush
Slicker brush
Electric trunk dryer
Shampoo
Mink oil
Spray
Diamondeye lotion or
    Eye-Brite
Ear powder
Steady table
Large grooming mirror

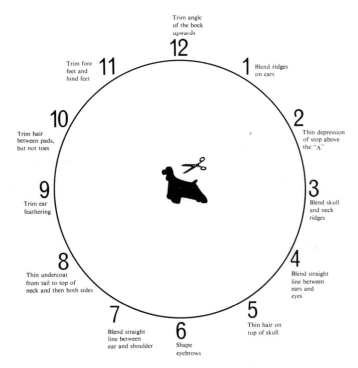

12 Trim angle of the hock upwards

1 Blend ridges on ears

2 Thin depression of stop above the "A"

3 Blend skull and neck ridges

4 Blend straight line between ears and eyes

5 Thin hair on top of skull

6 Shape eyebrows

7 Blend straight line between ear and shoulder

8 Thin undercoat from tail to top of neck and then both sides

9 Trim ear feathering

10 Trim hair between pads, but not toes

11 Trim fore feet and hind feet

ORDER OF TRIMMING THE AMERICAN COCKER

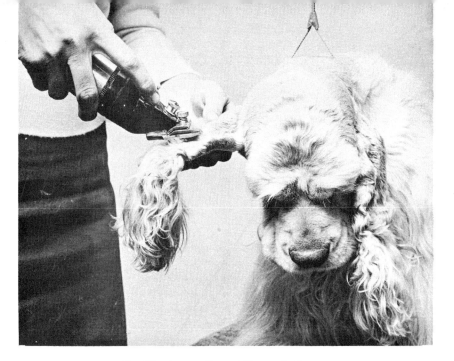

9. Clipping up the outside ear leather.

Photo: Anne Cumbers

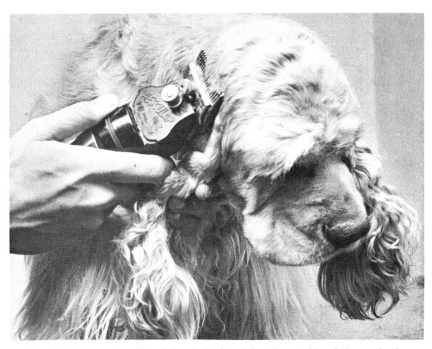

10. Continue up the side of the skull after doing the outside of the ear leather.

Photo: Anne Cumbers

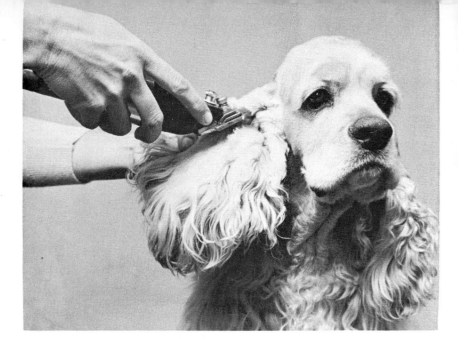

11. Clipping the inside ear leather.

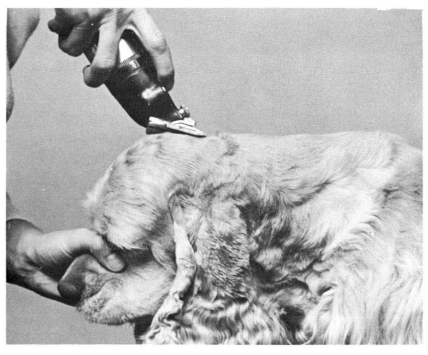

12. Shaping the crown.

CLIPPING AND TRIMMING THE AMERICAN COCKER
Change to 15 Blade.
Do the chiselling and "Λ" for stop

12

1 Oster A 5 with 10 Blade. Clip half way up ear leathers towards skull

11 Clip under tail, and rear end

2 Continue up with blade upright for one inch on side of head

10 Clip from nose to stop. Make inverted "Λ" in stop

3 Clip up the inside of ears cleaning out well

9 With blade upside down clip muzzle and plushy lip

4 Clip from top of skull down to neck, about one inch

8 Clip side of face from top of ear to outside corner of eye

5 Clip from top of brisket up chest, throat and do the mouth

7 Clip from top of ear to centre of the shoulder blade in one straight line

6 Clip neck and shoulders

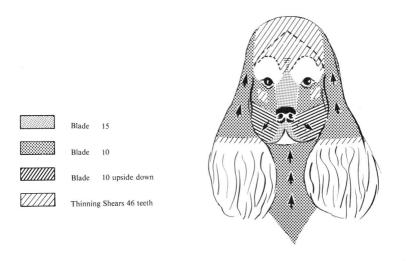

Blade	15
Blade	10
Blade	10 upside down
Thinning Shears 46 teeth	

As with the grooming of any long-coated breed, it is absolutely imperative to have the correct tools to attain the perfect finish. The American Cocker requires to be clipped with any good make of electric clippers, such as an Oster A5 with a no. 10 blade, whilst a no. 15 blade is required for the final touches only. Good thinning shears are also essential, and these should have at least forty-six teeth. Other essentials are well balanced, 7-inch French scissors either with one blade serrated or with normal blades, a cushioned Hindes brush with smooth wire bristles, a wide-toothed comb, an anti-mat comb and a curved-wire curry brush. It is particularly useful to have a large mirror behind the grooming table so that the whole dog can be viewed from time to time during the trimming.

For pet dogs where the coat has been allowed to become matted, an Oliver slant-tooth comb and an Oliver mat-and-tangle comb are useful for the difficult places; but they are not, of course, recommended to be used on a show dog, because too much hair would be removed and the coat could be ruined. As with all grooming procedures, it is essential to have a definite routine. The dog himself learns this routine and accepts it, whilst the person grooming the dog will not miss out important procedures.

All tools required must be collected together and laid out ready for use. The dog should be made to stand on command on a non-slippery surface and, until he is trained to do this, it is probably a good idea to have him tethered. This can be simply done by a collar and lead with the lead attached to something immediately above his neck. Canine control stands are useful for untrained dogs, but care must be taken never to leave a dog alone for one second, because it is not unknown for a dog to hang himself if left unattended. As with all clipping, it is important to have a good light and a steady table, and for the best effects the dog should always be bathed and dried first. Clean hair is easier to clip. It does not blunt the blades, and there is less likelihood of clipper rash. Make certain before starting to clip the dog that he has been well brushed and combed out and that the coat is completely free of tangles or mats.

SUGGESTED ORDER OF CLIPPING

1. *Outside of Ears.* Clip from half way up the leather towards the top of the ear going against the growth of the hair. At the top of the ear continue upwards for about an inch,

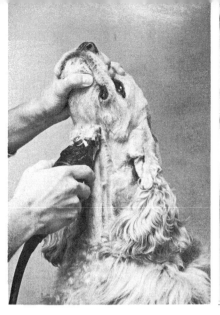

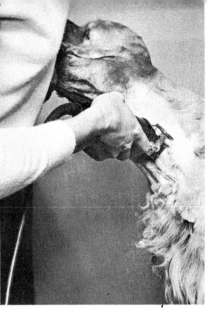

13. Clipping the front.

Photo: Anne Cumbers

14. Clipping a straight line from the top of the ear leather to a point halfway between the withers and the front prominence of the shoulder blade.

Photo: Anne Cumbers

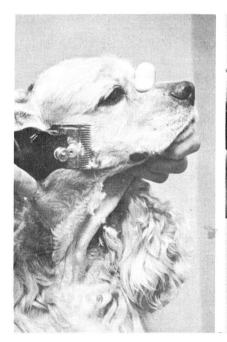

15. Clip the side of the face from the top of the ear to the outside corner of the eye.

Photo: Anne Cumbers

16. Clip from the top of the nose to the stop making an inverted V in the stop.

Photo: Anne Cumbers

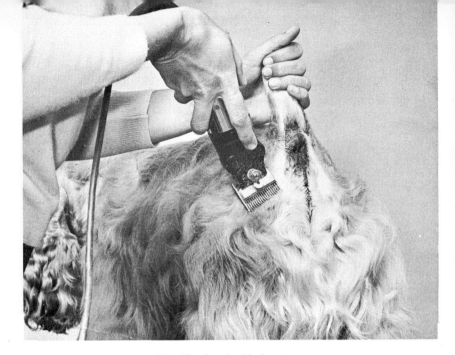

17.   Shaping the hindquarters.

Photo: Anne Cumbers

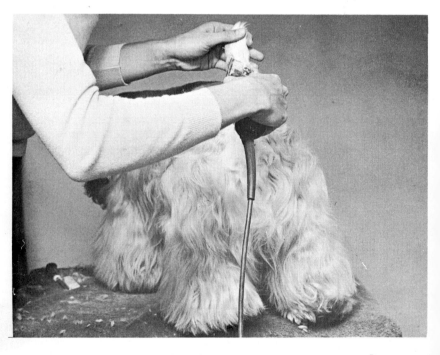

18.   Clip under the tail.

Photo: Anne Cumbers

placing the blade flat against the skull and continuing straight until the blade is in the air. *On no account should the blade follow the dome of the skull.* When doing the edges of the ear only use the edge of the blade, taking great care not to nick the skin in the vulnerable area. Care requires to be taken too to clean out the hair well on the back of the ear where it curves just before joining the skull.

2. *Inside the Ears.* The ears are clipped upwards against the growth, taking care to clean out all the hair round the entrance of the ear canal, and at the same time preventing any cut hair from entering the ear orifice. Clipping is commenced above the tiny ear flap which is found just a little farther up than the middle of the ear leather. This can so easily be caught if the blades are used carelessly. Clean the inside of the ear for about an inch beyond where it joins the head, so that everything is neat.

3. Repeat for the outside of the opposite ear.

4. Repeat for the inside of the opposite ear.

5. *Skull.* Where the skull joins the neck there is a slight depression which emphasizes the arch of the neck. Clip down an inch from the top of the skull towards this depression and then continue into the side of the neck for about an inch, gradually turning the clippers downwards.

6. *Chest and Throat.* Starting from the top of the breast bone, clip straight up the centre of the chest and throat as far as the chin and lips. Continue until the whole of the front of the dog is evenly clipped, ending in a blunt V-shape at the breast bone. Clip carefully round the mouth, especially at the folds in the lower lip where long tufts of hair can cause sores. Use only the edge of the clippers and stretch the skin straight with the thumb.

7. *Neck and Shoulders.* Make certain that the dog is standing correctly on all four legs. Then measure from the point at the top of the withers to the opposite side of the shoulder blade where there is a prominent bony structure. Mark a point exactly halfway between the two. Clip down in a straight line from the point where the ear joins the back of the skull to the centre of the point marked on the shoulder blade. Continue on downwards for about an inch, bringing the clippers downwards and slightly forwards towards the brisket, lifting the blade slightly until it is in the air so that no

 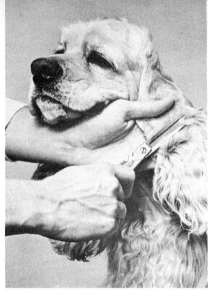

19. With the blade held upside down, bring it from the top of the muzzle downwards and forwards towards the upper lip.

Photo: Anne Cumbers

20. Blending the ridges on the ears.

Photo: Anne Cumbers

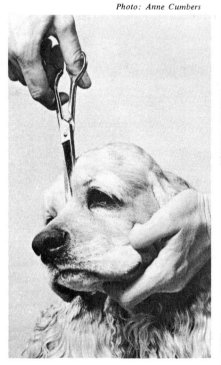 

21. Accentuating the stop with the thinning shears.

Photo: Anne Cumbers

22. Blend the ridges on the skull with the thinning shears.

Photo: Anne Cumbers

hard ridge is left. Finish off the clipping between this area of the neck and shoulder, and the throat, where the hair grows in various directions, so that it is neat and tidy.

8. *Side of Face.* Take a straight line from the top of the ear leather where it joins the skull to the corner of the eye and clip in a straight line. Continue the side of the face, carefully clipping under the eye and towards the nose but not extending this area much farther than about an inch beyond the line from the stop to the mouth.

9. *Muzzle and Plushy Lips.* With the blade held upside down and at right angles to the area to be clipped (as if on its 'toes') gently draw the blade downwards over the muzzle and in the direction of the growth of the hair. This produces a lovely, velvety, plushy look. Repeat on the other side of the face.

10. *Nose.* Clip from the nose to the stop against the growth of hair, stretching the skin at the outside corner of the eye backwards and upwards, so that the eye is automatically closed to avoid cutting it.

11. *Stop.* Clean out the stop by creating a V, using the corner of the clippers to penetrate into the stop as far as they will go.

12. *Tail and Rear End.* Holding the tail upwards, clip from the anus up the underside of the tail. Then clip downwards with the growth of the hair to just below the anus, forming a U-shape with the growth and colour of the coat.

13. *Change to no. 15 Blade.*

14. With the dog facing you remove any long hairs from the upper lip by clipping upwards from its centre towards the nose.

15. *Chiselling the Cheeks.* This is to emphasize the plushiness of the muzzle and only a very small area is scooped out or chiselled out in what could best be described as the hollow of the cheek bone.

16. Clip again from the nose to the stop, working in the same pattern for the inverted V of the stop, previously made with the no. 10 blade.

These are the only areas of the American Cocker which are clipped, although some lazy people will clip the hair on the pads of the feet instead of cutting the hair out correctly with scissors. Dogs which have very good heads are sometimes clipped all over the head except for the eyebrows, but this produces rather a hard effect. Pet dogs are frequently

E

clipped down the back to the end of the tail. There is an erroneous belief that, if a dog has his hair clipped on his back, it will never grow correctly again. This in fact, is not true, provided that, as the hair starts to grow, the woolly under-coat is removed carefully with thinning scissors. The hair will then eventually grow straight, but if the undercoat is left, then the top hair will automatically grow in an upward direction.

Thinning

The American Cocker next requires his coat to be carefully thinned.

This can be hard on the fingers unless thinning is done regularly. How I wish that someone would invent electric thinning shears! In heavily coated dogs it is recommended that the undercoat should be removed weekly.

1. The ridge between the clipped hair and the long hair on the ears must be blended together.
2. Thin the hair right into the depression of the stop above the inverted V made by the clippers, at the same time pulling forward the long hairs immediately above the inverted V and thinning behind them in order to create a softer appearance.
3. Blend in the clipped edge between the skull and the arch of the neck.
4. Blend in the hair clipping ridge formed by the straight line between the ears and the eyes.
5. Thin the hair on the top of the skull by first raising it with one hand and thinning the undercoat, gradually moving forwards towards the eyebrows. Leave the longer hair on top, which grows naturally in the shape of a fan. Do this all over the skull until the undercoat is removed. Then, using the thinning shears in all directions but mainly with the growth of the hair, tidy up so that the head looks soft and neat. Do not leave on excessive bangs of hair on the head, as these merely look untidy. If the eyebrows are too long at the sides, they may require thinning extra carefully, until they are flat with the sides of the head.
6. *Eyebrows.* The eyebrows are shaped in a curve, which should be in the same shape as the curve of the skull between the ears, which ideally is rather broad. The eyebrows should not

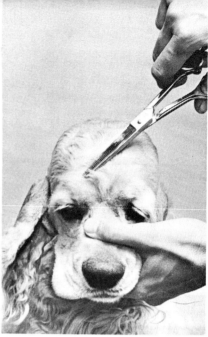

23. Thinning the undercoat on the skull.
Photo: Anne Cumbers

24. Shaping the eyebrows and 'top-knot'.
Photo: Anne Cumbers

25. Blend the straight line between the ear and shoulder with the thinning shears.
Photo: Anne Cumbers

be left too long, as this gives an untidy appearance. In tri-colours or blacks and tans, however, the tan eyebrows may be left a little longer to accentuate the brilliant colour.

7. The thinning shears must next be used on the straight edge between the ear and the centre of the shoulder blade made by the clippers.

8. *Undercoat.* Thinning the undercoat. Start at the tip of the tail. Lifting the hair with the left hand, thin the undercoat for a couple of inches, then lift the next line of hair and continue thinning in this method, removing the undercoat right up the back to the top of the neck. Continue to do this on either side of the backbone.

9. Then thin the undercoat from the sides by lifting up the long hair and taking out the undercoat against the direction of the growth.

10. Form a blunt-ended V or open U on the thighs and thin out the shoulders in a similar but smaller shape.

11. The neck and body, shoulders and hind quarters are now finished off by using the thinning shears on top of the coat, working in the direction in which the coat naturally falls. Cut the hair from the top of the back outwards and down-wards so that it gradually gets longer and blends into the long belly coat and leg feathering. On no account should a dog have a centre parting nor should he be plucked any-where: it is much kinder to use thinning shears.

Scissoring

1. *Ear Fringes.* Brush the ear feathering down and trim the edges neatly.

2. *Pads.* Trim the hair out between the pads on all four feet by lifting the feet backwards. Spread the pads with the thumb and cut out all the long hairs. Do not cut the hair between the toes.

3. *Forefeet.* Trim the forefeet. In order to get a good result it is essential that the dog should be standing correctly balanced on all four legs. The hair should not be trimmed above the nails. First comb the hair down to the skin in all directions, finishing with the hair being combed in the correct and final position required.

4. *Pattern.* A pattern is then cut. Place the scissors at the edge of the toe nails. Taking a straight line up from this, proceed to cut the topmost layer of hair only, then cutting a circular

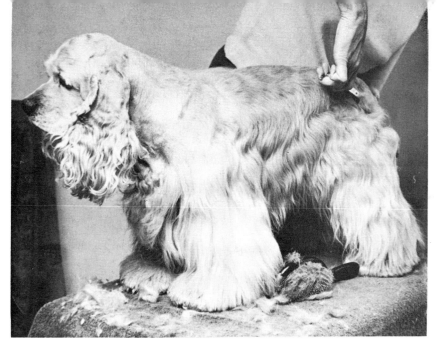

26. To take off more long hair the shears may be used on top of the coat working downwards.

Photo: Anne Cumbers

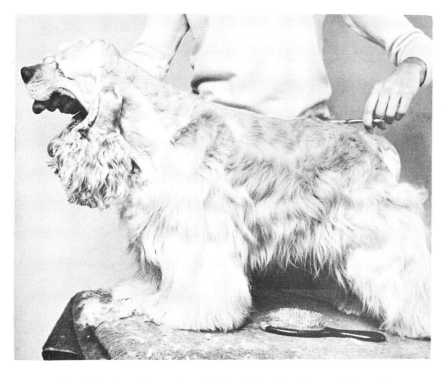

27. Thin the undercoat from the tip of the tail to the top of the neck.

Photo: Anne Cumbers

AMERICAN COCKER SPANIEL
CLIPPING THINNING AND TRIMMING

Area
Clipped with
an Oster A 5
Blade No. 10

Clipped area
with Oster A 5
Blade No. 10
Thinning with
fine thinning
shears 46 teeth

Clipping with Oster A 5
10 blade
upside down

Clipping with
Oster 15 blade

Trimming area

Tools Required:— Oster A 5 Blades 10 15
Scissors with 7″ blades
Thinning Shears 46 teeth

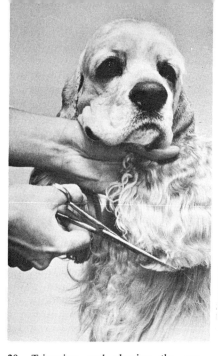

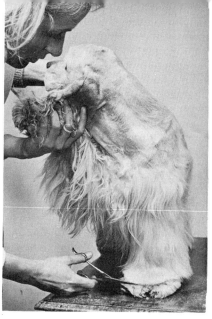

28. Trimming and shaping the ear feathering.

Photo: Anne Cumbers

29. Making the pattern for the foot by first scissoring a thin layer of the topmost hair vertically above the end of the toe nails.

Photo: Anne Cumbers

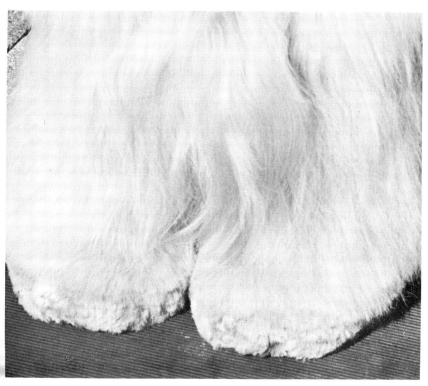

30. The trimmed fore feet.

Photo: Anne Cumbers

31. Two of the author's American Cocker Spaniels immaculately prepared for the show ring.

Photo: Sally Anne Thompson

pattern in the shape of the foot. To create the thick, padded-foot shape, proceed to cut the rest of the hair following the pattern layer by layer until reaching the ground. Finally make certain that the foot hair is about a quarter of an inch off the ground. The top hair from the legs is then brushed down but must not be longer than the pattern. If it is, cut if off by using the thinning shears. Occasionally, the feathering on the back of the forelegs may require thinning out and the ends made neat by scissoring, so that the line continues round from the front pattern, inclining slightly upwards.

5. *Belly Coat.* Occasionally, some dogs have such a profuse coat that the hair under the belly reaches the ground. This should be scissored off so that there is some 'daylight' seen under the body, because this much improves the look and movement and balance of the dog. Some dog puppies may require to have the long hair on the sheath trimmed to the same length as that of the belly coat.

6. *Hind Legs.* The feet are shaped in exactly the same way as the forefeet, except that the angle of the hocks require to be emphasized.

7. Stand the dog with its hind legs on the edge of a table, taking care to comb the coat from the hocks downwards. Cut any hair which falls below the table in a straight line. Pick up the entire coat from the hocks downwards in the left hand and cut in a straight line from the bottom of the foot to about 2 inches below the hock, cutting the hair at an angle with the leg. This greatly improves the look of the hind movement when the dog is moving away from the judge.

Puppies

Puppies require their first clip at the age of six weeks using a no. 10 blade only. If the coat on the back is thinned regularly from this age, there will be no heavy difficult coat thinning to do.

An American Cocker Pet Clip

Many people love the American Cocker Spaniel temperament and charm, but they are not interested in showing, and therefore cannot be bothered to spend the time or the money on keeping the dog in perfect show trim. There are various styles in which the pet American Cocker may be trimmed and clipped to make him into a neat, tidy and easily kept dog.

E*

SUGGESTED ORDER OF CLIPPING

The dog may be clipped all over the head, throat and shoulders and the clip can be continued down the back and half way down the sides. The long coat and feathering can be cut neatly so that they are off the ground, and the coat can be well thinned out and even the tummy coat can be clipped until it is about an inch long. People who prefer even less work to do on their Cocker can have the hair on the legs trimmed right down to a ¼ of an inch from the skin, perhaps leaving a small amount of feathering at the back. This should be cut at an angle, so that the legs resemble those of setters. It creates a slightly softer effect on the dog and balances the long, attractive ear feathering.

If the coat has not been cared for for a number of months, particularly during the moulting periods, the coat will be found to have matted extremely badly, particularly in the dogs which have a soft woolly undercoat. When a dog gets into this state, the mats must be cut out. The clippers should only be used in the direction of the growth of the hair, and the hair will have to be clipped over quite a number of times before the desired effect is reached. It is quite a good idea to trim the whole dog down for a general effect and then to repeat the process as often as is required. I would never recommend anything but electric clippers. Pet owners, when buying an American Cocker puppy, would be well advised to buy some electric clippers with a no. 10 head and the fine, 46-toothed thinning shears, unless they intend to take their dog to a beauty parlour regularly every three to six weeks.

A QUICK GUIDE TO PREPARING AN AMERICAN COCKER SPANIEL

1. *Shampooing*

    Shampoo the dog and rinse well. Dry thoroughly, brushing the coat straight.

2. *Clipping*

    (*a*) With an Oster A5 blade no. 10, clip half way up the ear leathers towards the skull.

    (*b*) Continue up until the skull is reached when the blade is held upright, clipping for 1 inch on the side of the head. Do not follow the line of the skull.

    (*c*) Clip up the inside of the ears to the top.

(d) Clip all round the top of the skull down to the neck for about 1 inch all round.

(e) Clip from the top of the brisket up the chest, throat and to the end of the bottom jaw including the lips.

(f) Clip a straight line from the top of the ear leather to a point halfway between the withers and the front of the shoulder blade, rounding off at the end of the clipper line.

(g) Join the clipped area between the side of the neck and the brisket.

(h) Clip the side of the face from the top of the ear to the outside corner of the eye in a straight line. Clip along the cheek and under the eyes.

(i) Clip from the top of the nose to the stop making an inverted V in the stop.

(j) With the blade held upside down, bring it from the top of the muzzle downwards and forwards towards the upper lip. This makes the muzzle plushy.

(k) Clip under the tail, along the base of the tail, and round the anus.

(l) Change to a no. 15 blade, chisel a small area under the eyes and work the inverted V in the stop. A small area is clipped beneath the nose on both sides of the lips.

3. *Trimming*

(a) Using the 46-toothed thinning shears, blend the ridges left by the clippers on both ears.

(b) Thin the hair behind the longer hair in the depression above the inverted V in the stop.

(c) Blend the skull and neck ridges, and also the straight line between the ears and the eyes.

(d) Thin the undercoat on top of the skull, and shorten the hair if necessary by raising the shears whilst still cutting.

(e) Blend the straight line between the ear and shoulder on each side.

(f) Thin the undercoat from the tip of the tail to the top of the neck, working the shears through the longer coat and removing the undercoat whilst progressing.

(h) Repeat this on either side of the backbone.

(i) Thin out the undercoat working up and slightly forward for about 2 inches below the previous thinning line.
If the coat is excessively long, raise the shears whilst cutting.

(*j*) To take off more long hair, the shears may be used on top of the coat working downwards.

(*k*) Thin the undercoat and top coat over the rump, making a curved contour over the hip, which balances the curved clip line on the shoulder and brisket.

(*l*) Thin the coat over the shoulder to balance the contour on the hind quarters.

4. *Scissoring*

(*a*) Trim round the ear feathering, tidying off the edges.

(*b*) Trim the hair between the pads, but not between the toes.

(*c*) Trim the forefeet by cutting a thin layer of hair immediately above the end of the toe nails, creating the pattern to be followed for the rest of the forefeet. This gives the padded-cushion look.

(*d*) Repeat a similar pattern for the hind legs.

(*e*) Stand the dog with his hind legs on the edge of the table and cut any hair which falls below the edge, in a straight line.

(*f*) Comb out the hock feathering with the thumb and first finger. Gather it all into one hand, and cut the ends off in a straight line from the bottom of the foot to the top of the hock. This emphasizes the angulation of the hock when the dog is moving.

(*h*) Trim off the hair on the tail neatly.

(*i*) Shape the eyebrows if necessary.

5. *Excess Feathering*

If the dog is heavily coated, the fringes on the ear leathers may require thinning out. Also, the hair on the front of the forelegs may fall below the feet and, if so, this should be trimmed sufficiently so that the feet show. If the hair is too long on the rear part of the foreleg feathering, this too should be rounded off to correspond with the line of the hock scissoring. Occasionally, the body coat may reach the ground, in which case it is advisable to shorten it, so that some daylight may be seen beneath the dog. If the coat grows to the ground it spoils the look of the dog's movement. Show dogs may be put down in oil to promote coat growth.

AUSTRALIAN TERRIER

This is one of the short-legged terriers and originated in Australia.

In looks, it is similar to a Yorkshire Terrier, with a much shorter coat. The standard requires that the coat should be two to two and a half inches in length and that it should be of hard texture. There is practically no trimming necessary, but the coat requires regular combing and raking out of all dead hair, and brushing with a stiff brush.

SUGGESTED METHOD OF PREPARING AN AUSTRALIAN TERRIER

Tools and Equipment required

Stiff bristle brush	7-inch scissors
Wide-toothed comb	Nail clippers
46-toothed thinning shears	Mink oil

SUGGESTED ORDER OF WORK

1. *Body Coat.* Comb the hair thoroughly and rake out all dead hair.
2. Brush the coat vigorously.
3. *Topknot.* This should never be flattened in any way, but it should be trained upwards with the brush and comb.
4. *Stripping.* Strip off any straggly hairs on the neck, body, front and tail. Strip off long hairs growing on the ears, leaving a certain amount of hair on the inside to give the impression of high set-on ears.
5. *Scissoring.* The legs may be trimmed with scissors or thinning shears. The forelegs are trimmed up to the elbows on the front and sides, leaving the feathering on the back of the legs. The hind legs are cleaned up to the hock, and the breechings may require tidying, as will the feathering at the back of the tail. A little hair should be left on the tip of the tail. The feet are not normally scissored.
6. The hair under the eyes may be cleaned out with thinning shears or by plucking carefully. This improves the keen alert expression. The hair is also trimmed between the eyes, blending the hair into the topknot.

BASENGI

This is one of the most ancient breeds in existence and comes from the region of the Congo. The standard requires that the coat should be short and silky and the skin very pliant.

There are no particular grooming hints required. A short-bristle brush and a hound glove with a good finger massage applied over the body once a week will keep the skin soft and supple. A final polish, with a chamois leather or velvet pad or a good hand strapping will produce a good sheen. The white areas may be bathed the day before a show and rinsed in a white hair rinse, or chalked and well brushed out afterwards, but in general the Basengi seldom requires bathing.

BASSET HOUND

This is a short-legged hound with extra large, pendulous ears and some head wrinkle. The standard requires that the coat should be short and close without being too fine. The stern should have a moderate amount of coarse hair underneath. The hound should be given regular daily grooming with a short-bristle brush. This can be followed with a vigorous finger massage, hand strapping or a good grooming with a rubber hound glove. The pendulous ears will need frequent attention, because they are liable to get dirty after meals or in wet weather. Chaps may form at the tips, which can be treated with benzyl benzoate emulsion. The interior of the ears will require dusting once a week with a good ear powder. The eyes may be wiped round with a good eye lotion. The interior of the flews and folds in the lower lip require keeping clean and free from accumulated stale food. The hound may be bathed if dirty, but this would require doing several days prior to a show, in order to allow the coat to settle and regain its natural gloss.

BEAGLE

This is a small compactly built hound. There are two varieties: the smooth which has a dense, short, but not too fine a coat texture, and the rough variety which has very dense and wiry coat.

Coat maintainance is easy. A good daily brushing with a short-bristle brush, followed by strong finger massage, will keep the coat and skin in excellent condition. Before a show the white areas require to be washed, and the coat should be rubbed over with a chalk block while the hair is still damp. The chalk must be thoroughly brushed out before the hound is exhibited. Ears should have a dusting with a good ear powder. Nails must be cut and teeth cleaned when necessary.

BEDLINGTON TERRIER

The Bedlington Terrier is trimmed and clipped and presented in a most unique manner, although the finished result should look completely natural. The coat is best described as being thick, curly and rather linty in texture without being the least bit wiry.

Trimming the Bedlington Terrier consists of clipping and scissoring. Some breeders prefer to singe the coat by using a comb and a lighted taper to burn off the ends of the hair. Dogs with excessive length of hair generally require to be scissored first, although, if the singeing method is used, this should be done more frequently than the normal scissoring procedure. Provided that the coat is kept short enough, this method works well.

Singeing is useful all over the coat except on the head, ears and lower legs and feet. After the hair has been singed the dog requires a good bathing to remove all traces of the yellow burnt ends which are left after the singeing operation.

Scissoring

The best method of scissoring the coat depends on the length and texture. Some people prefer to trim the hair with long-bladed scissors held flat on the coat, using the entire blades at each cut. Others find it more satisfactory to part the hair in sections, making ridges of about an inch wide, drawing the comb through each ridge until the desired length is achieved, and then scissoring the hair in the comb with the blades held flat against it. This method ensures that the hair is maintained at an even length. Ridging is done along the body and neck in horizontal lines, and on the shoulders and sides the ridges are made and worked vertically.

The coat requires constant and regular attention and should be trimmed every six to eight weeks. The following is a suggested order of work:

Tools and Equipment required

Electric clippers Oster A5	Hindes pin brush or bristle brush
Blade no. 10 or no. 15 or no. 30	
7-inch scissors	Comb, 10 teeth to 1 inch
46-toothed thinning shears	Artery forceps

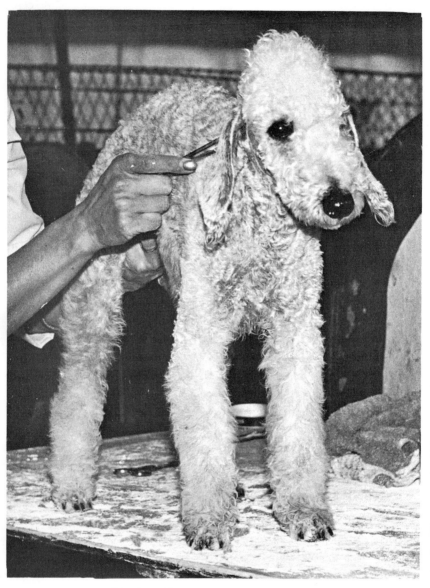

32. A Bedlington Terrier being groomed.

1. The Bedlington should be groomed in a good light and on a steady table, and standing on something which will prevent him from slipping. It is useful to have a large grooming mirror behind the table, in order to view the dog from both sides from time to time.

2. *The Coat.* This must be thoroughly combed out, making certain that it is free from all mats and knots. In cases where the coat has been neglected for some time, it may be necessary to work only a small area at a time before proceeding to the next section.

3. *Tassels.* A tassel is required on the outside of each ear. The apex of the triangular tassel starts 1½ inches from the tip of the ear leather. Brush the hair carefully down and scissor a line on either side of the tassel which is to be left.

4. *Ears.* Scissor the hair on the ear fringes sufficiently so that the edges and folds may be seen. This acts as a safeguard to prevent them from being nicked with the electric clippers.

5. Repeat this procedure on the other ear.

Clipping

6. *Inside Ear Leathers.* Using an Oster A5 clipper and blade no. 30 or no. 15, clip the hair up the inside of the ear leather, starting at the bottom of the ear and working upwards, taking particular care not to nick the edges or the folds, and work round the ear orifice carefully, making certain that no hair falls in. Repeat the process for the other ear.

7. *Outside Ear Leathers.* Clip the hair on the outside of the ear leather from the scissored tasselled line, moving up the ear leather and, taking care with the edges and folds, work up to the boundary of the ear. Do not clip above the cartilage line at the top of the ear, but clip in a straight line across this boundary. If the coat is thick, the ears should be clipped against the growth of the hair, but if it is fine, then the ears may be clipped with the growth of the hair. The apex of the tassel must be at an acute angle. Repeat the process for the opposite ear.

8. *Throat.* Using an Oster A5 blade no. 30 (or 15) proceed to clip from just below the adam's apple to the end of the lower jaw, taking care not to nick the sides or ends of the lips. The lips should be drawn taut and clipped with the edge of the blade, at the same time keeping the dog's mouth closed so

that the tongue is not nicked. Some dogs may look better if the clipping line commences at the adam's apple or a little above.

9. *Cheeks*. Next clip from the corner of the ear in a straight line towards the corner of the eye. It is extremely important that the hair should not be removed immediately round the outer corner of the eye, because the eye should have the appearance of being small and well sunken. The clipped line goes from a small distance away from the outer corner of the eye to the inner corner of the mouth. This line may be taken down in a straight line, which may then curve slightly towards the corner of the mouth for the last inch of the line. The actual shape depends very much on the shape of the dog's head. The side of the face is then clipped from a line running from the back of the ear to the already clipped line of the adam's apple.

10. *Tail*. Start to clip the top of the tail, commencing about an inch from the root and working carefully towards the tip. Next clip the sides of the tail working in the same direction; and finally, holding the tail up, start to clip once again about an inch above the root of the tail, working with the growth of the hair and clipping towards the tip. Make certain that all the hair has been removed evenly and neatly so that the tail now resembles that of a rat. Judicious clipping and trimming of the tail can camouflage an over-long tail or one that is too short.

11. *Stomach*. Clip from the groin to the chest using a no. 15 or no. 10 blade or this part may be scissored with the aid of a comb drawn through the hair to protect the teats. If clippers are used, the clipping should start just in front of the testicles or vulva, taking extreme care round the genital organs and especially round the teats.

Clipping must always be done with the growth of the hair and NEVER against it. The clipped area extends up to the beginning of the rib cage. Trained dogs will stand quietly on their hind legs with their forelegs held or supported. It may, however, be found to be easier to clip the dog while he is standing normally. One side is clipped first, holding the hind leg up and extending it backwards. Reverse the procedure to clip the other side. Only a very light pressure should be used on the clippers on this vulnerable area.

Scissoring

This may be done with scissors alone or with the 'ridge' method using a comb on the lower legs and feet.

(*a*) *Head.* The head scissoring is important as the head of the Bedlington Terrier has to be almost pear-shaped. The hair is first combed upwards towards a central point somewhere between the inner corner of the ear and halfway along the clipped line of the eye. The actual point depends on the shape of each individual dog. Study the head carefully and cut a line down from the dome at the selected angle. This first cut decides the final shaping of the head. Cut the hair in parallel lines from the central cut, continuing down the sides and gradually cutting the hair shorter. The amount of hair that is scissored on the muzzle depends very much on the shape and width of the skull between the ears and cheeks. Obviously, a dog with a wide head would require more hair left on the muzzle than a dog with a narrower head. The muzzle when scissored should be only slightly narrower than the skull. The line of the topknot starts to rise very gradually from the nose continuing above the eyes and over the top of the head in a line with the top of the ears. The head when completely trimmed requires to look smooth and even from any angle. The scissors must be held flat against the coat, making certain that the points do not dig in to the coat anywhere causing unsightly ridges and tufts. The trimming from the top of the head is blended in carefully to the dog's beautifully arched neck.

(*b*) *The Body.* Bedlingtons used to have their coat trimmed to about three-quarters of an inch all over, but the fashion now in Britain is for the shorter coat. Comb the coat out all over and fluff it up with the dog standing facing forward. Commence to scissor the coat to about half an inch in length, keeping the scissors held flat against the coat, and taking care not to dig the points in to the coat, as this causes tufts and ugly ridges. The ridging method may be found to be easier and partings may be made from the neck towards the tail using the comb as a guiding scissored line.

Back. With the dog facing forward, start to work a small section at a time, commencing about the middle thigh and working forwards along the top of the back to the top of

BEDLINGTON TERRIER

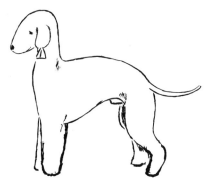

Clipped tail area

Quick guide to preparing a
Bedlington Terrier

Parting made on leg
before scissoring, using
the comb method

Clipped area of neck
and throat

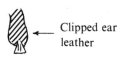

Ear Tassel

Clipped ear
leather

the withers, scissoring an area of several inches on either side of the spine.

(c) *Neck.* The hair on the neck is now required to be trimmed shorter than that on the body, in order to accentuate the fineness and length of the neck. The hair is gradually trimmed from half an inch to a quarter of an inch, and is gradually blended into the clipped line on the throat.

(d) *Sides of the Body.* Work forward from the middle thigh until the last rib is reached, where a little more hair is removed over the ribs to give a slightly flat-sided effect.

(e) *Shoulder.* The length of hair is gradually increased between the neck and the ribs, so that the hair on the shoulders is once again about half an inch in length, corresponding with the coat on the top of the back.

(f) *Chest.* With the dog facing you, commence to trim from the clipped line at the adam's apple, trimming the hair down the front of the neck to a length of about a quarter of an inch, gradually increasing the length of the chest hair until it is the same as that on the shoulders.

(g) *Forelegs.* Scissor neatly the hair between the forelegs, not cutting off too much, as this must be blended in to the slight fringe which is left on the bottom of the rib cage.

(h) *Chest Fringe.* The hair has already been clipped on the abdomen as far as the navel, which accentuates the tuck up. The hair must be trimmed round the tuck up to blend in with the clipped hair, and the length should gradually be increased underneath the rib cage in a slight fringe of a half to one inch in length, depending on the conformation of the dog, as this can accentuate the depth of brisket, but unless the coat is dense enough, it is often better scissored shorter.

(i) *Feet.* The standard requires the Bedlington to have hare feet, so that the foot is trimmed neatly in the shape of this animal's foot which is long and narrow. In actual fact, trimming follows the contour of the foot. Some Bedlingtons have cat feet, which are incorrect, and it is almost impossible to disguise this fault. The only hope is to cut the coat on the legs slightly shorter all round, but to lengthen the trim on the top of the foot. It is a matter of experimenting on each individual dog as to how best to camouflage this fault. But, whatever is done, it is unlikely to hoodwink a knowledgeable judge, should he think that the shape of the feet is more important than some other constructional fault.

(j)   *Hind Legs.* Comb out the leg hair thoroughly and start trimming the hind legs, commencing at the feet. Remove the hair from between the pads, holding up the leg opposite to the one being trimmed, scissor evenly up the leg following the contours and keeping the hair at the same length as the body hair of half an inch, work carefully on the inside of the leg, and then repeat the procedure for the opposite leg. The hind leg may be extended to facilitate the scissoring of the more difficult areas on the opposite leg.

BLOODHOUND

The Bloodhound is the largest variety of hound and is renowned for his fantastic olfactory powers. The Bloodhound standard must be the only standard where there is no mention of coat. The skin, however, is required to be thin and extremely loose. The best brushes to use are a bristle brush or a curved Addis. A thorough brushing should be followed by a good hand massage, to keep the skin supple. If the coat looks dry, a little mink oil sprayed on to a brush and brushed into the coat will bring up a good sheen. A final finish with a silk handkerchief or a velvet pad will really make the coat glow.

As with many hounds, the ears, being pendulous, and particularly the interior of them, require to be kept clean and dry. Chaps can be prevented by using a little benzyl benzoate emulsion. Ear powder, such as the recipe given in the general grooming chapter, should be dusted into the ears daily. Nails require to be kept short. The eyes should be wiped round with a good eye lotion, and eye stains dried off with boracic powder. If the eyes themselves look sore they may be bathed in normal saline. Wrinkles must be wiped dry daily and powdered with Johnson's baby powder. Pressure points require to be watched, particularly the elbows, hock joints and the end of the stern. These places are apt to become sore and bald, and to prevent this soft bedding is required and gentle, daily massaging of the areas with a little benzyl benzoate emulsion.

33. A Bloodhound. Wrinkles, folds of skin, eyes, pendulous ears and lips all require careful and regular attention, as do pressure points.

Photo: Anne Cumbers

BORDER TERRIER

This is another terrier which requires very little preparation and practically no trimming. A good brushing once a week, and normal care of ears, teeth and nails is all that is really necessary for this delightful breed.

BORZOI

This is a large aristocratic breed originating from Russia. The coat is exceptionally fine, but is not difficult to maintain. The standard demands that the coat should be long and silky and it should not, of course, have any tendency to woolliness. The coat may, however, be flat, wavy or even curly, and it should be short and smooth on the head, ears, and forelegs. The ruff on the neck must be profuse and rather curly. The chest and forelegs should be well feathered and there should be profuse, long feathering on the hind quarters and tail.

SUGGESTED METHOD OF GROOMING

Grooming Tools and Equipment

Hindes pin brush	Johnson's baby powder
Wide-tooth comb	Starch
Slicker brush	Mink oil
Blunt scissors for mats	Nail clippers.

Method
1. Brush the coat down to the skin.
2. Cut or file the nails monthly.
3. Bathing is required a day or two before being shown.
4. The coat may be cleaned with Johnson's baby powder or starch.

The coat is easily maintained, as it does not hold the dirt or mud The coat should be groomed daily for about ten minutes, in order to stimulate the skin. The hair is brushed in the direction in which it grows, except on the top of the back where it should be brushed gently forward. The fringes must be brushed or combed out carefully and any mats or tangles should be teased out with the fingers.

The dog should be brushed out extra carefully during the moulting period in order to prevent mats forming. Particular care is required when the puppy coat is coming out and the new coat is coming in. Mats of hair may appear behind the ears and under the joints. The tail and the hair round the anus are areas where mats and tangles are likely to appear unless these areas are groomed carefully. The only hard work about the grooming of a Borzoi is perhaps its size.

Borzois do require to be bathed before a show. Most exhibitors prefer to do this a day or two earlier, so that the white parts of the coat are really white and dazzling. There are several aids which may be used for whitening the coat. One of the whiteners for human hair is excellent for this. A Borzoi is never chalked, but the hair may be trimmed out from between his pads if necessary. As with all breeds, the ears should be given regular attention to prevent an infestation of ear mites. The eyes must be kept dry and clean and the teeth should be rubbed over with a little hydrogen peroxide, using a 10% solution mixed with a little milk in the proportion of half and half. If the nails become long, then they should be filed or clipped once a month.

Sometimes the area round the anus becomes soiled and this area may be washed and rinsed carefully. But if the faeces here have become hard and dry, they may be removed by breaking them up with the fingers and then brushing out the remains with a slicker brush.

BOSTON TERRIER

These dogs originated in the U.S.A. and came from Boston, as the name implies. The coat is short, smooth and fine in texture. A soft, short bristle brush is best for grooming. Finger massage keeps the skin supple and a final coat dressing should be given of a little mink oil sprayed lightly on to the brush for a final brushing over the coat. Eyes may be wiped over with a good eye lotion and stains removed with boracic powder caked on to the damp area and later brushed off.

Show dogs require to be bathed, their whiskers cut off, and any encroaching dark hairs which overlap the white areas should be cut off. General care of ears, teeth and nails should be carried out weekly and monthly.

BOXER

This compact, short-haired, sturdy dog is extremely easy to groom. The coat should be short and lie close to the skin, and it should always have a good sheen. Grooming should be done daily with a soft, short-bristled brush. Strong finger massage over the body keeps the skin supple and a good polish with a velvet pad or good hand strapping brings up a sheen. A little mink oil can be used very sparingly sprayed on to the brush to give a final gloss over the coat. Eyes should be wiped over with Eye-Brite lotion. Wrinkles and ear stains must be cleaned and dried. Boracic powder is useful for removing eye stains and Johnson's baby powder for keeping the wrinkles dry. Show dogs may be bathed if necessary and the white areas rinsed in white hair rinse or chalked whilst the coat is still damp. The latter must be well brushed out of the coat. Nails may be polished. The flews and the folds of the lips require to be kept free from any accumulation of food.

BULLDOG

The Bulldog is an easy breed with regards to its coat. The standard requires that the coat should be short, close, fine and smooth in texture. A soft-bristle brush and a rubber hound glove are useful. Finger massage should be given weekly to keep the skin supple especially over the pressure points. A little mink oil may be sprayed on to a brush for a final polish before using a chamois leather or velvet pad. The eyes require wiping over with a good eye lotion. Wrinkles must be dried and cleaned and powdered with Johnson's baby powder. Ears require regular weekly attention. They should be cleaned out with a cotton wool swab dipped in alcohol and then dusted with a good ear powder. The recipe for an excellent one is given in the grooming section. If the nose is dry a little vaseline should be applied. Nails require to be kept short by clipping and then filing. The flews and the folds of the lips require to be kept clean and free from any accumulation of stale food. Dogs should be bathed before a show and a white rinse may be used on the white areas. A chalk block may be used on the white areas while they are still damp, but the chalk must be brushed out thoroughly. Nails may be polished for shows, or wiped over with vaseline just before entering the ring.

BULLMASTIFF

This is a heavy breed often weighing 130 lbs. The coat is easy to keep in good condition. The coat should be short and hard, lying close to the body and giving good, weather protection.

A medium-soft, short-bristle brush is excellent, and a rubber hound glove and a velvet pad will bring up a fine polish. Many people only groom using a chamois leather over the coat. Finger massage keeps the skin supple and a hand strapping is excellent. Pressure points must be watched and regular attention given to ears, teeth and nails. Show dogs may be bathed, but a good walk in country rain is even better than a bath. The nose may be lightly greased with vaseline, and before entering the ring the nails may be highlighted by applying a little vaseline to each one separately or they may be polished. The eyes should be wiped round, and wrinkles cleaned and dried out with Johnson's baby powder. Eye stains can be removed with boracic powder pressed on to the area. The flews and folds of the lips require to be kept clean and free from accumulation of stale food.

BULL TERRIER

The Bull Terrier is described as the gladiator of the canine race. The standard requires a short, flat, rather harsh coat with a good gloss. Grooming is no problem. Rubber brushes or soft hand gloves are probably best for keeping the coat in good condition. Strong finger massage and good hand strapping keep the skin supple. Polishing may be done with a silk handkerchief or velvet pad. For shows the Bull Terrier requires a bath and a rinse in a special hair whitener. The coat should be rubbed over with a chalk block while still damp. Castor oil drops should be dropped into each eye to prevent chalk getting into them whilst brushing it out. Rechalking will be required on the legs and head just before entering the ring, but the chalk must be well brushed out. Attention to pressure points and to the ears, teeth and nails are the only other grooming requirements of the Bull Terrier.

CAIRN TERRIER

This charming terrier has a double coat, consisting of a soft, fur-like undercoat and a top coat which should be profuse and hard but not coarse. Daily grooming with a medium-hard brush is all that is called for. The ears require plucking to tidy them and, when the coat has 'blown', a general tidying up of the body, legs and tail should be done. Otherwise, there is little work required, beyond the normal attention to the ears, nails and teeth.

CAVALIER KING CHARLES SPANIEL

I cannot think why the Cavalier King Charles Spaniel is classified as a Toy breed when the standard weight is 10-18 lbs. Nevertheless, it is a most popular breed and it presents no grooming problems. The standard requires a long, silky coat, free from curls, though a slight wave is permissible. There should also be plenty of feathering.

Grooming should be done daily with a stiff brush and a hound glove, followed by finger massage to keep the skin supple. Feathering should be combed out carefully. Ears must be kept clean, particularly at the edges. The inside ear should be wiped round and cleaned with a cotton wool swab moistened in alcohol and then lightly dusted with ear powder. The eyes should be wiped round gently and kept dry. The mouth must be kept clean, particularly the flews and the folds of the lips, because food sometimes accumulates here. Teeth must be cleaned and scaled regularly. Nails must be kept short by cutting and filing.

The Cavalier King Charles is generally bathed before a show, and the final rinse should contain a hair-whitening preparation. Officially, there is no trimming or stripping required. There must, however, be few dogs which cannot be improved when tidied up with fine thinning shears (46-teeth), particularly the skull and the top of the ears. The hair growing between the pads should be cut, but not the hair between the toes.

CHIHUAHUA, LONGCOAT

This enchanting little dog is of Mexican and United States origin, the long coat having been obtained by crossing the Mexican smoothcoat with the Papillon and Pomeranian and probably other breeds at the beginning of this century. The standard requires that the coat should be of soft texture, either flat or slightly curly, with under-coat preferred.

Grooming is identical to that of the smoothcoat variety, except that the feathering may be combed out with a wide-toothed comb. Coat cleaning can be done with Johnson's baby powder. Bathing should be done the day before a show, and the coat can be helped with a good brushing with coat dressing and powder. A little mink oil sprayed sparingly on to a brush can be lightly brushed over the coat to give an added sheen. Hair should be trimmed from between the pads, and the feet should be trimmed round just below the nails. It is seldom necessary to trim the feathering, but it could be trimmed a week before the show. Whiskers may also be cut close but this is purely optional. I, personally, prefer the whiskers to be left on.

CHIHUAHUA, SMOOTHCOAT

This charming Toy dog is of Mexican origin and is the smallest of all breeds of dog. The standard requires a fine-textured coat, close and glossy, though heavier coats with undercoats are per-missible.

Grooming is obviously easy with such a tiny smooth-coated dog A soft-bristle brush or a Mason Pearson brush is best for normal grooming. This may be followed with gentle massage and light hand strapping with a final polish with a silk handkerchief.

Chihuahuas are apt to get stains under the eyes, particularly if they get into draughts. The stains should be dried with cotton wool, and boracic powder pressed on to the area, and later brushed off, will remove the stain.

Ears require to be brushed lightly, particularly at the end of the leathers. The edges of the ears get clogged up with dandruff, old hair and grease, and if this is not removed or prevented the edges eventually become crusty and dry. The best way to deal with such a situation is to cover the edges with vaseline overnight to soften the hard areas, and the ears can then be wiped clean; and this generally removes the clogged dirt as well as the old dead hair too. The hair will take about four to six weeks to grow in again.

34. A long coat Chihuahua, bred and owned by the author.

Photo: Anne Cumbers

35. A smooth coat Chihuahua, bred by
the author and now owned by Her Highness
Princess Manejeh Pahlavi of Iran.

Photo: Anne Cumbers

Chihuahua nails are apt to grow too long, and they will curl right round if they are not cut regularly once a month. Like most dogs, they dislike their nails being clipped, but owners must be strong-minded and make certain that this part of their toilet is not neglected. Teeth are often not as strong as they should be, and many Chihuahuas lose them at an early age. They should be cleaned regularly. Some Chihuahuas have extremely good teeth and it is very much a hereditary trait. Watery eyes can be helped by wiping them over with Diamondeye or Eye-Brite.

The Chihuahua has an idiosyncrasy in its tail. This should be furry and flattish in appearance, broadening lightly in the centre and then tapering to a point. The tail requires to be brushed carefully. Sometimes the hair becomes rather bald along the tail, in which case benzyl benzoate emulsion will soften the skin and allow the new hair to grow in quickly.

Chihuahuas should be bathed before a show, and a little Johnson's baby powder sprinkled on the coat keeps it clean and smelling fresh. The powder is also a useful grooming cleaning aid. Nails may be polished, and if the nose looks dry a little vaseline may be smeared on lightly.

CHOW CHOW

This is one of the breeds which originated in the east and is really one of the Spitz group. The Chow Chow has a great wealth of coat. The standard requires a double coat, the undercoat being soft and woolly, whilst the outer coat should be somewhat coarse in texture. The two coats together must not only be abundant and extremely dense, but they should also be straight and stand off the body.

The coat is easy to maintain, but particular care is required during the seasons of moulting, change of puppy coat, and with bitches after whelping.

SUGGESTED METHOD OF GROOMING

Tools and Equipment required

Brush with long bristles	Nail clippers
Wide-tooth comb	Artery forceps
Thinning shears	Shampoo
7-inch scissors	Electric trunk hair dryer

Method

Grooming should be started from the extremities, gradually working upwards and brushing the hair down layer by layer. If a trunk dryer is used at the same time, this helps not only to see any mats close to the skin but helps to separate the hair during the brushing. Hair should be removed from between the pads by scissoring. Extra long hair which grows on the feet or ears should be removed.

When the coat is coming out, it should be helped by combing. The coat should be brushed daily or at least twice a week, particular care being taken behind the ears and under the joints, where the coat is most likely to mat. The anal area may be scissored for the sake of hygiene as may the hair in front of the penis.

The Chow Chow coat does not become spoilt by bathing, and this is strongly recommended before a show.

Normal care of ears, eyes, nails and teeth.

COLLIE, BEARDED

This breed is treated in a similar manner to the Old English Sheepdog, except that the long tail requires combing out. These dogs may be bathed if dirty a week before a show. The hair on the muzzle is brushed downwards, whilst the beard is brushed forwards and the hair on the skull is brushed backwards. The eyebrows should be arched over the eyes, but they should not fall flat over the muzzle.

COLLIE, ROUGH

The standard for the Rough Collie requires a dense coat. The undercoat should be soft, furry and very close, so that it almost hides the skin; and the long outer coat should be harsh to the touch. The mane and frill are abundant. More hair is required at the base of the ears than on the top.

SUGGESTED METHOD OF PREPARING A ROUGH COLLIE

It will probably take about six to four weeks to prepare a collie for a show. It depends on the time of year and the condition of the coat. Preparation is similar to that of a Shetland Sheep Dog.

Tools and Equipment required

Long-bristle brush	Johnson's baby powder
Wide-toothed comb	Chalk
7-inch scissors	Coat dressing
Thinning shears, 46-toothed	Mink oil
Stripping knife	Bay rum

It is a matter of personal preference, whether the dog is taught to be groomed standing or to lie on a table or the floor. The coat should be brushed on alternate days with a good long-bristled brush with a handle, or with a Hindes pin brush. Brushing should commence from the extremities, holding the hair up with one hand whilst brushing it down with the brush in the other hand. If a blow dryer is used at the same time, each hair is separated as the grooming proceeds and the dust, dirt and scurf are blown out, and any mats or tangles will be visible. Extra care is required with the breechings, tail and mane, and particularly the hair just behind the ears, which will felt and ball unless attended to regularly. As with all breeds with undercoats, care must be taken not to remove too much whilst grooming. Feathering on the legs should be combed in the direction in which it grows.

A month before a show the hair on the back of the hocks may be trimmed closely, so that it is the correct length for exhibition. If the coat is too abundant behind the ears or on top of the tail, this may be stripped out with a knife or thinned out with fine thinning shears, until the desired effect is reached. The ears are not generally touched, but if the ear set is incorrect, judicious trimming may give the desired effect.

Ear Carriage. The desired ear carriage of tipped ears laid down for the show ring often requires aid during puppyhood. There are various methods used to make the ears tip in the desired position; powdered ash stuck on the ears with wax or something similar is probably the most popular method, combined with massage and continued bending of the ears particularly during early puppyhood. Most collies' ears would be completely erect naturally, but fashion has decreed that tipped ears are required and these often have to be assisted if not made. It is surprising how many show collies are exported, only to disappoint their new owners, who have not been initiated into collie ear procedure, and who find that all their litters of top show-quality collies have produced litters with erect ears.

F

COLLIE, SMOOTH

There is nothing special about this breed's grooming. It is similar to the grooming of any other smooth-coated breed of the equivalent size.

CORGI
(Cardigan and Pembroke)

These ancient Welsh cattle dogs are similar to each other. The Cardigan has a long tail whilst the Pembroke has a short tail. The standard requires that the Cardigan coat should be short or of medium length, and that it should be of hard texture. The Pembroke coat must be of medium-length and very dense. Brushing the coat should be done with a medium-stiff bristle brush every day. The coat should be combed through about once a week with a medium-fine comb. Finger massaging and hand strapping is strongly recommended. Many breeders do not advise much bathing, but it does depend very much on the dog's colour, particularly for a show. If the dog is bathed, it is probably better to do so a few days before a show. Only the normal canine care is required for ears, eyes, teeth and nails.

CURLY-COATED RETRIEVER

This is one of the oldest of the British gun dogs, and it is probably related to the poodle and to the Irish Water Spaniel. The coat, surprisingly, is extremely easy to manage. The hair on the head is naturally short and requires no trimming. Many dogs are shown having had little or practically nothing done to them. There are two schools of thought as to the correct preparation for showing.

The standard requires that the coat should literally be one mass of crisp curly hair all over, except half-way up on the skull and foreface. The coat on the tail should also be curly and the tail is required to taper to a point. The ear leathers are covered in short crisp curls.

SUGGESTED METHOD OF PREPARING A CURLY-COATED RETRIEVER

Many breeders prefer to use hand massage on the body and the coat is only brushed occasionally. It should, however, be brushed down to the skin when the puppy coat is changing. In fact, the less done to the coat the better.

Tools and Equipment required

Bristle brush	Artery forceps
Comb	Ear powder
7-inch scissors	Mink oil
Nail clippers	Shampoo
Tooth scaler	

Method
1. Regular massage helps to stimulate the skin and does not disturb the coat.
2. Clean the ears and powder them when necessary.
3. Clean the teeth.
4. Brush the coat and legs when necessary, paying attention to the ear leathers.

Trimming
1. Scissor any upstanding curls on the head, ears and body, so that they lie flat.
2. Scissor the curls on the tail quite extensively. The tail should resemble an otter's tail, being wide at the base and tapering to a fine point.

Bathing
Many people do not advocate this, unless it is really necessary, because it tends to soften the coat, and this is required to be crisp. If the dog is bathed, this should not be done less than three days before a show. A shampoo similar to JDS is recommended. The tight curls require careful and thorough rinsing.

Just before the coat is quite dry, a little mink oil may be rubbed through the curls in a circular motion, so that they become well set.

DACHSHUND, LONG-HAIRED

Being a small breed, these delightful little dogs are no problem to groom. They do not require scissoring or trimming, although too heavy a coat is considered a fault, and exhibitors of such dogs might well thin and trim the coat down to the desired density and length.

The coat being fine and silky requires brushing with a good bristle brush, a small cushioned brush is best. A medium-fine comb is used for brushing out the fringes on the ears and the leg feathering. The coat is brushed along the back and down the body more or less in the direction in which it falls naturally. The flag (that is, the tail) is brushed straight down the top and from the root of the tail to its tip. The hair underneath is then combed out forming a beautiful fringe. The feathering on the hind legs is also combed out carefully, making certain that the area round the anus is clean.

The straggly hair between the toes should be trimmed out and the foot made to look neat and round.

Ears require regular attention to prevent an infestation of ear mites. *Eyes* must be kept dry and clean.

Teeth may be cleaned with hydrogen peroxide, using a 10% solution diluted half and half with milk. It is probably better to wipe the teeth over with a small piece of flannel or cotton material rather than to use a brush. *Nails* require trimming or filing once a month.

Dachshunds are, unfortunately, apt to produce follicular, or demodectic, mange. Any signs therefore, of balding patches or scabs should be watched for, and if discovered treatment should be commenced without delay.

DACHSHUND, SMOOTH-HAIRED

This charming little dog is of German origin. The standard requires that the coat should be short, dense, smooth and strong. The hair on the underside of the tail (or should it be stern?) should be coarse in texture. Grooming is simple: a short, soft brush should be used, with a final polish with a silk handkerchief. Ears should be powdered weekly and nails must be kept short and teeth clean.

Dachshunds are rather liable to demodectic mange, and a watch must, therefore, be kept for bald patches. This type of mange is not particularly catching, but an anti mange drug applied to the skin as directed by the veterinary surgeon will probably stop any further spreading of the mange mite.

DACHSHUNDS, WIRE-HAIRED

This is similar to the other varieties of dachshund, but the standard requires that the coat should be short, harsh and even, except on the jaw, the eyebrows and the ears, and there is an undercoat. The eyebrows should be bushy, there should be a beard on the chin, whilst the hair on the ears should be soft. The coat requires stripping twice a year when the coat has 'blown', and it takes approximately six to four weeks after a dog has been stripped before he is in show condition. Daily grooming with a rather stiff brush and a medium-fine comb will keep the coat in good order. Occasional in-between stripping may be necessary to keep the dog tidy. Once a week the ears should be cleaned out with a cotton wool swab moistened in alcohol and then powdered with a good ear powder. Nails must be kept short, and teeth scaled and cleaned when necessary.

DALMATIAN

This is the only all-over spotted dog and he was widely used when carriages were fashionable in the last century. Grooming is simple as the breed has neither wrinkle nor trimming to deal with. The standard requires a short, fine, dense, hard and sleek coat. A medium-bristle brush and a hound glove are best for grooming and a velvet pad for polishing the coat. Brushing should be done every day, so that the spots are kept clear from the encroachment of neighbouring white hairs. Good finger massaging keeps the skin supple and pliable and good hand strapping excellent for the coat gloss. Normal attention is required for the ears, nails and teeth. The ears should be kept clean with a gentle rub round with a cotton wool swab moistened in alcohol. The interior of the ears should be dusted with ear powder and an excellent recipe for this can be found under the grooming section. Dalmatians seldom require bathing, only extra grooming before a show. The nose may be gently wiped over with a little vaseline to make it shine, and so can each toe-nail, or the latter may be polished.

DANDIE DINMONT TERRIER

The Dandie Dinmont Terrier is named after the well known character in Scott's *Guy Mannering* and is one of the short legged terriers. The chief characteristics of the breed include the head covered with a very soft silky hair; the lighter the colour and the silkier this is the better. The coat is most important and consists of harsh and soft hair which gives a feeling of crispness when touched. The outer coat, however, should not be wiry, and the standard describes it as "pily and pencilled"—whatever that may mean. The hair on the under part of the body is softer and lighter in colour. If the dog is to be shown, the coat is required to be from 1½ to 2 inches in length. The normal method of preparing the dog for a show is by stripping or plucking with finger and thumb.

The hair on top of the ears is left long. It is brushed up into the topknot and should be of the same colour as that, and feathering is required on the ears starting about 2 inches from the tip. Many dogs do not, however, grow this feathering until they are about two years old. Some breeders prefer to scissor this fringe into a tassel. This is purely a matter of personal preference, as it is not mentioned in the standard, and fashions change.

The Dandie Dinmont should not be bathed unless this is really necessary, because it is apt to soften the coat. The topknot and tassels, however, require washing the day before a show and they are then whitened with chalk or powder while still damp.

SUGGESTED METHOD OF PREPARING A DANDIE DINMONT

It takes about eight weeks to prepare a Dandie Dinmont for a show. The coat is plucked, scissored and thinned in various stages, due to the different lengths of hair required and also to the difference of the rate of growth of the coat on different parts of the body.

Tools and Equipment required

7-inch scissors	Grooming table
46-toothed thinning shears	Grooming mirror
Bristle brush	Artery forceps
Wide-tooth comb	Ear powder
Nail clippers	Chalk
Johnson's baby powder	Shampoo
Electric hair dryer	

SUGGESTED ORDER OF WORK

STAGE I—*Eight weeks before the Show*
Body Coat. With finger and thumb pluck or strip the body coat. There is no reason why the neck and shoulders should not be stripped at the same time, because this certainly makes the dog look more groomed, but the latter will require re-doing.

STAGE II—*Two weeks before the Show*
1. *Neck and Shoulders.* The old coat should be plucked from the neck and shoulders, graduating the length of hair into the body coat.
2. *Ears.* The hair on the top of the ears is left long and brushed up into the topknot, to give the effect of a wide skull.
3. Leave a fringe of hair 1 to 1½ inches on the edge of the lower tip of the ear to form into a tassel.
4. Strip the hair from the inside of the ear, that is the underside of the ear leather, so that the ear will lie close to the cheek.
5. Strip the hair on the ears between the long hair left to join the topknot and the fringe hair which forms the tassel. It is quite a good idea to scissor the shape of the tassel. The apex of the triangular tassel should start about 1 to 1½ inches from the centre of the tip of the leather.
6. *Tassel.* Comb the tassel hair down, and trim the ends off into a straight line.
7. Dogs with sensitive ears may have the ear hair thinned out with fine thinning shears, working underneath the longer hair from the bottom of the ear towards the top. This is much kinder and just as effective.
8. *Muzzle.* Strip any long hair from the top of the muzzle, working from the nose towards the eyes.
9. *Stop.* Emphasize the stop by plucking the hair from between the eyes, but do not overdo it.
10. *Eyes.* The hair round the eyes should be trimmed to emphasize their size and to show the black pigmentation round the lids. It is important to keep the trimming round, because otherwise the expression would be lost.
11. *Face.* It is important not to over-trim the face, both on the top of the muzzle and round the eyes. The custom has always been to pluck the hair, but thinning shears with fine teeth

worked under the coat, and gradually drawn away from the hair while still cutting, produces a very good effect and has the added advantage of causing no discomfort at all to the dog.

12. *Tail.* The tail is required to be thick at the base and tapered to a point. The feathering on the underside of the tail is left, but it generally requires tidying. All the hair that grows at the end of the tail beyond the last bone must be removed, either with a stripping knife or with thinning shears. The final tip should be graduated so that it looks natural.

13. *Forelegs.* The hair is stripped on the front and inner sides of the legs. A light feathering is left at the back of the legs.

14. *Hind Legs.* The hair is removed reasonably short from the hocks down, and the breechings from the root of the tail to the hocks are left long, but they may require tidying. The breechings help to emphasize the length of the body.

15. *Feet.* The nails require to be short, the long hair should be removed from between the pads, and the feet themselves should be scissored neatly and rounded.

16. *Under-body Coat.* This should be trimmed from the end of the last rib and the hind legs, to emphasize the tuck up and to show a waist.

17. *Topknot.* This should be trimmed facing the dog. Brush the hair from the top of the ears to join the topknot, and either shorten any untidy hair with a stripping knife, or scissor neatly to give the effect of density.

STAGE II.—*One day before the Show*

1. *Topknot and Tassels.* These should be shampooed and rinsed well the day before the show. While the hair is still damp, the hair should be well chalked. When using chalk, eye drops should be used afterwards to clean the eyes in case particles of chalk have entered them.

2. *General Grooming.* The whole coat requires a good grooming and, if there is any last minute tidying up required, this should be done at this time.

STAGE IV—*Day of the Show*

Brush all the chalk out of the topknot and tassels; comb the face and ear hair upwards and also lift the hair from the neck; comb the tassels out neatly. The hard daily brushing which should have gone into the preparation of the show Dandie Dinmont Terrier will now pay its dividends.

Chalk rots the coat in an insidious manner and it is therefore essential that the topknot and ear tassels should be well washed after the show. For daily use the topknot and ear tassels could be prepared with Johnson's baby powder.

DEERHOUND

The Scottish Deerhound is a breed which has altered little over the years. The standard requires that the body coat should be three to four inches long and should be harsh and wiry. This applies to the neck and to the hair on the quarters. There should be a slight, hairy fringe on the legs. The hair on the breast and belly is softer than elsewhere. A woolly coat is a fault, the correct coat being is thick close lying, ragged, and harsh and crisp to the touch. The tail hair should be thick and wiry on the inside and somewhat longer on the outside. The ears should be covered in soft mousy-textured hair. Grooming is easy and requires a good brush once a week, the usual attention to the ears, the nails and the teeth. Show dogs require the long hair to be trimmed or plucked off the ears and the long hair off the toes, but otherwise the coat is just generally tidied up, bearing in mind that the dog requires to look shaggy.

DOBERMANN

This breed is generally known in other countries as the 'Doberman Pinscher'. They were named after the man in Germany who started the breed.

With regards to grooming, this is an easy breed. The standard requires the coat to be smooth-haired, short, hard, thick and close-lying. Daily brushing, followed by some good finger massage to keep the skin supple, and then by a good hand strapping, makes the coat gleam. A final finish with a velvet pad will make the coat really shine most beautifully. Scurf may be treated with Rotenone oil. The ears must be kept clean and dusted with ear powder once a week.

If the coat is scurfy just before a show, the dog should be bathed in Tetmosol soap, which will also help the condition. Nails and

F*

nose may be smeared over with a little vaseline to make them shine if they look dry, or the nails may be polished. Normal care of ears, eyes and nails are necessary.

ELKHOUND

This is one of the Spitz group of dog and like most Spitz varieties it is hardy and sporting. The standard requires that the coat should consist of two coats. The undercoat should be light-coloured, soft and woolly. This should be covered with an abundant, thick, coarse, weather-resisting outer coat, whose length is longest on the neck, chest and hind quarters, behind the forelegs and on the underside of the tail. The head should be covered with short hair, as should the front of the legs. The hair should also be short from the hocks down. The top coat consists of long and short hair. The tail hair must be thick and close.

The coat is not difficult to maintain, but it is better if groomed regularly every day. Bathing is only recommended when the dog is really dirty, in which case bathing should not be done less than a week prior to a show, because it softens the coat. Piecemeal bathing is often necessary and this is similar to that described for the Keeshond.

SUGGESTED METHOD OF GROOMING

Tools and Equipment required

Short-bristle brush	Nail clippers
Medium-fine steel comb	Ear powder
Hound glove	Shampoo
Artery forceps	Spirit shampoo
Tooth scaler	Electric trunk hair dryer
Fuller's earth	Mink oil.

Method

The Elkhound should first be combed thoroughly all over with a medium fine-toothed comb, and then brushed in a similar manner as described for the Keeshond. A little mink oil sprayed lightly on a brush will give a good sheen, especially if worked on the coat with a good, hard hand strapping. Nails may be polished for shows. Normal care is required for ears, eyes, teeth and nails.

ENGLISH SETTER

The English Setter is one of the most handsome of breeds. He is very friendly, although he is naturally quiet-natured. He is essentially a gun dog with a keen game sense.

The standard requires that the coat should be slightly wavy and long and silky from the top of the neck between the ears and all over the body. The legs should be well feathered down to the feet except on the hind legs below the hocks. There should also be extensive feathering on the breechings.

The coat is easy to maintain with regular daily brushing lasting about ten minutes, or grooming twice a week for half an hour. The coat does require a little stripping on the head and neck and some thinning of the feathering. Thinning shears can be used to good advantage on the throat before a show.

SUGGESTED METHOD OF GROOMING AND SHOW PREPARATION

In the U.S.A. setters are clipped from the adam's apple to the end of the lower jaw with a no. 5 or no. 7 blade against the growth of hair, or with a no. 10 or no. 15 with the growth of hair. The clipped area includes the hair on the side of the neck along the cheek from the inside corner of the ear to the outer corner of the eye. The ear leather is cleaned out from halfway up the leather both on the inside and on the outside. All the clipped areas are then blended by careful stripping or by the judicious use of fine thinning shears.

Tools and Equipment required

Hard brush	Nail clippers
Soft brush	Artery forceps
Wide-tooth comb	Ear powder
Fine-tooth comb	Whitening to aid stripping
Stripping knife	7-inch scissors
Thinning shears, 46-teeth	Mink oil
Oster A5 (U.S.A. only), with	Chamois leather or velvet
no. 10 blade	polisher

Method

Any clipping should be done about a week before a show in the U.S.A., depending on the state of the coat. If clippers are used in Britain they should be used about two months before a show, so that the hair has time to grow to the correct length and look natural.

Grooming

1. Brush the coat vigorously in the direction in which the coat grows, starting gently at the head.
2. Comb out the feathering on the legs, making the dog extend his forelegs so that any mats may be reached between the legs.
3. Comb the tail feathering carefully.
4. Use a fine-toothed comb all over the body when the dog is moulting, carding the coat as you work.
5. Wipe the eyes.
6. Clean out the ears with a swab of cotton wool moistened in alcohol and powder weekly with ear powder.
7. Spray a brush lightly with mink oil and brush into the coat.
8. Polish the coat with a velvet pad or use the hands.

Stripping

1. Strip the hair on the top of the head if necessary.
2. Strip the hair on the neck and anywhere required on the body, particularly during the times of moulting and the change of puppy coat.
3. Fine thinning shears are kinder than stripping the head and can be used instead of plucking, provided that the blades are kept close to the skin and underneath the top coat.

Trimming

1. Trim round the ear feathering.
2. Remove whiskers (optional).
3. Trim the ends of the feathering in a straight, diagonal line.
4. Trim the tail feathering in a similar manner.
5. Trim or pluck the hair from the hocks downwards, but do not trim it too short.
6. Remove the hair from between the pads.
7. Scissor round the feet.
8. Clip the nails, if required.

Bathing

1. This is necessary if the dog has been trimmed recently.
2. Use a whitening rinse.
3. Cover the coat with a thick towel and pin it to keep the coat lying flat.

ENGLISH TOY TERRIER
(Black and Tan)

This English breed is a smaller edition of the Manchester Terrier. Grooming, and general grooming procedures for both breeds are identical.

FINNISH SPITZ

This is one of the Nordic group of dogs. The grooming is not difficult and is similar to that of the Keeshond. The standard requires a light-coloured, short, soft, dense undercoat, covered with a coarse top coat. The hair on the head, the front of the legs and from the hocks down should be short and close lying. The coat on the body should be semi-erect or erect and somewhat longer, particularly on the shoulders and especially in males. This body coat should also be coarse. Along the back of the thighs and on the tail the coat must be dense. Daily grooming is probably best, but some dogs are better if only groomed thoroughly once a week. It very much depends on the individual dog, the type of coat and the time of year.

SUGGESTED METHOD OF GROOMING

Tools and Equipment required

Medium-stiff brush	Fuller's earth
Nylon comb	Ear powder
Steel comb for cleaning brush	Shampoo
Artery forceps	Spirit shampoo
Tooth scaler	Electric trunk dryer
Nail clippers	Mink oil

Method

The use of the comb, except when the dog is changing his coat, should be discouraged. Grooming procedure is similar to that for the Keeshond.

FOX TERRIER, SMOOTH

This breed is similar in conformation to the Wire-Haired Fox Terrier. The standard requires that the coat should be smooth, flat and straight, hard and abundant. Grooming should be done with a short-bristle brush or a hound glove. This should be followed with finger massage to keep the skin supple and a good polish with a chamois leather. For show purposes the dog should be bathed and rinsed in a hair-whitening rinse. Whilst still damp the feet and legs can be chalked. Considerable trimming is necessary with fine thinning shears (46-teeth). In Britain however, Smooth-Haired Fox Terriers are more often plucked or stripped. The ears should be made to look as small as possible. The ruff round the neck should be thinned, particularly at the sides, and the elbow hair generally also requires thinning out well. Nails must be cut short or filed and may be polished before being exhibited. If the nose looks dry, a slight smearing of vaseline will make it shine. If there is no time to bath the dog, a good brush over with a coat dressing will clean him up quickly. Normal care is required for ears, eyes, teeth and nails.

FOX TERRIER, WIRE

The Wire-Haired Fox Terrier is a most attractive breed, particularly for the show ring, but there is no short cut in obtaining the perfect results which are absolutely essential if top honours are to be won at shows. The traditional method of dealing with show Wire-Haired Fox Terriers is stripping with a knife, or plucking the hair out with the finger and thumb.

It may seem rather far fetched to say that a mediocre Wire-Haired Fox Terrier prepared by an expert will always 'go over' a much more perfect specimen prepared by an amateur. In these days thinning shears, clippers and razor combs, etc., are not unknown to be used on some of the show specimens, particularly in the U.S.A., but these methods never give quite the same results, although the work is certainly accomplished more quickly. It would doubtless surprise many of the old diehards what good results can be obtained with the help of fine thinning shears. The Wire-Haired Fox Terrier requires two months of preparation before a show, worked in three stages on certain areas of his coat.

The pet Wire-Haired Fox Terrier naturally has to be dealt with in a more practical manner, and these dogs are generally clipped and scissored instead of being subjected to the traditional plucking and stripping, which should be done—from a dog's point of view—when he is casting his coat, which in terrier parlance is known as when the coat has 'blown'.

Preparing a Wire-Haired Fox Terrier for a show probably re-

36. Combing out the knots from the coat.

Photo: Anne Cumbers

37. Correct angle of stripping knife in action, the dog being controlled with the left hand.

Photo: Anne Cumbers

quires the greatest art and the most skill and knowledge of coat and coat textures of any breed. This applies to some of the other terriers, particularly the Airedale, but to the Wire-Haired Fox Terrier most of all. The desired coat of the Wire-Haired Fox Terrier, as with the desired coat of all breeds, must initially be bred for, fed for and above all cared for; and on top of this, in order to obtain perfect results it must be prepared for correctly over a period of time.

FOX TERRIER, WIRE

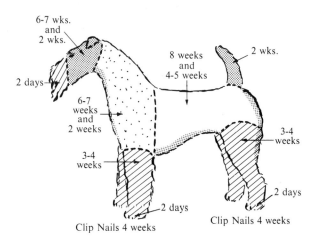

Areas plucked before a show

Rear legs
well arched

Blended front
legs into body coat

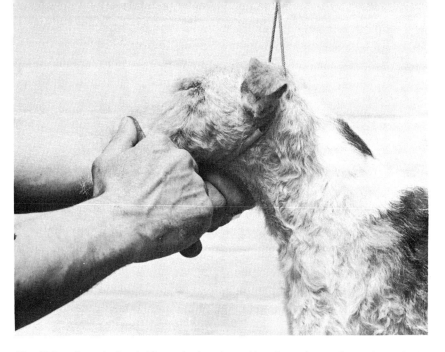

38. Using the stripping knife on the beard, working from the eye forward. Strip the skull really close from above the eyebrows.

Photo: Anne Cumbers

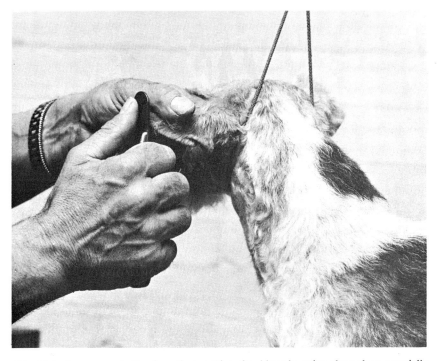

39. Stripping an ear, starting from the top. They should not be stripped too close, especially in winter, as this is liable to cause chaps, which are extremely difficult to cure. Ears are never clipped, because clipping removes the colour.

Photo: Anne Cumbers

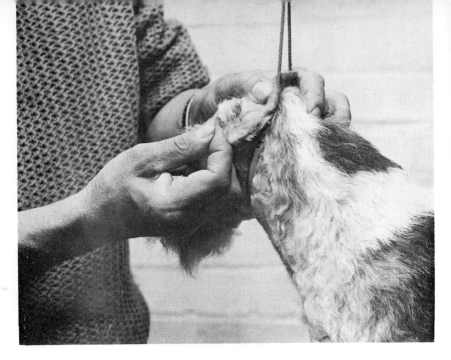

40.   Plucking out the hair growing in the ear canal.

Photo: Anne Cumbers

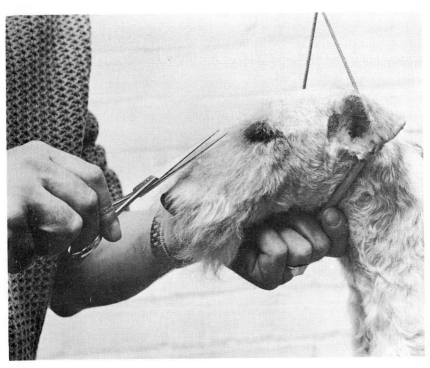

41.   Scissoring into the hair below the eyes, snipping to leave sufficient undercoat to pad the face.   The scissors are held parallel to the top of the muzzle.

Photo: Anne Cumbers

HOW TO LEARN THE ART OF PREPARING A WIRE-HAIRED FOX TERRIER

Practical experience is worth more than reading a hundred books on the subject, particularly if the aid of an expert can be enlisted. The best method of all is to watch an expert prepare one side of a dog, taking notes while this is being done, and remembering to ask suitable questions at the right moment. The novice should then try to prepare the other side of the terrier in the same manner, and it will be surprising how much of the expert's work will have gone unobserved.

The expert will be able to work fast without becoming tired, and he will naturally make the preparations look extremely simple, though this, of course, is far from the case. The novice must take heart and should realize that the expert too was once a novice; and the expert must have patience with the novice and should try and remember far enough back to the stupid mistakes he made in setting out to learn the difficult art of terrier preparation.

But where there is a will there is always a way.

Before being able to prepare a Wire-Haired Fox Terrier correctly, it is absolutely essential to understand the standard and the various coat textures which are to be found in the breed. It is important, too, to learn how each should be dealt with to obtain maximum results. It is a good idea to study photographs of top Wire-Haired Fox Terriers, to try to view them in the ring, and if possible to talk to terrier people at a propitious moment at a show, when they are actually doing the last preparations before entering the ring. The more good dogs that are looked at and the more different textures of coat that are studied—not forgetting to observe the different stages of growth that the coat undergoes throughout the year— the quicker the novice will learn this new and fascinating art.

The standard of the Wire-Haired Fox Terrier requires that the coat should be dense, wiry-textured, like coconut matting with a tendency to twist. The hair should be so dense that, when it is parted with the fingers, it should not be possible to see the skin. Under the top coat is a shorter growth of fine soft hair which is known as the undercoat. The coat is always harder and wirier on the back and quarters than it is on the sides. It will often be found that the hardest coats are crinkly or slightly wavy, but they should never be curly.

The hair on both jaws should be crisp and sufficiently long to give added strength to the foreface, and on the forelegs is dense

42. Measuring the head.

43. Continuing the use of the dolling-up pad.

and crisp. The standard states as a guidance that the coat should be three-quarters to one inch long on the shoulders and neck, lengthening to one and a half inches on the withers, back, ribs and quarters. Although the standard states that colour is of little or no importance, in actual fact it is, because if the ears are clipped instead of being plucked there will be loss of colour, which will not correspond with the markings on the body; and this is why the ears are plucked and scissored and never clipped.

Stripping and plucking a show Wire-Haired Fox Terrier

A professionally 'put down' Fox Terrier for showing has to be stripped and plucked by hand, because this undoubtedly produces the best results, which cannot be produced by mechanical methods. For the true professional it would be unheard of to use electric clippers or fine-toothed thinning shears. Nevertheless, if these mechanical aids are used, and used with care and intelligence, very good results can be achieved in far less time. The secret is that, after using clippers, as soon as the hair begins to grow, fine-toothed thinning shears must be used extensively to remove the undercoat as it comes in, because if this is not done the outer coat will grow upwards instead of lying flat as is required.

It takes about eight weeks for a Fox Terrier coat to grow in, and the coat is prepared during this time in three main phases. At approximately six to eight weeks before the dog is to be shown, the first stage of preparations must be started. This consists of stripping out the terrier's body coat when it has 'blown'; in other words when the old hair is dead and is in the process of moulting. The coat at this stage stands out from the body and can easily be removed with absolutely no discomfort to the dog.

Luckily for exhibitors, it is not absolutely essential to remove the coat as soon as it has 'blown'. It may indeed be left for several weeks, so that the coat may be got ready for a particular show. During this period the terrier will look very rough and untidy indeed.

At the first stage, the body coat is removed from the withers to the elbow and back to the hind quarters between the root of the tail and the hips and rump. At the second stage, which should take place somewhere between one and two weeks later, the coat from the top of the neck to just above the elbows is stripped. The third stage includes the stripping of the skull, the ears, the front, the tail and the area between the root of the tail and just above the hocks

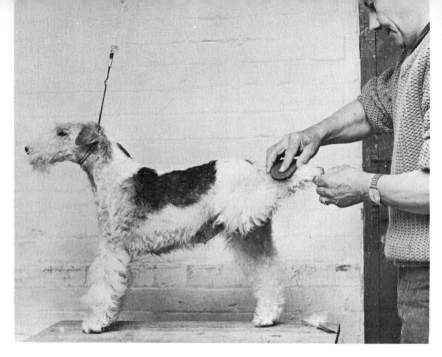

44. The position of the hind leg when using the dolling-up pad. The dog is controlled by a slip collar and leash attached to a hook in the ceiling which is regulated by a lead weight.

Photo: Anne Cumbers

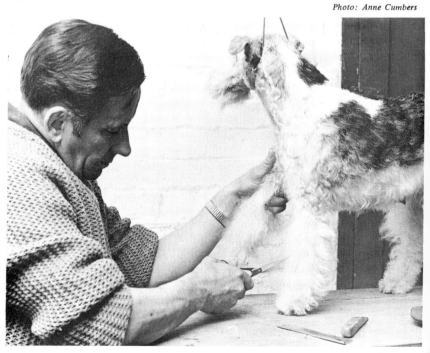

45. Correct positions when scissoring the fore legs. The scissoring is done by snipping carefully into the coat.

Photo: Anne Cumbers

46. Trimming one foot. The other foot is meanwhile held off the ground to **prevent** the dog moving the foot being trimmed.

Photo: Anne Cumbers

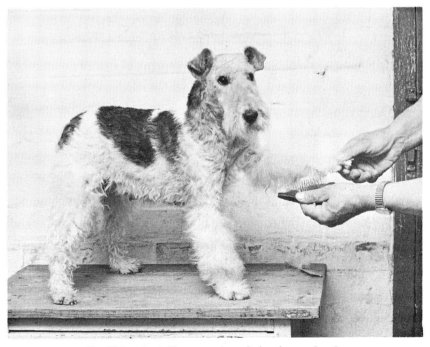

47. Using the dolling-up pad or pin brush on a fore leg.

Photo: Anne Cumbers

and also underneath the body between the forelegs and the tuck up.

The reason why stripping has to be accomplished in three stages is because of the varying rate of growth of the hair. This differs quite considerably on different parts of the body and, when stripping is performed correctly in the three stages, the end result is a coat of uniform length and texture.

STAGE I

Body Coat. The day before stripping, chalk the coat on the body between the withers and the elbows and back to the root of the tail and the loins. This is purely optional. Chalk dries out the natural oils in the hair and makes it easier to hold when stripping. If pre-ferred, the coat may be stripped from the neck including the shoulders down to the elbows at this time, but it will require doing again at stage two. The body coat generally takes between four and five weeks after stripping to reach the correct length for exhibition, whilst the hair on the head and quarters only requires about two weeks to reach the desired length. There is one advantage in doing stage one and stage two at the same time, and that is that the dog as a whole will look more presentable during this period.

1. *Chalking.* Chalk the body and the coat from ears to elbow, if stage one and stage two are to be plucked at the same time. Chalking should be done twenty-four hours before plucking. Many breeders, however, do not bother to chalk the coat at this stage at all.
2. *Combing.* Comb the coat carefully and thoroughly. Insert the comb and comb the coat downwards, using what may best be described as a rolling action without actually removing the teeth from the coat. This is called 'carding'. Do not clean the hair accumulating in the teeth but continue the rolling action. The object is to remove the woolly undercoat, as it is this soft, downy undercoat which is so undesirable, and this coat prevents the growth of the new live hair coming in. If there are any knots or mats, try and separate these by dividing them into three or four with the fingers, and comb out with the end tooth of the comb.
3. *Stripping.* With the stripping comb, held at the correct angle as previously described under stripping, commence to strip the coat from the top of the neck, removing only a small quantity

of hair at a time and making certain that it is stripped out and not cut out. The movement is similar to that of plucking a chicken, but the twist of the wrist should not be too sudden, since this will inevitably cut the coat instead of plucking it out. The coat is stripped out all over the body, following the direction in which the coat grows. If chalk has been used to aid the stripping procedure, it is essential to bath the dog to get rid of the chalk, as chalk rots the hair in a slow, insidious manner.

STAGE II

Ten to fourteen days later, strip the neck and shoulders as far as the elbows. This must still be done, even if this area was stripped at the time when the body coat was stripped.

STAGE III

This takes place about a week later.

Skull and Ears. The skull and ears are extremely sensitive areas, and they are plucked as closely as possible without hurting the dog. The hair is plucked out with finger and thumb and should only be done when the coat has 'blown'. It is quite a good idea to scratch the hair forward gently and then to pluck it out. If there is difficulty, a stripping knife may be used. The ears are never clipped because this causes them to lose their colour, and they have instead to be stripped carefully, in order to avoid removing the darker outercoat. The ears must never be plucked too close especially during the winter months. Plucking the ears causes irritation to the ear leather, and the dog will then automatically shake his ears and, if he catches them on anything, chaps will be caused and these splits are often difficult to cure. They quickly become extremely sore, and this will inevitably affect the ear carriage. Zemol powder or benzobenzoate emulsion will help the chaps. In cases where there is a previous history of chapped ears, it is probably better to use the fine, thinning shears, removing the underneath soft coat on the ears, because this produces the same effect as plucking them and does not remove the colour of the longer hair.

Throat, Shoulders, Quarters and behind Tail. These areas, including the skull and ears, are plucked closer than anywhere else on the body. After stripping, these areas should be smeared with a little vaseline, taking particular care with the ears. If the skin, as it generally does, looks pink and irritated, then it should be coated with a little baby oil or mink oil to prevent it from drying and eventually flaking off. The undercoat is generally left in at this stage, and, depending on the individual dog's coat, it should be raked out regularly about twice a week, so that the desired gloss and colour of the markings may be enhanced.

Legs. Three or four weeks before the show the legs should be worked on for the first time. If they are played about with before then, the valuable undercoat may easily get destroyed and lost in the process, so that three weeks is probably the best time to 'pick over' the leg hair. The legs require to have a padded look, so that practically no undercoat should ever be raked out, as is constantly required on the body. In terriers lacking in undercoat on the legs, every hair will count in producing the desired shape. If, on the other hand, the undercoat is really dense, then a great deal of unwanted fluff must be plucked out by hand, in order to avoid the incoming new coat from being choked. If this undercoat is not controlled, the leg hair will automatically 'blow', and it will take several months before the leg coat is up to show standard again.

The use of hairdressing scissors is better for dogs who lack a dense growth of hair on the legs. This is a method which requires a great deal of practice. The leg shape must be maintained and only the very tips of the scissors should be used to snip the hair, the points of the scissors being kept at the same angle the whole way up the leg. It is essential that the leg, when finished, should not have either a scissored or a clipped appearance.

STAGE IV—*Two Days before the Show*

Head. The dog now requires his final shaping and clever trimming. The requirements are a long, lean skull, a narrow front, a well-scooped throat accentuating a reachy neck, and small V-shaped ears. Comb down the hair from the eyebrows towards the nose and scissor the hair carefully as required. With the scissors held parallel to the bone structure on top of the muzzle, carefully snip the hair as you go, taking care not to remove too much under the eyes, which causes a snipy effect. Continue snipping the hair, leaving an undercoat to pad the cheeks. Comb the beard forward and scissor neatly to the desired effect.

Eyebrows. Scissor the eyebrows so that they are longer at the inside corner, cutting them with one straight diagonal cut, from the outside towards the muzzle. Pick out the hair dividing the eyebrows so as to accentuate them.

Beard. Scissor the beard to conform with the rest of the head.

Ears. Scissor the edges neatly.

Leg Furnishings. These are finished off with the fingers and the dolling-up pad. If the coat is sparse, the legs should be finished by careful scissoring. Shape the feet with scissors. The perfectionist, at this stage, will chalk and powder the dog exactly as he should be done for the show, making any corrections necessary to the outline for the perfect terrier. This might entail scissoring from the tuck-up to just beneath the elbow. All chalk must be removed to avoid ruining the coat.

STAGE V—*One Day before the Show*

Shampoo. Wash the legs and face in a good shampoo and rinse well, partly dry and whiten the coat by rubbing in precipitated white.

Sacking the Coat. Place a towel, folded in half, over the body, and pin the folded end over the brisket. Pin under the body just behind the elbows and again at the tuck up. This will help to flatten the coat until it is dry. During this time it is best to keep the dog in a warm, confined area, to prevent him from catching a chill.

Brushing out the Chalk. This must be done thoroughly all over the coat with a good bristle brush.

Polishing the Coat. Polish the coat with a hound glove.

STAGE VI—*Day of the Show*

Damp the coat and chalk it. Smear the legs with a very little vaseline and chalk the furnishings. Chalk the eyebrows with the head held down, so as to prevent chalk particles entering the eyes.

Eye Drops. Drop some soothing eye drops into the eyes in case any chalk powder has got into the eyes.

An hour before entering the Ring. The terrier is given his final preparations on a table specially prepared for whitening terriers. The routine remains the same, and according to Kennel Club regulations all signs of chalk must be removed from the coat before the dog is exhibited.

COMPLETE PREPARATION OF A WIRE-HAIRED FOX TERRIER

The preparation of a Fox Terrier for the show ring consists of a number of procedures which take place over a period of six to eight weeks according to the quality and texture of the coat.

1. *Plucking.* The coat is plucked at three different stages and areas, as the coat growth varies on different parts of the body.

2. *Building the Coat.* This consists of a daily grooming routine when the dog is in full coat.

3. *Topping the Coat.* Topping the coat consists of removing only the worst of the top coat with the finger and thumb so as to save the coat to enable the dog to be shown when the coat is about to 'blow'.

4. *Carding the Coat.* This is done on the furnishings with a wide-tooth comb which is inserted diagonally into the hair and it is then levered up into a perpendicular position. This rolling movement is continued from the top of the furnishings to the bottom, using only a gentle rolling action all the way. The hair which accumulates in the teeth of the comb should not be removed.

5. *Plucking out the Hair in the Ear Canal.* This should be done weekly, using ear powder and artery forceps. Tweaking out the hair with a rapid rotary action.

6. *Nail Trimming.* This requires to be done monthly depending on the dog. The nails should be clipped or filed with special attention to the two centre nails.

7. *Scissoring.* Scissors are used on the feet, the edge of the ears, the eyebrows and the beard. They are also used on the leg furnishings if they are not dense.

8. *Shampooing.* Shampooing is generally only required on the head, legs and feet before a show.

9. *Vaselining.* A very light smear of vaseline is used on the furnishings to hold the chalk. Vaseline may also be used instead of baby oil on the skull, ears, throat, shoulders, and behind the tail and quarters, because these areas are plucked shorter than anywhere else. Some people prefer to use baby oil or to spray mink oil on these areas instead of applying the light smearing of vaseline.

10. *Chalking.* The coat is whitened with precipitated white, which is put on to a damp coat. Block chalk is used when the coat is dry. Chalk rots the coat in a most insidious manner and it is essential that all traces of chalk be brushed out of the coat before the dog is exhibited. It is absolutely imperative that the coat should be bathed and shampooed and rinsed well the day after the show to eliminate any chalk which

may have adhered to the coat, particularly the areas on the furnishings which were greased with vaseline.

11. *Polishing.* This is accomplished with a hound glove to create a beautiful glove.
12. *Dolling Up.* This is the work done on the furnishings with a dolling up pad or a pin palm. It is worked in small circles drawing the pins outwards and downwards taking great care not to remove any hair in the process.

SUGGESTED METHOD OF PREPARING A SHOW WIRE-HAIRED FOX TERRIER

Tools and Equipment required

Bristle brush	Chalk
Steel comb, wide-tooth	Steady table
Razor comb	Good light
Nail file	Ear powder
Dolling-up pad	Artery forceps
Stripping knife	Hound glove
7-inch scissors	Large mirror
Nail clippers	Vaseline

SUGGESTED ORDER OF WORK WHEN STRIPPING AND PREPARING A WIRE-HAIRED FOX TERRIER

As with all grooming procedures, it is essential to have a definite routine. The dog learns this routine and accepts it, and the person grooming the dog will not miss out or forget important procedures. All tools must be collected together ready for use, the dog should be placed on a steady table with a non-slippery surface, and he should be trained to stand on command. It is probably safer to have the dog tethered with a corded lead round his neck, which is adjustable and may be attached to a hook on the ceiling immediately above the dog. It is better still if it can be worked on a pulley. If the dog is tethered, he must on no account be left even for one second, because he could easily accidentally hang himself if he tried to jump off the table. It is almost essential to have a large grooming mirror on the wall, placed so that the whole dog can be viewed at the same time. A good light is also essential, and a container to take the removed hair, which prevents it from getting blown about and from mixing with the dog's own coat.

1. Stand the dog on a firm, non-slippery table.

2. Have a grooming mirror behind the table.
3. Provide a good light.
4. Stand behind the dog and start stripping from the top of the neck downwards over the body.
5. Stand in front of the dog when doing his ears and face.
6. When working on the leg furnishings on the forelegs, hold the leg up which is not being worked on. This makes the dog stand still and keeps him balanced. As each stage of the coat is worked, it is extremely important to take great care in blending the coat from one area to another. This is particularly important on the front furnishings above the elbow and on the inside and outside of the hind legs. When viewed from behind, this should form a Gothic arch without the apex.

A QUICK GUIDE TO WIRE-HAIRED FOX TERRIER PREPARATION

STAGE I—*Eight weeks before the Show*
Body Coat. This is ready for preparation and is 'BLOWN', and it may remain in this stage for another two weeks.
   (*a*) Pluck the body coat with the finger and thumb.
   (*b*) The skull, neck, and shoulder may be done now if preferred, as it makes the dog look tidier.

STAGE II—*Seven to Six weeks before the Show*
Skull, Neck and Shoulders. These require to be stripped closely, blending them into the body coat.

STAGE III—*Four weeks before the Show*
Body Coat. Correct the length of the body coat, if necessary using a BLUNT knife. Bad coats require CARDING or RAKING twice a week from now onwards. Really bad coats require raking almost daily to remove the woolly undercoat. This is most important because the woolly undercoat chokes the growth of the top coat. Do not tamper with the legs.

STAGE IV—*Four to Three weeks before the Show*
Leg Furnishings. These require to be 'PICKED OVER' for the first time.

STAGE V—*Four weeks before the Show*
Nails. These require to be filed short, particularly the two centre ones.

STAGE VI—PLUCK Skull, Ears, Throat, Shoulders, behind the Tail and the Quarters. These areas are plucked closer than anywhere else. Rub a thin smear of vaseline or mink oil over these areas.

STAGE VII—Two days before the Show
Leg Furnishings. Shape the furnishings with the finger and thumb, or scissor them, depending on the quality of the coat.
  (*a*) Shape the feet by scissoring.
  (*b*) Trim the ears, eyebrows and beard.
  (*c*) Apply vaseline and chalk to the furnishings, and ascertain that all is correct.
  (*d*) Brush out all traces of chalk.

STAGE VIII—One day before the Show
Washing and Chalking
  (*a*) Shampoo the face and legs and rinse well, and partly dry them.
  (*b*) Dampen the body coat and apply whitening.
  (*c*) Sack up the body coat.
  (*d*) Lightly vaseline the face and leg hair and fill up with fine chalk or precipitated white.
  (*e*) Brush out all the whitening.
  (*f*) Polish off with a hound glove.

STAGE IX—Day of the Show
  (*a*) Chalk the eyebrows with the head held down.
  (*b*) Soothe the eyes with eye drops.
  (*c*) Comb the eyebrows and beard forward in one sweep.
  (*d*) Re-trim the eyebrows if necessary.
  (*e*) Pick the hair out of the stop between the eyebrows.
  (*f*) Trim the beard if necessary.
  (*g*) Trim under the body, ears and tail if necessary.
  (*h*) Brush out all traces of chalk from the body coat before entering the ring.
  (*i*) If the dog is excessively thirsty, water him with a syringe placed into the side of the mouth.

GERMAN SHORT-HAIRED POINTER

The coat is short, flat and coarse to the touch. Grooming is the same as for the Pointer.

GORDON SETTER

The Gordon setter is certainly a dog with great style. The standard requires that the coat should be short and fine on the head, front of the legs and on the top of the ears. The coat should be of moderate length on the rest of the body being almost free of waves and curls. The ear feathering should be long and silky and the feathering on the legs breechings and underline should be long and fine. All the feathering is required to be as straight as possible.

Grooming and stripping and all coat procedures are similar to that of the English Setter except for rinsing.

GREAT DANE

The Great Dane is one of the largest breeds of dog. Grooming is easy except perhaps for the great area which must be covered. The standard requires that the hair should be short and dense and sleek-looking. Brushing should be done with a soft brush, followed by good finger massage and then hand strapping to bring up a sheen on the coat. For shows this may include a final rub over with a chamois leather or a silk handkerchief.

Ears should be cleaned weekly with a swab of cotton wool moistened in alcohol and held with a pair of artery forceps, but care must be taken never to dig down into the ear. The ear should then be dusted with a good ear powder, for which a good recipe will be found in the chapter on Grooming. Lip folds must be cleaned and teeth cleaned and scaled when necessary. Nails must be kept short by clipping and filing and may be polished before a show. Bathing should only be done when the Dane is really dirty. A good walk in heavy country rain cleans the coat better than bathing. Nose and nails may be rubbed with a slight smear of vaseline to make them shine. Ear leathers may get dirty and should be washed and well rinsed. If there are signs of chaps, benzyl benzoate emulsion will help to heal the split ends.

Pressure points are often a serious problem with large dogs. These areas include the elbow joints and the hock joints, and the end of the tail frequently becomes sore from constantly hitting hard objects when it is being wagged. Benzyl benzoate and skin massage helps to soften the skin, which allows the new hair to grow through quickly. Tails may require a tail shield, whilst the sore area is healing.

GREYHOUND

This is one of the oldest breeds of dog. The show Greyhound differs considerably from the racing Greyhound. The standard requires that the coat should be fine and close. Grooming should be done with a medium-hard, dandy brush, followed by ten minutes' finger massage. The suppleness of the skin will greatly improve, if massage is given twice a day. The ears, feet, eyes and teeth require the usual canine care.

48.   A Puli.

G

49.   A French Bulldog.

GRIFFON BRUXELLOIS

This is one of the most enchanting of the Toy breeds. The Griffon is the only Toy which is wire-haired. The standard requires that the coat should be harsh and wiry and free from curl. The coat has to be stripped or plucked to prepare a dog for show. As with all wire-haired breeds, preparation takes time and is performed over a period of weeks, though individual dogs vary in the time they require. Dogs with excellent harsh coats can be almost ready for exhibition at any time, whilst others may take a number of weeks to prepare. Pets should be stripped twice a year, after the coat has 'blown'.

The hair should be longest on the crest of the neck, along the back and quarters and at the back of the forelegs. It should be less long on the sides of the neck and on the shoulders, and the same applies to the brisket flank and thighs. The length of hair continues to decrease in length on the throat and on the front part of the forelegs. The hair is stripped shortest of all on the legs below the hocks. The hair on the stomach should be trimmed off with scissors and blended into the hair on the brisket.

There is some controversy over the head trimming, more hair being removed now than in the past, although some breeders still prefer that the hair on the skull and cheeks should be at least $\frac{1}{2}$ an inch in length, gradually increasing on the eyebrows, which should merge into the cheeks. The cheek hair should in turn increase in length merging gradually into the still longer hair on the neck. The whiskers, the moustache and the beard should be as long as possible forming part of a large ruff. The hair is trimmed reasonably short on the muzzle leaving it thick at the stop and forming a small fan between the eyes. The hair just beneath the eyes must be shortened. The ears are plucked until the hair is short and velvety in texture, and the edges of the ears are scissored as short as possible.

SUGGESTED METHOD OF PREPARATION FOR SHOWING

Tools and Equipment required

Brush with medium-length bristles	7-inch scissors
Wide-tooth comb	Ear powder
Stripping knife	Artery forceps
Nail clippers	Grooming mirror

SUGGESTED ORDER TO WORK

STAGE I—*Eight to Six weeks before the Show*
Strip the hair on the legs and ribs.

STAGE II—*Six to Four weeks before the Show*
1. Strip the back, quarters and rear, neck and forelegs.
2. Cut the nails.

STAGE III— *Three to Two weeks before the Show*
Strip the hair on the ears, skull, side of the neck, shoulders, brisket, flank and thighs. Scissor the stomach.

STAGE IV—*One week before the Show*
1. Trim the hair under the pads and round the feet. Do not remove too much hair from the top of the toes.
2. Trim or file the nails.
3. Trim the fan of hair above the nose and the hair round the eyes. Work on the head and ears, if necessary. Allow the eyebrows to blend into the cheeks, the hair being about ¾ inch in length on the eyebrows.
4. Tidy up the tail stump and anal area.
5. Scissor round the ears, and pluck the hair until the ears are velvety.

STAGE V—*Day before the Show*
1. Groom thoroughly. The coat may be cleaned if necessary with a dry cleaner. A little mink oil sprayed on the brush and lightly skimmed over the coat will give a good sheen, especially if the coat is polished afterwards with a chamois leather.
2. Powder the interior of the ears.
3. Clean the teeth.

Note. Griffons should not be bathed unless they are really dirty, because this softens the coat.

The undercoat should not be visible except on the throat and front of the neck.

Pet Dogs
These only require stripping twice a year, or they may have their coat clipped and the undercoat removed with thinning shears.

The ears can also be dealt with in the same manner. Only the whiskers beard and moustaches should not be touched, and they should be left as large as they will grow.

GRIFFON BRABACONS

These are similar to the rough variety except for their smooth coats. Grooming should be done with a soft brush, polishing with a chamois leather. General grooming care is similar to the other variety. Bathing is suitable for this coat. Nails may be polished for shows.

IRISH SETTER

The Irish setter is a delightful breed. The standard requires him to be racy, full of quality, and kindly in expression. The coat is required to be of moderate length flat and free from curl. The hair on the head is required to short and fine on the head front of the legs and on the top part of the ear leathers. The fringes on the ears should be long and silky and the fringes on the tail breechings and legs should be long and fine. The tail feathering should be moderately long tapering towards the tip of the tail.

Grooming and coat preparation is similar to that of the English setter except for rinsing the coat after bathing.

IRISH TERRIER

This is one of the easier terriers to prepare for show, as his coat is not nearly so profuse as that of other similar terriers. The standard requires that the coat should be hard and wiry and reasonably short. There is also a soft undercoat.

The preparation for showing is not nearly so extensive as that for the Wire-Haired Fox Terrier. In fact, there is very little work to be done on the coat, but the Fox Terrier principles of preparation, except for chalking, could be followed.

The Irish Terrier Head

The standard requires that the head should be wider between the ears than between the eyes. The stop should be hardly visible except in profile. The hair is swept forward from the eyebrows down the muzzle. The eyebrows may be trimmed and the beard squared off.

IRISH WOLFHOUND

The Irish Wolfhound originated in Ireland, as the name implies. The breed should not be so large as the Great Dane. The coat should be rough and hardy on the body and legs and on the head. It should be especially wiry and long under the lower jaw and over the eyes. The tail should also be well covered. Only a little tidying-up stripping is required and a good brushing daily with a stiff brush. Pressure points should be watched and normal care taken of nails, ears and teeth.

ITALIAN GREYHOUND

This is a most elegant Toy breed and much resembles the Greyhound, but in miniature. The standard requires the coat to be thin and glossy like satin. Grooming is done with a soft brush, finger massage and a silk handkerchief. Ears must be kept clean and eyes wiped over gently. Nails should be trimmed regularly once a month and they can be polished for shows.

JAPANESE

The Japanese is one of the prettiest of the Toy breeds and, like a number of other Toys, it originated in China before becoming a Japanese breed. In looks the dog is somewhat similar to a Pekingese, but he has long legs and a domed skull, and he is always particoloured. The standard requires that the coat should be long, profuse and straight, and it should have a tendency to stand out. There should be profuse feathering on the tail, and there should be a good frill.

Grooming this delightful breed is no problem. The coat can be cleaned once or twice a week with a little Johnson's baby powder sprinkled into the coat, and then well brushed out with a Hindes pin brush, followed by a good brushing with a Mason Pearson brush. Feathering should be combed out with a medium-wide comb.

The ears require cleaning with a piece of cotton wool moistened in alcohol. They should then be dusted with a little ear powder. The eyes require careful wiping over with something like Diamondeye lotion. The wrinkle on the face and the stop must be cleaned and dried carefully. Staining can be removed with boracic powder left on the area over-night. It must be carefully removed in the morning and the wrinkled area should be powdered with Johnson's baby powder. Hair between the pads should be cut out carefully, but the feet should be feathered. Nails require cutting once a month, and teeth should be scaled when necessary and cleaned daily with cotton wool moistened in hydrogen peroxide and milk or ordinary human tooth paste.

Show requirements are simple: a good bathing in a cream Shampoo or J.D.S. followed by a whitening rinse, the day before the show, and a little coat dressing brushed into the coat. A sprinkling of baby powder well brushed out just before entering the ring will make the coat stand out. The coat should lie flat on the head and back. It should be brushed forward on the chest, the frill should be brushed up and the breechings well out, and finally the ear feathering should be combed forward.

KEESHOND

This is one of the Spitz breed of dogs. The coat is not difficult to maintain but, nevertheless, it does require fairly regular grooming, especially during moulting. The standard requires an off-standing coat typical of all Spitz breeds. The undercoat should be light-coloured, soft and thick. The outer coat should be dense and harsh. There should be a good ruff, profuse trousers and good feathering on the legs. There should, however, be no feathering below the hocks.

Keeshonds may be bathed if really dirty, but it does tend to soften the coat, so that a dog prepared for a show should not be bathed less than a week before being exhibited. It may, however, be necessary to bath the light areas of coat the day before a show. This would only include the legs, feet and tail. Any good shampoo is suitable, provided that the coat is thoroughly rinsed afterwards.

A long enamel jug is a useful utensil for piecemeal bathing, the dog being made to place one leg at a time in the jug. The areas can be dried quickly with a trunk hair dryer or a chamois leather. The rest of the coat may be cleaned with a spirit shampoo. When quite dry the coat should be given a thorough grooming down to the skin. As with all Spitz breeds, it is important not to remove the undercoat whilst grooming, except when the dog is moulting.

SUGGESTED METHOD OF GROOMING

Tools and Equipment required

Hinds pin brush	Ear powder
Soft brush	Shampoo
Wide-tooth comb	Electric trunk hair dryer
Scissors	Mink oil
Artery forceps	Fuller's earth or powder
Tooth scaler	Spirit shampoo
Nail clippers	

Method

Some dogs require daily grooming, whilst others are better when only being groomed once a week. It depends very much on the density and texture of the coat. It is useful if the dog can be taught to lie on each side whilst being groomed, as it makes the more inaccessible areas easier to reach. But whether the dog stands or lies down, the principles remain the same.

Brushing

1. Brush the coat up in a forward direction, starting at the top of the neck. Work only a fine layer of hair at a time, flicking each layer forward with the brush and proceeding steadily down the back to the root of the tail.
2. Brush from the extremities in the same manner towards the spine, working 3-inch wide strips from the shoulder to the hind quarters.
3. Repeat the process for the other side.
4. Brush the breechings and leg feathering.
5. Part the tail down the centre and brush from the tip forward and slightly to the side. Do both sides of the tail.
6. Lift one hind leg and brush the inside of the opposite one thoroughly.
7. Repeat for the other hind leg.

8. Brush the coat from the chin to the forelegs.
9. Extend one foreleg and brush carefully, brushing the inside of the other foreleg at the same time.
10. Repeat the procedure for the other leg.
11. Brush the ruff working right down to the skin working the ruff upwards and forwards.
12. Brush the ears both inside and outside the leathers, taking care to remove any scurf or grease from the tips.
13. Brush the head with a soft brush.

Combing
1. Comb the foreleg feathering.
2. Comb the hair out from behind the ears.
   These are the only two places where a comb should be used. A comb is useful, however, for cleaning the brushes whilst grooming, since they quickly become furred up.

Coat Cleaning
This may be done with Fuller's earth or with a spirit shampoo.
1. Take a flannel and dip it into a spirit shampoo.
2. Rub the coat over in the same order as for brushing, working the spirit well into the coat.
3. Brush the coat out vigorously.

General Cleaning
1. Scale and clean the teeth, if necessary.
2. Put ear powder in the ears once a week.
3. Wipe round the eyes with damp cloth.

Trimming
1. Trim hair from between the pads when necessary.
2. Cut or file the nails monthly.
A trunk hair dryer set at 'Cold' is excellent to use whilst grooming. The strong current of air blows right down to the skin, separating the hair and blowing out dust, dirt and scurf, and it also makes a space for the brush to work up from the skin.

KERRY BLUE TERRIER

The Kerry Blue Terrier is of Irish origin. The coat is soft and wavy and it has no undercoat. It is a quick-growing coat, and it requires regular and frequent trimming with good long-pointed scissors. The coat has one great advantage in that it is not shed but grows out, and it is therefore removed when trimming. The standard requires that the head should be long, lean, and flat over the skull with very little stop. The eyebrows are brushed forward over the eyes and are blended into the foreface hair and beard.

It is a matter of personal preference as to which is the best method of trimming the Kerry Blue Terrier. Whichever method is used the basic requirements are the same. The coat is short on the skull and the front of the neck, increasing gradually at the bottom of the neck to one inch in length on the back. This is continued over the hips, and the coat is gradually increased in length down the sides to two inches. The hair is slightly shorter over the shoulders, and it is then blended in with the longer hair at the sides and the full hair on the legs. Whilst being trimmed, the coat requires to be constantly brushed or combed in the direction in which it grows or is to lie.

Trimming may be done with scissors alone, and this is easy where there is a dense coat. Some people prefer to use the ridging method where the coat is parted in inch-wide ridges. The comb is drawn through the ridge and scissored off to the required length. Partings are made down the neck and back horizontally, but on the sides the partings should be made vertically. In the U.S.A. and for pet trims, the Kerry Blue is frequently clipped on the skull, throat and sides of the neck.

SUGGESTED METHOD OF TRIMMING

Tools and Equipment required

Electric clippers Oster A5, with no. 10 blade	Grooming table
	Grooming mirror
7-inch scissors	Nail clippers
Hindes pin brush	Artery forceps
Wide-toothed comb	Mink oil
Slicker brush	Electric trunk-hair dryer

SUGGESTED ORDER OF WORK

METHOD 1—*Scissoring*

1. Bath the dog with a good shampoo.
2. Brush or comb the coat thoroughly, so that it lies in the correct directions.

G*

3. *Head.* Comb the eyebrows and beard forward. Scissor a line from the outer corner of each eyebrow either to the corner of the mouth or the angle of the jaw, depending on the individual dog and the profuseness of the eyebrows and the beard.

4. *Skull.* Trim the hair from the top of the eyebrows to the occiput as closely as possible, and from the outer ear to the corner of the eye.

5. *Cheek.* Trim down the cheek to the beginning of the beard.

6. *Side of Neck.* Measure the distance between the top of the withers and the bony prominence at the front of the shoulder and take a point half way between the two. Scissor a line from the outer corner of the ear to this centre point.

7. *Throat.* Scissor an area from the breast bone to the beard, forming a V at the apex of the breast bone, and scissor the area closely, joining up the scissored areas and being careful to blend the shorter coat into the longer coat where this is required.

8. *Back.* Brush or comb the coat upwards on the back and scissor it off to an inch in length.

9. *Sides.* Continue brushing the coat up, gradually increasing its length until it is two inches at the sides.

10. *Hind Quarters.* Scissor the coat closely under the tail and about one inch over the hips, gradually increasing the length over the lower thighs and blending the coat into the side of the body.

11. *Brisket.* Scissor the hair neatly between the legs so that it blends with the coat under the body.

12. *Body Coat.* Scissor the body coat from the tuck up to the forelegs, leaving a fringe neatly trimmed to the contours of the lower rib cage.

13. *Tail.* Scissoring requires to be graduated, so that the tail is slightly pointed at the end and carried erect. A low set tail may be cleverly camouflaged by leaving the coat a little longer on the back at the root of the tail. The hair may be scissored more closely on the underside of the tail than on the sides and top.

14. *Forelegs.* Brush the leg hair in all directions and fluff it out and tidy any stray ends, taking care to blend the longer hair on the legs with the shorter coat on the front and sides.

15. *Hind Legs.* Brush the coat down, fluff it out and trim off any stray ends.

16. *Feet*. The nails require to be short, and the hair should be removed from between the pads. With the dog standing four square, trim the hair round the feet and trim any leg hair which is too long.

17. *Hocks*. Stand the dog on the edge of the table and trim off any hair which falls below the edge of the table. Comb down the hair from the hocks and hold the ends pointing downwards between the finger and thumb. Trim off the hair at a slight angle so that a little more is cut off at the bottom than at the top. This emphasizes the angulation of the back, particularly when the terrier is moving.

18. *Ears*. Trim the ears as close as possible on the inside, the outside and on the edges. Powder the ears with Ryotin or any good ear powder and tweak out not more than a few hairs at a time if they grow in the ear canal.

19. *Blending*. Blend in carefully the different lengths of hair which have been trimmed. They are more easily blended together with 46-toothed thinning shears.

20. *Beard*. Comb the beard and eyebrows forward and square off the ends, giving the required strong jaw and foreface.

21. Spray a little mink oil lightly on to a brush, and gently brush over the coat, giving it a beautiful sheen, and polish it with a hound glove.

METHOD 2—Clipping

If this method is to be used, the dog should be clipped about a week before the show, but this very much depends on the density of the coat and its rate of growth on each individual dog. Only the ears, skull, side of neck, throat and anal area should be clipped. But there is no reason why the stomach should not be clipped as with a poodle for the sake of hygiene, particularly in the case of a male. Clipping is not normally advocated in England, but in many countries where dogs are exhibited clippers are used.

1. *Skull*. Leaving an inverted V on the top of the skull above the eyebrows, clip the skull back between the ears to the occiput.

2. *Ear to Eye*. Clip a line from the outside corner of the ear to the outer corner of the eye.

3. *Eye to Jaw*. Clip a line from the outer corner of the eye to the angle of the jaw, or, if preferred, this line may be taken to the corner of the mouth.

4. *Ear to centre of Shoulder.* With the dog standing, clip straight down from the outer corner of the ear to the centre point between the withers and the shoulder prominence at the chest.

5. *Brisket to Throat.* Clip up from the brisket to the already clipped line of the commencement of the beard. Join all the clipped areas together and blend the longer hair on the neck, sides, legs and chest with thinning shears.

6. *Ears.* The ears require clipping either with the growth of the hair towards the tips or from the tips of the ears to the boundary. Depending on the thickness of the hair on the ears, a no. 15 blade used with the growth of the hair produces a better sheen than a no. 10 blade used against the growth of the hair. The rest of the Kerry Blue Terrier is trimmed and thinned with scissors.

7. *Feet.* There is no reason at all why the feet of a Kerry Blue should not be trimmed in the same manner as that for an American Cocker Spaniel.

    The preparation of all show dogs often changes quite radically over the years, as new people come into a breed from other breeds bringing with them new ideas and different interpretations.

KING CHARLES SPANIEL

This charming little dog was named after King Charles II, who was very fond of the breed. The standard requires that the coat should be long, silky and straight. A slight wave is permitted but the coat should not be curly. The ears, legs and tail should be well feathered.

Coat. This requires a good brushing every day with a Hinds pin brush, followed by a brushing with a medium-hard-bristle brush. All feathering should be combed carefully, taking care not to break the hair. A nit comb is useful for going through the coat, and finger massage keeps the skin supple.

Ears require quite an amount of attention, as the ends are apt to get dirty, especially after feeding. The ears can, however, be protected during meals by putting an old stocking or sock over them with the foot cut off. The edges of the ear leathers sometimes become chapped, and benzyl benzoate emulsion will help this trouble to heal quickly. The ear feathering requires careful brushing and combing to keep it free of mats and knots. The interior of the ears should be cleaned weekly by wiping them round with a cotton wool swab moistened in alcohol, and then dusting with ear powder to prevent ear troubles, which are not uncommon in breeds with pendulous ears.

Eyes should be wiped round daily with Diamondeye lotion. The stop must be kept clean and dry and should be dusted over with Johnson's baby powder. The teeth should be cleaned carefully and scaled when necessary. The mouth and particularly the flews and the folds of the lips require to be kept free from any accumulation of food.

Feet may sometimes be a problem as many King Charles Spaniels have webbed toes. The hair should be cut between the pads and trimmed round the feet. This prevents the feet from becoming extra wet and from bringing unnecessary mud into the house.

Nails must be kept short by cutting and filing.

Bathing. A bath before a show is necessary owing in particular to the white areas of the coat. Bathing with a good cream shampoo, or J.D.S., followed by a rinse in a special white hair preparation, makes the coat whiter than white. On the day of the show a good hand strapping will help to bring the natural oils back into the coat.

LABRADOR RETRIEVER

This is a well known and popular gun dog. The coat is easy to maintain and requires normal grooming procedures.

The standard requires a dense short coat with a weather-resisting undercoat. The texture of the coat is rather harsh, and it should be free from any sign of wave.

Grooming should be done daily or at least twice a week, followed by a good hand and finger massage. The procedure for golden retrievers could be followed. Nails may be vaselined or polished for shows.

LAKELAND TERRIER

This is a splendid little dog, but one which, unfortunately, requires a great deal of work to be done on his coat, to bring him up into perfect condition and show standard.

The coat is dealt with in exactly the same manner as that for the

Wire-Haired Fox Terrier, except that the coat is not chalked. The head is also trimmed in a different manner.

The Lakeland Head

The standard requires that the length of head from the occiput to the stop should be the same as that from the stop to the nose. The skull should be flat and the muzzle broad with powerful jaws. More eyebrow is left over the eyes than with the Fox Terrier. The eyebrows are trimmed diagonally to expose the eye, but they are not divided at the stop, and they are combed forward in a fall between the eyes. The beard and hair on the foreface, including the eyebrow fall, are all swept forward and the beard is squared off.

LHASA APSO

This is a charming little dog, very similar to the Shih Tzu, but he has a longer muzzle. Both breeds originated in Tibet. Preparation of the Lhasa Apso is similar to that of the Shih Tzu, except for the head style, which is prepared more like that of the Skye Terrier, the hair being combed gently forward over the eyes.

It is strongly recommended that pet dogs should be allowed to have the hair drawn back from their eyes into an elastic band, so that they can see properly.

Many pet owners find these dogs hard to keep clean and tidy. It is quite a good idea in these circumstances to cut the coat about one inch all over, except the tail, the back, the leg feathering on the back of the legs, and the feathering on the ears. These may be left long or trimmed. The ear feathering looks attractive, if it is cut straight across like a square fringe. The moustaches and whiskers may also be trimmed off squarely to go with the ears. The coat, in fact, is kept like it was originally when the dog was a puppy. It is certainly better than having an untidy dog, covered in felted mats, which not only attract fleas but also lice and other parasites.

MALTESE

The Maltese is one of the most ancient of the Toy breeds. It is renowned for its all-white, long, silky-textured coat. A good Maltese has no undercoat and the long hair should be straight and as long as possible and not wavy. The coat should in no way be woolly. In actual fact, the standard states that any self colour is permissible, but that it is desirable that a Maltese should be pure white. Slight lemon markings should not penalize. The standard does not mention the skin, but many breeders find that if there is dark pigmentation of the skin underneath the white coat, the dogs generally have extra good dark pigmentation of the nose and eyes.

The pet Maltese can look most attractive if the coat is trimmed an inch short all over, with long ears cut squarely at the ends, and a long tail. But to keep a Maltese in show condition requires constant care and attention. Maltese are generally exhibited with a centre parting from the nose to the stop, a parting on either side of the head from the corner of the ears to the corner of the eye, with another parting between the ears. The hair included within these partings is known as the topknot and is gathered up in to a bow or it may be plaited. The parting continues down the neck to the root of the tail, the coat being brushed straight down on either side. Some breeders prefer to exhibit their dogs with a parting straight down the centre from nose to tail with no bows or adornments. Others prefer to draw the hair back into two plaits, whilst others prefer one plait.

The hair should be drawn back at as young an age as possible and placed in an elastic band. Once it is long enough, the hair of the topknot should be plaited, because this drawing back and plaiting of the hair helps it to grow more quickly. If the hair is very fine, as it is on most puppies, the plaits may be reinforced by using a thin strip of cotton with each braid of hair, this also gives added bulk for tying the bow on the ends of the hair or fixing an elastic band. Elastic bands should always be cut when being removed and never pulled off as this only breaks the precious hair.

Some judges make a great furore and demand that the dogs should be exhibited under them in one bow, two bows or plaits, and in some cases it has even been known for the exhibitor to be made to remove the offending adornments, I cannot help feeling that these judges should be judging the dogs and not be so taken up with such a minor matter. What they should really be looking for is real faults of conformation like foreleg plaiting.

Tools and Equipment required

Brush with medium-length bristles, and with a handle

Boracic powder for eye stain or eye-stain remover

Comb with handle and medium teeth. This must be smooth-ended

Elastic bands or ribbon

Paper curlers

Otodex or Ear-Rite

Mink oil

Ear powder

Artery forceps

Johnson's baby powder

Blunt-ended surgical scissors

Cotton for plaiting

SUGGESTED METHOD OF GROOMING

1. With the dog standing, make a parting from the nose to the stop, and from the centre of the stop to the corner of each eye. A parting is also made from the inner corner of the ear to the outer corner of the eye. Another parting is made from the top of the head to the root of the tail, stretching the skin slightly as the parting is made, so that it is absolutely straight. Dogs may then be groomed lying on a table or in the lap according to preference.

2. *Eyes*. Comb out the hair beneath the eyes and place on boracic powder or stain remover beneath the inner corner of the eyes.

3. *Ears*. Remove a few hairs from the ear canal with artery forceps, having previously powdered the ears with Ryotin or a similar ear powder. Clean the ears out with twists of cotton wool. If the wax is dark cheesy brown use Otodex drops.

4. *Chest*. It is a matter of preference whether the dog is groomed lying on a table or in the lap. With the dog lying on his back in your lap, with his hind legs towards you, start by brushing the hair, layer by layer, picking up a small portion of hair in one hand, and brushing it down with a slight twist upwards, working slowly up the chest layer by layer until the chin is reached.

5. Reverse the procedure, starting at the chin, and work downwards, taking care to brush out the coat under the forelegs.

6. *Side of Dog*. With the dog lying with his back towards you, start by working from the bottom upwards holding the hair in one hand and brushing the hair downwards with a flick of the wrist upwards, working right down to the skin. Continuing layer by layer, working eventually from the foreleg up to the neck.

7. *Ribs*. Take another strip of hair at the bottom and gradually brush up to the parting layer by layer, teasing out any knots as you work.

8. *Hind Leg to Back*. Holding the hair between the hock and the foot, brush out layer by layer working up the leg and body once again, until the parting is reached. Some Maltese are inclined to have an undercoat on the top of the back just above the tail, a wire slicker brush or a fine comb is useful for removing this.

9. *Tail*. Brush the tail feathering from the skin downwards. A parting may be made down the centre of the tail. Hold the feathering near the roots to prevent breaking the hair and then comb carefully.

10. Turn the dog on the other side and reverse the procedure, always starting to brush the coat out from the bottom, working slowly and gently all the way up the coat until the parting is reached.

11. *Ears*. Hold the ears in one hand and brush the feathering out carefully on both sides making certain that the edges of the ear leathers are reached with the bristles of the brush.

12. Repeat the procedure on both sides of the other ear. Brush out the eye stain powder beneath the eyes.

13. *Muzzle*. Straighten the parting from the muzzle to the nose and make a parting from the corner of each eye to the top of the parting forming a V. Then brush or comb the moustaches downwards and forwards. Make another parting from the outside corner of the eye to the inside corner to the top of the ear and another parting from the top of the ears right across the head.

14. *Topknot*. Comb the topknot upwards and divide it equally into three. Plait it neatly, drawing the hair backwards. If the hair is rather fine or short, braid each of the three sections with a strip of cotton to reinforce it and secure the ends with an elastic band. The latter must be removed on alternate days and must always be cut off.

15. The topknot may be parted from the nose parting to the parting between the ears and the hair plaited on either side into two plaits.

16. The topknot may be simply combed back and secured with an elastic band or a small bow on the top of the head, and the rest of the topknot then combed out backwards. Plaiting the hair on the topknot helps the hair to grow longer and should be started at the earliest possible age.

17. Check whether the hair requires trimming between the pads, or whether nails require cutting.
18. Stand the dog on a level surface, and brush or comb the coat downwards, starting from the bottom and working upwards. Spray the coat, if necessary, with water or a coat dressing.

Show Dogs. Show dogs require to be very carefully groomed, so that *almost no hair* is lost in the process. In order to prevent the ends from breaking, the coat should be parted in strips from the centre parting downwards, each strip being two or three inches in width. Each strip should be put into paper and secured with an elastic band. The coat may be put into a light oil occasionally, such as mink oil or almond oil, which are excellent if the dog has been bathed frequently for exhibition.

Paper Curlers. Tissue paper or toilet paper or fine polythene may be cut into oblong strips about four inches by three inches, and each hair strip is then placed lengthwise in the centre of one and the curling paper folded lengthwise into three. One side covers the hair strip, and the other side covers the paper strip. This is then folded from the bottom upwards, again into three, the bottom going a third of the way up, and the fold at the bottom being folded forward to the top, so that the strip of hair is also divided into three. The whole strip is secured firmly at the top with a small elastic band. The tail may also be divided into two strips, and so can the hair on the front of the chest. Paper curlers may be used for the topknot ear fringes and one on each side for the top moustaches. This helps to keep them unstained after eating. The papers should be removed on alternate days, because, if they are left longer, the silky-coated hair quickly felts. See diagrams on page 26.

Cleaning Aids. Johnson's baby powder is useful for cleaning the coat and leaves it nicely scented. Starch is also a useful cleaner, any cream shampoo is excellent for Maltese. The coat should be shampooed once a month, and it is surprising how clean it will keep if regularly brushed. Maltese do not look well when the coat has been put down in oil, because the oil quickly attracts dust and dirt, and this is very noticeable on a white coat, whereas it is hardly noticed on an oiled Yorkshire Terrier, owing to its colour. There are any number of conditioners and dressings for coats, but initially the coat length is hereditary, and no amount of aids will be of any avail unless the basic coat is already there. On the other hand, an excellent-coated dog can have its coat ruined in a matter of days from neglected grooming, rough brushing and combing, or being bathed with mats left in, or through leaving the hair in paper strips for more than two or three days. Young puppies must be kept separately, because they will play and chew each other's coats. Never keep a show Maltese on newspaper, as the print is liable to turn the coat grey, particularly, just after bathing.

MANCHESTER TERRIER

The Manchester Terrier should not resemble the Whippet in conformation. The coat is short, smooth, close and glossy. There are no grooming problems at all. All that is required is a chamois leather and no brushing. A little mink oil may be applied to the top of the muzzle and to the ears if they look dry. Finger massaging keeps the skin supple. The breed does suffer occasionally from dandruff, but a preparation, obtainable from the veterinary surgeon, helps this condition considerably. Some show dogs may require the hair on the tail to be thinned out. Nails, ears and teeth require normal attention. Nails may be vaselined or polished for shows.

MASTIFF

The Mastiff is one of the oldest of the British breeds, it is also one of the largest. The standard requires that the coat should be short, close-lying, but not too fine over the neck, shoulders and back. Grooming presents no problems, except for the expanse of coat which has to be covered.

Coat. There is no mentoin of an undercoat in the standard but all mastiffs have an undercoat. This must be raked out or combed out with a fine-tooth comb when the dog is moulting. Grooming with a good hound glove every day, followed by a finger massage and some good strong hand strapping, will bring the coat and skin into good condition. A final finish with a chamois leather is all that is required for the actual coat.

Ears must be cleaned with a cotton wool swab moistened in alcohol, and then dusted with ear powder. Teeth must be scaled and cleaned regularly.

Nails must be kept short by clipping and filing.

PRESSURE POINTS must be watched carefully, and the area of

50. Adult Chinese Crested dogs which now have acquired hair on the head.

Photo: Anne Cumbers

the hock and elbow joints must be massaged with benzyl benzoate emulsion.

Wrinkles. The loose skin or wrinkles on the face should be powdered and kept dry.

Eyes may be wiped round with Diamondeye lotion.

Lips, particularly the flews, require cleaning after meals.

MINIATURE PINSCHER

The Miniature Pinscher is a German breed and used to be called a Reh Pinscher. The standard requires that the coat should be smooth, hard and short. It should also be straight and lustrous, adhering closely to the body, and it should be uniform all over.

There are no grooming problems. The eyes, teeth and ears must be kept clean, and the nails short. A soft brush for grooming and some finger massage keeps the skin supple, and a polish with a chamois leather will make the coat gleam. Rotenone oil is useful against dandruff. Miniature Pinschers may be bathed before a show, and their nails look better if they are polished.

NEWFOUNDLAND

This is one of the largest breeds of dog. He is by nature a water dog and he is often used for life saving. Lord Byron wrote a famous poem to his Newfoundland dog Boatswain, who is buried at Newstead Abbey. It was written in 1808, and it is inscribed on the dog's tombstone.

The breed, being large, requires considerable work on the coat, in order to maintain it in good order. The standard requires that the coat should be flat and dense and coarse in texture. The coat is also oily by nature, so that it is water-resistant. The standard also states that, if the coat is brushed up the wrong way, it will automatically fall back into place immediately. The legs and breechings should be well feathered. The tail should be fairly thick, but there should not be a fringe.

SUGGESTED METHOD OF GROOMING

Tools and Equipment required

Hindes pin brush   Spirit shampoo

Soft brush   Ear powder
Wide-tooth comb   Shampoo
Scissors   Electric trunk hair dryer
Artery forceps   Nail clippers
Tooth scaler

Method

This is similar to the Pyrenean Mountain Dog, including good finger massage. Newfoundland dogs, being black, clearly do not require the processes for whitening the coat that the Pyrenean goes through, but in all other respects the coat can be treated in a similar manner.

NORFOLK TERRIER

This is another of the terriers which requires the minimum of tidying up.

NORWICH TERRIER

This is another of the terriers which officially requires no trimming. Nevertheless, a little judicial trimming and tidying up of the coat, legs, feet and tail, and even scissoring of the ears, will give the final well-groomed finish.

OLD ENGLISH SHEEPDOG

The Old English Sheepdog is often referred to as a 'Bobtail', and it was originally used for sheep. The standard requires a profuse, hard-textured coat, which must not be straight but should be shaggy and free from curl. There is a dense undercoat, and the two coats together make an excellent weather-resistant coat. Clearly, a breed with such a wealth of coat requires a great deal of coat maintenance, particularly for show purposes. On the whole, bathing is not advocated, because it not only softens the coat, but removes the natural oils which help to keep it clean.

There are two schools of thought as to how much brushing an Old English Sheepdog requires. If the coat is over-brushed, then a great deal of the undercoat will be removed in the process. If the dog is not groomed sufficiently, then the coat will not only tangle but will form heavy felted mats. Grooming should therefore be done in accordance with each individual dog, depending too on the time of year. During moulting and after a bitch has whelped the old coat should be removed to allow the new coat to come in.

Some breeders prefer to spend one hour a week brushing the coat out carefully, whilst others prefer to deal with the top coat only two or three times a week and perhaps spend as much as three hours on the grooming before a show. The coat is brushed with a Hindes pin brush or any long-bristled brush. The coat is brushed down to the skin, working from the extremities, holding the coat up in one hand and brushing it down in layers with the brush in the other hand. On the back the coat is brushed up and forwards from the bobtail towards the withers, forming a pear-shape. The areas of the coat which are white may be powdered with something like Johnson's baby powder or ordinary starch. If chalk is used before a show, then the coat must be washed out afterwards as the chalk will rot the coat if left in.

SUGGESTED METHOD OF PREPARATION FOR A SHOW

Tools and Equipment required

Long-bristle brush	Nail clippers
Wide-toothed comb	Artery forceps
Thinning shears	Shampoo
7-inch scissors	Electric trunk hair dryer

In hot weather, the Old English Sheepdog is liable to slobber and pant, and so his coat may require protecting with a bib.

Feet. The hair should be removed regularly between the pads by scissoring, because, otherwise dirt and mats of hair form balls between the pads and toes. The feet are not normally trimmed for show purposes, but it is strongly recommended that the hair should be trimmed on all four feet so that it is just off the ground; otherwise the feet become dirty and stained, and if the dog is a house dog large wet paws obviously make more dirt than trimmed ones. The only other place that the dog might be trimmed is round the anal area from a hygienic point of view and, in the case of a male dog, the coat could be trimmed short just in front of the penis, this prevents staining and a most unpleasant smell.

Ears. The ears must be kept clean and free from hair.

Topknot. The topknot is brushed forward over the eyes blending with the hair on the muzzle and cheek.

Eyes. These must be kept clean and the area round them free from staining.

Pet Old English Sheep Dogs. These are probably happier if the topknot is combed back and kept in an elastic band so that they can see; or, where the owner is not prepared to give sufficient time to grooming, the coat may be trimmed short all over including the head, so that it resembles that of a young puppy at its most attractive stage. For extra adornments the hair on the ears could be left long and perhaps also the beard and moustaches. Enterprising owners could invent their own Bobtail Trim, which could perhaps include clipping them like an American Cocker Spaniel

PAPILLON

The Papillon, or Butterfly Dog, is somewhat similar to the Longcoat Chihuahua, except that there should be no undercoat. The standard requires an abundant, flowing coat, which should be long, fine and silky, and it should fall flat on the back and sides. There should be a profuse frill and well feathered legs, breechings and tail, and the ears should be heavily fringed. There are no grooming problems, and grooming procedures are similar to those described for the Longcoat Chihuahua, except that the ear fringes should be brushed or combed outwards, so that the effect of the ears is like a large butterfly.

PEKINGESE

This charming and adaptable Toy dog originated in China and has the most profuse coat of all the Toy breeds. The coat is, however, not difficult to maintain provided that it is groomed regularly. The standard requires that the coat should be long and straight, with a profuse mane extending well over the shoulders, forming a cape or frill right round the neck. There should be profuse feathering on the ears, legs, thighs, tail and toes, whilst additionally the feathering on the tail must be straight and long. The undercoat is required to be thick. The coat on the various areas of the dog requires special treatment, and it is therefore important to use the correct grooming tools.

SUGGESTED ORDER OF GROOMING

Tools and Equipment required

Brush medium stiff with
  1½-inch bristles
Wide-tooth comb
Medium-tooth comb
Nail clippers
Scissors

Johnson's baby powder
Coat dressing or bay rum
Ear powder
Cotton wool
Artery forceps
Electric trunk hair dryer

Method
GENERAL CLEANING
1. Wipe the eyes, using a clean cotton wool swab for each eye.
2. Dry out the wrinkles, wipe clean, and use either Johnson's baby powder or a little boracic powder.
3. Examine the ears. Clean them out with alcohol on a cotton wool swab and put a little ear powder in the ear orifice.
4. Clean the teeth with cotton wool moistened in hydrogen peroxide and milk or some other tooth cleaning preparation.
5. Cut or file the nails, if necessary.
6. Remove hair from between pads, if necessary.
7. Clean round the anal area, if necessary.
8. Rub in bay rum or coat dressing, and then powder coat with Johnson's baby powder mixed with a little flea powder.

Grooming procedure with Brush and Comb and Electric Trunk Hair Dryer
The dog should be taught to lie on a table or on your lap.
1. With the dog lying on his back, start by brushing the hair layer by layer under the chin, holding the hair in one hand and flicking a layer or hair forward with each stroke. Be sure to brush each layer right down to the skin. Work from the chin to the hind legs.
2. With the dog next lying on his side, start at the bottom of the foreleg and work up the body strip by strip to the neck.
3. Work from the bottom of the rib cage up to the spine.
4. Work from the hind leg up to the root of the tail.
5. Brush out the breechings.
6. Turn the dog over on to his other side and repeat the process.
7. Remember to clean the brush out with the comb as you work.

8. Brush out the tail feathering carefully.
9. With the dog facing you, brush out the ear feathering, making certain that there are no mats behind the ears.
10. Comb the hair back carefully on the head.
11. Comb out the ear feathering.
12. Comb the hair beneath the ears forward towards the eyes.
13. Comb out the foreleg feathering.
14. Comb out the breechings so that they lie straight.
15. Part the tail down the centre and comb the feathering on each side, taking care to hold the hair near the roots in order to avoid breaking it. Place the tail over the back, so that it falls over the body.
16. Finally, brush the coat up from the sides to emphasize the width of the ribs. Brush the bib downwards and the ear feathering forward with a soft brush. The coat on the back from the waist to the root of the tail should be brushed flat in the direction in which it grows. The hair of the bib and chest should hang straight down. Leg feathering must be brushed back in line with the body. The hair on the head must be as flat as possible and the ear feathering must be brought forward. The hair should be encouraged to stand up at the corner of the mouth. It should then be lightly combed forward, giving the affect of extra width of face and emphasizing the flatness of the skull. Wipe over the eyes and stop, if necessary.
17. After the elaborate grooming and vigorous brushing, do not forget to praise the dog for his patience and for looking so glamorous.

PHAROAH HOUND

This is an ancient breed and has recently been imported to the U.S. from Malta, (via Britain) where it is known as Tal Fenek, which means 'rabbit dog'. It is a delightful breed with no grooming problems. Brush the coat vigorously with a short-bristle brush, and finish off with a hound glove, velvet pad or silk, to bring up a good sheen on the coat. Once a week a good finger massage all over will keep the skin supple, and occasionally a good hand strapping will keep the hound in excellent coat. The ears, nails, teeth and pressure points require normal canine attention. Nails may be vaselined or polished before showing. Pressure points should be well massaged.

POINTER

This is a most attractive gun dog built on setter lines, only with a short coat. The standard requires a smooth, straight, short, fine coat, evenly distributed with a good bloom. Grooming is no problem. Use a medium-stiff bristle brush, followed by a hound glove and give a final polish with a velvet pad or silk. A good hand strapping and weekly finger massage will keep the coat and skin supple. Pressure points require to be watched. Otherwise give normal canine care to the teeth, ears and nails. The latter may be vaselined or polished before a show. Flews and lip folds must be kept clean and pressure points watched.

POMERANIAN

The Pomeranian is one of the Spitz group of dogs. It has a profuse coat, which consists of a soft undercoat and an overcoat which should be perfectly straight and harsh in texture. This overcoat covers the whole body and is particularly abundant around the neck and fore-part of the shoulders and chest, where a profuse frill is formed which extends over the shoulders.

The tail is characteristic of the breed and is turned over the back and carried flat and straight. The hair on the tail should be profuse, long, harsh and spreading. There is nothing in the standard which says that the coat must be brushed up over the body in the opposite direction to which it grows, but this is one of the unwritten laws which has been accepted as part of the correct grooming procedure and has been followed for nearly a century. There is also no mention in the standard that the ears must be trimmed, nor that the coat should be tipped and the tail and feathering shaped. Nevertheless, this is always carried out for all dogs exhibited at shows.

Grooming. In spite of the Pomeranian's great wealth of coat, it is extremely easy to keep this in good trim with comparatively little time spent on the actual grooming except before showing. Pomeranians moult twice a year, and bitches lose most of their coat after whelping. Although puppies start life with a quickly growing, fluffy, puppy coat, this comes out and the puppy is left looking a long-legged, ugly duckling, until the new profuse coat comes in at about the age of eight months.

51. A Pomeranian in show trim.

Photo: Sally Anne Thompson

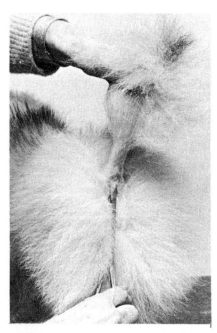

52. The hair on the hindquarters has been trimmed in a circle and brushed forward. The anal area is trimmed short for the sake of hygiene.

Photo: Anne Cumbers

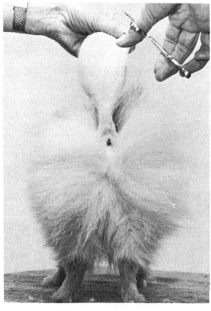

53. The tail being trimmed. Two inches at the base of the tail is trimmed short and also a small triangular area immediately in front of the tail with its apex pointing towards the head.

Photo: Anne Cumbers

Too much brushing is not recommended as this results in much of the undercoat being lost. The only time that the coat should be brushed and combed is when it is coming out, because it is important to get rid of all the old hair, so that it does not spoil the new coat coming in.

Most breeders agree that a good brushing once a week is enough. Combs are mainly used for keeping the brushes clean or for removing the coat when moulting. They are also useful for teasing out the occasional knot or mat after they have been divided by the fingers.

Johnson's baby powder or Fuller's earth is useful for cleaning the coat; Vaseline or Nivea Cream can be used on the ear leathers if they become dry. Bay Rum is frequently used to brighten the coat and is, technically speaking, a sort of dye.

SUGGESTED METHOD OF GROOMING AND TRIMMING

Tools and Equipment required

Two bristle brushes with handles

A comb for keeping the brushes clean

46-toothed thinning shears

Trimming scissors, 7-inch blade and 5-inch blade, for ears, tail and coat.

A spray bottle containing water

Electric trunk hair dryer

Brushing

Either use a brush in each hand and brush the coat with alternate brushes, or the coat may be held with one hand and brushed out with the opposite hand. It is a matter of personal preference whether the dog is trained to be groomed lying on a table or in a lap.

1. With the dog lying on his back in your lap between your knees, start by brushing the hair downwards layer by layer, brushing right down to the skin, from the stomach to the chin. Then start again under the chin and brush the coat forwards layer by layer.
2. Brush the breechings and feathers out on each leg.
3. With the dog's head facing forwards turn him on his front, start grooming from the tail and work upwards towards the head, brushing down layer by layer. In very heavily coated dogs, it may be necessary to part the hairs with a comb. The hair must be brushed from the roots slowly and gently, in

order to remove as little undercoat as possible. Repeat the procedure on either side.

4. Brush the tail out layer by layer, then place it over the back and brush the hair gently forwards. Tease out any knots with the fingers.

5. Stand the dog on something firm. Then, starting to brush from the top of the head, brush the coat forwards and continue down the whole body to the tail and breechings.

6. Spray the coat with a fine spray of water or eau de cologne and sweep the hair forward for the final time, laying the tail on the back and gently brushing it out to lie flat and spread out like a fan over the back. If the coat is found to be slightly matted behind the ears or on the breechings or the tail, sprinkle Johnson's baby powder on and brush out carefully. A little mink oil may be sprayed on the brush and lightly brushed over the whole coat so as to give it a sheen.

Trimming

Trimming should be kept to the minimum required to make the dog look neat, tidy and well-groomed, and should be done a few days to a week before a show depending on the individual dog.

1. *Ears.* With the dog facing towards you hold the tip of the ear leather between the thumb and forefinger in order to protect it. With the tip of the trimming scissors cut a straight line across the tip of the ear. Then cut the hair on the inside of the ear leather a little less than half an inch in length and parallel to the tangent to the dome of the head where the other ear meets the skull. Round off the lower end of this cut. This produces the optical illusion of a small ear. The line of cutting should not be in line with the ear leather.

2. The second trim of the outside of the ear is cut a little longer than the inside, about half an inch in length, depending on the size of the dog. The angle, again, is the same as for the inside of the ear, the line of cutting never being an equal distance from the ear leather all the way down. This is most important. The bottom of the cut should be rounded off as before

3. Repeat the trimming for the other ear. Some breeders prefer slightly rounded ears, so that the angle is less acute at the top.

4. Fold the ear in half at the tip, and taking great care not to

snip the ear leather, trim any hair neatly away that comes above the already cut lines.

5. Any ridge that may have been formed by this trimming can be neatly thinned away using only the 46-tooth thinning shears, and the tips of the ears may also be thinned out at the back, if necessary, using the same shears.

6. *Head and Neck.* Brush the coat forward from the neck up and tip the hair between the ears very carefully layer by layer in a semi-circle. Brush the hair from time to time in all directions and finally forwards to avoid making unsightly ridges.

7. *Ruff.* Brush the ruff down, and then brush a thin layer of hair upwards, with a good light behind the dog. Tip the ruff layer by layer very carefully until the whole effect is a circle from the top of the head to the bottom of the ruff. It is surprising how tipping off the stray ends of the coat makes it look much thicker. It is occasionally necessary to remove as much as an inch of coat from the tips to give the affect of a denser coat.

8. *Anus.* Turn the dog round, brush the coat forwards and, with the scissors held flat, trim the hair about an inch below the anus for the sake of cleanliness.

9. *Tail.* Hold the tail upright and trim the hair off all round and up the tail for one and a half to two and a half inches from the root.

10. *Back.* Brush the hair up from the root of the tail forwards and slightly outwards and trim a line up the backbone about two inches to two and a half inches in length. Trim the hair off to a point on the back from either side of the root of the tail, pull the tail gently forward and brush out. The scissoring of this part of the tail gives the impression of a very short back.

11. *Breechings.* Brush the breechings forwards and upwards layer by layer and trim off the stray ends against a good light, so that the trimming of the back is also circular. Make certain that there are no ridges. As with the ruff it is occasionally necessary to remove as much as an inch of hair to give the effect of a denser coat.

12. *Tail.* Brush the tail in the direction in which it grows, making it as flat as possible; then hold the tail in one hand and trim the sides in a straight line to a point at the tip of the tail, so

that the hair spreads out in the shape of a fan with the tail lying flat on the back.

13. *Foreleg Feathering.* Brush or comb the leg feathering and trim in a diagonal straight line from the elbow to just above the extra pad. Use only one cut if possible, because this line requires to be straight, but it should be considerably wider at the elbow than at the bottom. The front and sides of the foreleg require to be trimmed, but this should not be done too closely. It may be done with scissors, snipping only a little coat off at a time. It is much easier to trim the legs with the fine 46-toothed trimming shears, because then no ridges are left and the hair on the legs looks neat and even. The hair is cut close to the leg at the back from the feet to the first joint.

14. *Toe Nails.* These require to be cut reasonably short, and the hair between the pads of the feet should be removed, taking great care not to nip the pads in the process.

15. *Hind Legs.* The hind legs are trimmed close at the back as far as the hocks with thinning shears, and scissors. The sides and the front of the legs may be thinned out, if necessary, with the fine thinning shears.

16. *Feet.* With the dog standing, the hair is neatly trimmed round the feet so as not to expose the nails.

17. The whole coat may be lightly sprayed with water and brushed carefully into position.

POODLES

Poodles have been known for a number of centuries in France, Germany and Russia. It is interesting that the Russians preferred black poodles, and the French white poodles, whilst the Germans went in for the brown poodles. The origin of the breed seems to have come from the Irish Water Spaniel and the Portuguese Water Dog (Cao d'Aqua). There is no doubt that through the centuries the poodles of the large variety were used primarily for work whilst the smaller varieties were bred and kept as pets or used for truffling.

Large poodles were particularly used for retrieving game from water, but owing to the density and growth of their coat, it became easier to remove this coat, because it was found to be a hindrance rather than an asset for their work. Obviously, a long coat collected

4. A Poodle puppy wondering if he will ever have a coat like the white Standard Poodle
e is admiring.

Photo: Anne Cumbers

briars, burrs and parasites and took a long time to dry, and so, for the sake of convenience, sportsmen cut off much of the unnecessary coat. This was removed on the legs, and later it became the custom to remove the coat on the hind quarters too, because it was thought that this made it easier for the dog when swimming. Later still it became customary to leave the hair long on the joints, firstly probably for the protection of the joints, and secondly because it probably helped if the dogs were liable to get rheumatism in their old age. Whatever the reason may have been, the custom of clipping poddles and leaving bracelets quickly became fashionable, particularly for the pet variety. The original lion trim can be seen in may old paintings and sculptures throughout Europe. Prince Rupert's famous white poodle dog is portrayed on the front page of a parliamentary broadsheet dated 1642, sporting a typical lion trim which has changed little from the way the Portuguese Water Dog is trimmed to this day.

From these early beginnings clipping the poodle in numerous patterns progressed from the days when the French aristocracy had their poodles barbered with their own coat of arms to modern accepted show trims which have become an unwritten law and to the innumerable varieties of fancy pet trims.

The standard required for preparing a show poodle is an acquired art, but no one can clip and barber a poodle well, or to the dog's best advantage from the show point of view, unless they really understand the poodle standard and can also interpret the standard correctly. Artistic people with photographic memories and good co-ordination will always produce the best results on their poodles.

Before a novice starts to learn the art of clipping, trimming and presenting a poodle, it is absolutely imperative that the standard should be fully understood and, having mastered this, photographs of outstanding dogs should be studied. Then lastly, poodles should be studied by observing top poodles from the ring-side at a specialist or championship show. If possible, become on good terms with the owner of an outstanding poodle and hope that he may pass on some of his knowledge to a novice. Probably the only way to learn this is to buy an expensive dog from him! There is no doubt that the best method of learning to clip and trim any breed is to watch an expert do one half of the dog, at the same time taking notes on what is done. The novice should then try to clip and trim the other side of the same dog in a similar manner under supervision. This will teach him what to do and what not to do more than reading 500 books on the subject.

55. A Miniature Poodle—Lion Trim.

Photo: Sally Anne Thompson

THE PUPPY CLIP

Puppies may be initiated into their first clip as early as five or six weeks. It cannot be stressed how important it is at this first clipping that the puppy should not be frightened in any way. He must be introduced to the noise of the running clippers for a few minutes before they are actually used on him. The puppy must feel secure and at home in his surroundings, and he is best held in somebody's arms. The clippers should then be rested on his legs or body so that the puppy gets the feel of the vibration of the clippers without, of course, any hair actually being clipped at this stage.

I prefer to start with the face, but this is purely a matter of opinion. The temperament and disposition of the puppy will be shown up in his reaction to this first clipping. It cannot be stressed too strongly that on no account must the puppy be frightened, and, if he is nervous, then the procedure must be taken gently and slowly until his confidence is gained. If he is frightened or hurt at his first clipping, he will probably never be completely at ease while he is being clipped. This also applies to an older dog who has had his scrotum clipped, nicked or hurt; he will never forget or forgive, which is not really very surprising.

The puppy's tail is another vulnerable area. If his tail is grabbed roughly and pulled or hurt, he may get a tail complex, and he may possibly never carry his tail correctly again. This, of course, is important in the case of a show dog, and it is usually preferable to scissor the tail neatly in the case of a very young puppy. The following is a suggested order of work:

Tools and Equipment required

Electric clippers Oster A5	Hindes pin brush
Blades no. 10 and no. 15	Electric hair dryer
7-inch curved scissors	Bath spray attachment
Comb	Shampoo
7-inch trimming scissors	Curved slicker brush

SUGGESTED PROCEDURE FOR THE PUPPY CLIP
(For details see pages 243-251)

Clipping
1. *Face.* Clip the face with a no. 10 blade, remembering that the skin is sensitive here, and clip against the growth of hair. For a Show Trim, the face must be completely clipped, but many pet owners prefer to have their puppy's moustache left on, since this gives a somewhat softer line.
2. *Feet.* Clip the feet to just above the end of the toes. This should not include the ankle area.
3. *Tail.* Depending on the length of the tail, which again is dependent on how much has been docked, the tail is clipped against the growth of the hair on top of the tail to the approximate base of the tail and also on both sides. The underside of the tail is clipped with the growth of the hair clipping from the root of the tail to the pompon. If it is the puppy's first clip, it is probably better to scissor the hair all round the tail from the root to the base of the pompon.
4. *Pompon.* It is quite a good idea to trim the pompon roughly at first, so that the proportion of how the tail should be trimmed may be gauged in relation to the whole dog.
5. It is probably better to use a no. 10 blade for the first few clips, although later a no. 15 blade may be used to better advantage.

Scissoring
It is important that the finished shape of the puppy be constantly borne in mind.

1. Stand the puppy in a show stance, and look at him from all directions; then decide what requires to be trimmed, so that the puppy will have a good, unbroken line, with all the stray ends removed.

2. *Base of Tail.* Depending on the size of the puppy, it is a good idea to scissor a small area completely round the base of the tail. This gives the impression of shortening the back, and emphasizes the angulation of the hind quarters. The scissored area should now be continued below the anus, gradually tapering to a point. This is not done only for hygienic reasons, but it also improves the shape of the hind quarters.

3. *Pompon.* The pompon is trimmed next. Comb the hair upwards and gather it in the hand; then, drawing it up from the clipped area, cut the top hair in a straight line. Release the hair, and it will fall naturally and fan out.

4. Proceed to trim the pompon from the base, working right round in a complete circle and not forgetting to comb the hair out frequently as you work.

5. The pompon must now be completed by carefully trimming the circle in the opposite direction, that is, starting the scissoring from the back of the pompon and working towards the front. Comb the pompon once again in an upwards direction and trim off any stray ends, making certain that the pompon is completely spherical.
   Trimming the pompon is extremely easy where the coat is dense and of the correct texture. In soft, sparse coats it is naturally not so easy to obtain good results. However, the proportion of the pompon is more important than its density.

6. Tails which have been docked too short or have been left too long can be cleverly camouflaged by the positioning of the pompon. Where the tail is too short, the pompon should be started at the end of the tail. Where the tail is too long, the top of the pompon can end almost at the stump of the tail, but where the length is correct, the stump of the tail should be in the centre of the pompon.

7. I feel strongly that the docking of dogs' tails is a barbaric practice and is merely a passing whim of fashion. The poodle would look just as attractive if he had two pompons topiarized on his tail!

8. *Hind Legs.* With the puppy still facing away from you, com-

mence by working from left to right starting at the bottom of the leg.

9. Comb the hair downwards and outwards and trim the hair in a slight curve just above the foot, continuing up the leg and working all round the leg too, holding the scissors flat against the coat as the work progresses and tipping only the ends as you work. Scissor upwards until the area round the anus is reached, graduating the length of the hair so that no ridge is formed. If the puppy is inclined to fidget and not stand still, lift the leg that is not being trimmed, so that he has to maintain his balance by keeping the leg that is being scissored on the ground.

10. Repeat the procedure for the other leg, making certain that each leg is trimmed to the same size and has the same gentle curves.

11. *Body Coat.* Comb the body hair in an upwards and outwards direction and scissor the hair carefully around the hind quarters, emphasizing the natural curve, which in turn emphasizes the angulation of the hind legs.

12. Continue scissoring forward round the entire body including the chest and neck, just tipping off any unruly hairs.

13. *Forelegs.* Turn the puppy so that he is now facing you, and comb the hair on the forelegs in a downwards and outwards direction.

14. *Feet.* Trim the hair above the feet in a slight curve similar to that on the hind leg. Trim each leg equally all round until the chest is reached. If the puppy fidgets and will not stand still, hold the foot of the leg not being worked on, so that the puppy has to stand on the leg that is being scissored.

15. The same procedure should be followed for the other foreleg making certain that both legs are trimmed equally. In fact, all four legs should be similar in width from above the feet to an imaginary line drawn from midway between the hock and the stifle parallel to the top of the back.

16. *Ears.* Comb the ear feathering through to the skin carefully, but do NOT trim.

17. *Topknot.* Comb the hair on top of the head in an upward direction. When the puppy gets older, it will require the top-knot hair to be held in place by a rubber band, but this would not apply to a young puppy.

18. Make a parting from the inside corner of the top of the ear

across the head to a similar point on the opposite ear, gather the front portion of hair in one hand and put on an elastic band of small enough dimensions for it not to require twisting more than two or three times. The object of the elastic band is to keep the hair out of the poddle's eyes. The band should not be put on so tightly that it drags the hair up from the eyes. For the correct method of putting on a rubber band see below

19. *Elastic Bands.* An elastic band should be removed from the topknot by slipping a blade of the scissors underneath one strand of the band and cutting carefully, avoiding cutting any hair in the topknot. Dragging the elastic band off the topknot is apt to break or split the hair. Elastic bands should be removed daily.

20. *Pet Puppies.* Pet puppies do not require such elaborate care in trimming. The hair is generally scissored to an even length all over, including the hair on the head, the topknot being scissored so that the hair is short enough to prevent it from falling into the eyes, as this would cause irritation to the eyes, and this in turn can cause quite serious troubles, such as eye ulcers.

21. *Hair in the Ear Canal.* Poodles are one of the unfortunate breeds which grow hair in the ear canal. This requires to be removed regularly, tweaking out a few hairs ONLY each day or perhaps once a week. It is quite a painful performance, and naturally dogs do not like this being done to them. Some form of ear powder, such as Ryotin or canker powder in a puffer, makes the hair brittle and dry and it is then easy to remove. The hair is always more easily tweaked out with artery forceps rather than with eye-brow pluckers, which are commonly used by many owners. The use of artery forceps is also easier than using the finger and thumb, especially with Toy Poodles and puppies. The hair is also not so likely then to drop back into the ear canal with all the complications that this may cause.

How to put on an Elastic Band

A number of the long-coated breeds require to have the long hair on the head held back, in order to prevent it from constantly falling into the eyes, or, in the case of a very profusely-coated dog, to allow them to see.

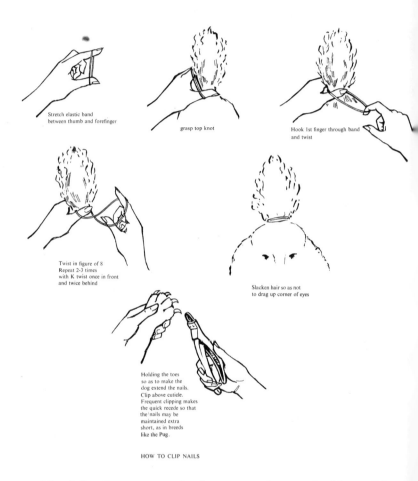

HOW TO PUT ON AN ELASTIC BAND

Stretch elastic band
between thumb and forefinger

grasp top knot

Hook 1st finger through band
and twist

Twist in figure of 8
Repeat 2-3 times
with K twist once in front
and twice behind

Slacken hair so as not
to drag up corner of eyes

Holding the toes
so as to make the
dog extend the nails.
Clip above cuticle.
Frequent clipping makes
the quick recede so that
the nails may be
maintained extra
short, as in breeds
like the Pug.

HOW TO CLIP NAILS

Elastic bands are easy and safe to use, and are preferable to slides, as dogs are apt to swallow these if they come off. Bows or ribbons are probably best of all as they do not damage the hair. Bias binding is good, being cheap and available in various colours, but both ribbon and bias binding are somewhat difficult to keep in place and they also take longer to put on. If ribbons are used for high days, holidays and shows, it is important that the colour chosen for the ribbon should be fast, as it is not unknown for the dye to stain a white dog. Nylon ribbons are preferable to silk.

It is important that the width of ribbon used should be in proportion to the size of the dog. The ends of the ribbon should be cut. One method is bending the ribbon in half length-wise, and cutting it at an angle, which gives an attractive double point at the ends. The other method is simply to cut the ends of the ribbon on the cross, which gives a single point at each end, and when the bow is tied it is neater if the points at the end face the same way. Bows require to be wound twice round the hair to keep them on, and it is probably better to fix an elastic band round the hair first, and then to apply the bow, if it is required to stay in place all day.

Another method is to attach the bow to the elastic band before starting.

THE LAMB CLIP

This is sometimes called the Utility Clip or the Kennel Clip. The Lamb Clip is so called because the coat resembles a young lamb. It is a popular trim because, not only is it easy and rapid to clip a dog in this manner, but it is also easily maintained, and the dog looks well cared for and perhaps more natural than in some of the more exotic trims. This clip is used on poodles of all sizes and of all ages. It is particularly suitable for old poodles, who perhaps cannot stand the long grooming sessions required for the more exotic trims, and it is very useful for country dogs.

Tools and Equipment required

Electric clippers Oster A5	Hindes pin brush
Blades no. 10 and no. 15	Curved slicker brush
Blades no. 4 and no. 5	Electric dryer
7-inch trimming scissors	Bath spray attachment
Comb	Shampoo

SUGGESTED PROCEDURE FOR THE LAMB CLIP

Clipping

The face, feet and tail are clipped in accordance with the instructions given for the Dutch Clip on page 233.

1. *Face.* Clip the face using a no. 15 blade under the eyes and on the muzzle, but use a no. 10 blade on the sides of the face and up the throat.
2. *Feet.* Clip the feet using a no. 15 blade.

H*

3. *Tail.* Clip the tail using a no. 10 blade.
4. *Stomach.* Clip with a no. 15 blade.
5. *Body Coat.* With the dog standing, use a no. 4 or no. 5 blade so that the body coat will be clipped to ½ to 1 inch in length. If a longer coat is required, the coat should be scissored. Commence to clip from the base of the skull going right down the back to the top of the root of the tail.
6. *Back and Neck.* Clip the sides of the neck starting at the base of the skull and continue all along the back. This clipped area should continue from the necklace in an almost straight line to the root of the tail. The clippers should not be used below the hips and shoulders.
7. *Shoulders to Hips.* This clipping shapes the trousers. Commence to clip down from the necklace in a slight curve to the bottom of the rib cage, clip along the line of the rib cage working towards the tuck up. Just before the tuck up a slight curve should be made going up towards the underside of the root of the tail. This curve corresponds to the curve of the clipped line on the shoulders.

Scissoring

8. *Hind Legs.* With the dog facing away from you, comb the coat out and fluff it up and commence to shape the trousers by scissoring. The width and shape of the trousers will depend on the size and conformation of the individual dog. Fat dogs look better with thinner trousers, and thin dogs with full trousers. The amount of hair left on the trousers also very much depends on the density and texture of the coat.
9. *Ankle Trim.* With the dog still facing away from you, commence to work from left to right, starting at the ankle. Comb the hair downwards and outwards and trim the hair in a slight curve just above the foot, continuing up the leg and at the same time working all round the leg too. The scissors must be held flat against the coat as the work progresses, so that the points of the scissors do not dig into the coat making ugly ridges. Continue scissoring a small area at a time from the ankle to the hips, and make sure that the trousers have an equal amount of hair all round the leg.
10. *Blending the Hind Trouser Leg into the Body Coat.* As the scissoring progresses up towards the hip, the trouser coat

must be gradually blended into the shorter coat of the body, and the coat requires to be constantly combed and fluffed out. When all is evenly shaped, repeat the procedure for the opposite hind leg, making certain that both hind legs are equal in shape and size in every respect.

11. *Forelegs.* With the dog facing towards you, comb the coat out and fluff it out as before. Commencing at the ankle, comb the hair downwards and trim off the ends in a slight curve. The trousers of the forelegs should be roughly the same size in width all round as those of the hind legs. This is not always possible but the important point is that there should not be a great dissimilarity in size and shape between the trousers on the forelegs and those on the hind legs. Continue to scissor up the leg doing only a small area at a time and working gradually all round the leg in a similar manner to the scissoring on the hind legs.

12. *Chest.* Comb the chest hair downwards and fluff out, and scissor neatly between the forelegs. The length should be consistent with that of the coat on the rest of the body.

13. *Blending the Foreleg Trousers into the Body Coat.* As the scissoring progresses up the leg and towards the shoulders the foreleg trouser coat must be gradually blended into the shorter coat of the body. The coat must be constantly combed and fluffed out as the scissoring progresses. When all is evenly shaped, repeat the procedure for the opposite leg.

14. *Chest and Necklace.* Continue to scissor the coat on the chest from between the forelegs up to the necklace, blending in the hair on the shorter-clipped neck area, and working gradually towards the shoulders and body.

15. *Topknot.* Comb the topknot upwards and forwards and fluff it out. A round topknot is probably more becoming than a square one, since the rest of the dog will have been trimmed in curves and circles. Long-bladed, curved scissors are excellent for this, and, whichever shape is chosen, it is important to blend the hair into the shorter-clipped coat on the neck.

16. *Ears.* Any ear style is acceptable, but normally the hair on the boundary of the ears is trimmed shorter in order to accentuate the rounded topknot, and this also gives the impression of longer ears. The ear fringes should finally be combed out and scissored neatly.

Completely Scissored Coat

On some occasions, particularly in winter or with elderly dogs, it may be considered better for the poodle to have a longer coat. In these cases the whole coat should be scissored only, and the basic shaping of the body coat, trousers, chest and neck is the same as for the Lamb Clip only longer.

Some people prefer to use just the scissors while scissoring, but it is quite a good idea to use a large wide-toothed comb in conjunction with the scissors. The coat is parted in one inch ridges and combed up from the skin so that the comb lies parallel to the body and the hair is then trimmed off with the scissors laid flat against the side of the comb. This comb and scissor method should, as before, be worked progressively along each ridge.

This ridging method is generally worked by parting the body coat from the neck to the tail along the back and the top of the sides. The shoulders, hind quarters and legs are parted vertically. The forelegs are parted down the centre and the coat is brushed upwards and outwards and then scissored.

ENGLISH SADDLE CLIP OR THE LION CLIP

This consists of a long topknot, a large mane, long-fringed ears, a bracelet on each foreleg with the legs clipped above the bracelet to the elbow, a belt clipped behind the mane, which is joined by a scissored pack on the hind quarters, a pompon on the tail and two bracelets on each hind leg, separated by a clipped garter line between the two bracelets and between the top bracelet and the pack. The tail is clipped from the root to the base of the pompon.

The English Saddle Clip is known as the Lion Clip in Europe. It is the traditional, accepted trim for adult poodles of all three varieties, the Standard, the Miniature, and the Toy. This clip is sometimes loosely called the Show Trim and there are a number of variations of it which are acceptable in the show ring.

SUGGESTED METHOD OF CLIPPING AND SCISSORING

Tools and Equipment required

Oster A5 electric clippers with blades nos. 6, 7, 10 and 15	Electric hair dryer
	Hair spray
Thinning shears, 46-toothed	Nylon mane cover

7-inch scissors with open-ended
   shank
Hindes pin brush
Slicker brush
Wide-toothed comb
Steady non-slippery table

Elastic bands
Ear papers or polythene wraps
Mink oil
Grooming mirror
Shampoo

Mane Cover

Before proceeding to clip and scissor the dog, the mane should
be protected with nylon net or some similar light-weight material.
The protection of the mane prevents the cut hair from mingling
with the long hair of the mane and it also prevents the mane from
being accidentally cut during trimming. The mane cover requires
to be wide enough to cover the entire mane and it must also be
long enough to fit the dog. There should be two holes for the forelegs. The mane is gathered up into the cloth and pulled up until it
is above the poodle's elbow. The ends should be tied together with
tapes or pinned above the neck and withers.

Clipping

The face, feet, tail and stomach are clipped in the same way as
for the Puppy Clip. Instructions for this will be found on pages 216
and 243-251

SCISSORING

Pattern for the English Saddle Clip or Lion Clip

1. *Mane.* With the dog facing away from you, push the mane
   forward with the hands or brush and make a parting all round
   the dog just below the last rib (this is the nearest rib to the tail).
   Some people prefer to use a tape tied lightly round the dog
   to set the pattern. A dark tape should be used on light dogs,
   and a light tape on dark dogs. The exact position can be
   varied by an inch or two according to the length of the dog's
   back.

2. *Mane Cover.* This should be placed over the mane and secured
   lightly.

3. *Hind Legs and Quarters.* These are first basically scissored in
   exactly the same fashion as for the Puppy Show Trim or
   Lamb Trim. The pack on Toy Poodles is scissored to about
   $1\frac{1}{2}$ to 2 inches in length, on Miniatures to about 2 inches, and
   on Standards to about 3 inches.

With the dog facing away from you, comb the coat, fluff it up and commence to shape the pack by scissoring. Working from the root of the tail towards the mane or, if there is a belt line, towards the belt, shape the pack, starting from the lower thigh and taking care to hold the blades of the scissors flat against the coat to avoid making unnecessary ridges.

CLIPPING
Belt Line
1. First, scissor a line all round the dog where the clipped belt between the mane and the pack is to be made. Using a no. 15 blade, clip the width of the belt, which depends upon the size of the dog, right around the dog's body, and work against the growth of the hair towards the head. The scissored line can be used as a guide, and if the scissored line requires correcting, this may be done with the clippers without spoiling the width and placement of the belt. The width of the belt is generally about ½, 1, and 2-3 inches in Toys, Miniatures and Standards respectively.
2. *Hind Leg Bracelet Pattern.* This should not be set on the hind legs. There are two bracelets, one above and one below the hock. The first bracelet starts at the ankle, and the second ends at the stifle joint.

SCISSORING AND CLIPPING
Lower Band or Garter
To set the pattern for the lower bracelet, a band of hair called the garter should be scissored in a straight line from just above the hock joint to the centre of the same joint on the inner side of the leg. This automatically makes the correct angle between the two bracelets. This scissoring goes completely round the leg. The garter band slopes towards the front, fitting in with the angulation of the joint. Using either a special narrow cutting blade or a blade no. 15 or no. 30, clip across the scissored area so that the blades of the clippers are working up the leg with each stroke. The leg should be clipped in short even strokes making the width of the garter band between the bracelets a ½-1 inch wide, depending on which variety of poodle is being clipped. It will be noticed that the skin is loose just above the hock joint, and when clipping the outside of the leg, it will be found convenient to place the first finger of the hand not holding the clippers into the hollow on the inside of the

leg covered by this loose skin. This pushes the skin out on the opposite side and makes the clipping of the garter band easier. When clipping the inside of the leg, the finger is pressed on the opposite side, in order to achieve a similar effect.

Top Band

To set the top band, feel for the little bone which protrudes at the stifle joint, and scissor a line right round the leg, making certain that the line is parallel to the lower bracelet or garter band, clipping, of course, up the leg as previously. Short strokes should be used with the clippers, and the band is generally made about ¼-¾ of an inch in width depending entirely on each individual dog. The width between the two bands, however, should generally be equal, but this depends on the conformation of the dog. Repeat the procedure exactly for the other hind leg, making certain that the patterns for the bracelets and garter bands are uniform. The best way to view these is to stand the poodle with his hind quarters facing you.

SCISSORING

Bracelets—Hind Legs

The scissors should be held flat against the hair, cutting only a small quantity of hair off at a time, it is important that the points of the scissors should never be dug into the hair, as this will give an uneven finish. The bracelets should be constantly combed and re-combed in all directions while scissoring, in order to get a perfect finish. The hair on the bracelets is naturally straight and not curly.

Bottom Bracelets—Hind Legs

The bottom bracelet is roughly oval in shape and is now scissored by combing the hair down and scissoring off any that falls below the clipped line of the ankle. Next comb the bracelet up over the garter band and scissor off any hair that extends above the hock joint. The bracelet should now be fluffed out with a comb or a curved slicker brush, working towards the centre of the bracelet. The hair is then scissored into shape. The hair left on the bracelet should be 2, 3 or 4 inches long, according to the variety of poodle and in accordance with the conformation of the dog.

Top Bracelet—Hind Legs

The top bracelet is scissored in a similar manner to the bottom bracelet, except that the front and the back of the bracelets are shaped to follow approximately the contour of the leg, whilst the line above the hock curves slightly outwards and then forwards from the bottom. Obviously, the contours of the bracelet on all sides of the leg must be equal in every respect. When looking at the dog sideways, the lines of the top bracelet and the band follow the slant of the top of the lower bracelet and garter band.

The Pack

The pack is the area of coat round the hind quarters from the belt to the clipped band at the stifle joint. Comb the hair down from the belt to the stifle joint in the direction in which it grows. The hair on the pack is generally scissored to 1 inch on Toy Poodles, 2 inches on Miniatures and 2-3 inches on Standards. The actual length is governed by the texture and the curl of the coat of each individual dog, and the finished effect must be like astrakhan.

Starting at the band at the stifle joint, having already combed the hair down, scissor off the stray ends of hair which hang over the clipped band. It is important to emphasize the effect of strong, rounded hind quarters and good angulation, and to do this, the hair must be scissored in a gentle curve, starting just above the top bracelet and working up the pack and round towards the root of the tail. This gives the buttocks their rounded effect. The length of the coat is gradually tapered towards the root of the tail and the line carried round to the belt, gradually increasing the length of hair so that it is longer at the belt. When viewing the hind quarters from behind, the pack must be even on both sides and should generally be tapered slightly towards the root of the tail, depending entirely on the muscle and conformation of the individual dog. It is important when viewing the dog from the rear and from the sides, that the bracelets, the pack and the pompon should all be well proportioned one to another.

Foreleg Bracelet Pattern

The foreleg bracelets, which are slightly larger than the hind leg bracelets, are set with the dog facing towards you, the actual size depending on the variety of poodle being clipped. The depth of the bracelets should be roughly $2-2\frac{1}{2}$ inches, $3-3\frac{1}{2}$ inches and about $4-4\frac{1}{2}$ inches on Toys, Miniatures and Standards respectively.

Foreleg Clipping

First, make a scissor line just slightly below the elbow joint, cutting a horizontal line straight across and parallel to the ground, and continue this line right round the leg. Since the hair grows in opposite directions on the forelegs, the hair requires to be clipped in two directions. Clip from the top of the bracelet on the inside of the leg and also on the front of the leg as far as the scissored line, but without actually uncovering the elbow.

Next, clip from slightly below the elbow joint, so that the elbow itself is not uncovered, and clip down the leg to the top of the bracelet. With the dog standing facing you, make certain that the clipping pattern will be identical on each leg. Scissor the line at the elbow to correspond with the opposite leg. The clipping is now finished, and the rest of the poodle is then scissored.

SCISSORING

Foreleg Bracelet. The foreleg bracelet is round in shape, and an equal amount of hair is therefore left on all round the leg. The bracelets are also slightly larger than those on the hind legs. The hair is first combed down over the feet and the ends are trimmed off in a straight line parallel to the ground. Next, comb the hair up over the clipped part of the leg and scissor off the ends neatly all round. Then, comb the hair outwards and towards the centre and finish off the final shape of the bracelet.

Mane or Ruff

The mane or ruff is now dealt with. First remove the mane covering, the poodle should then lie on his side while the long mane hair is brushed carefully and gently in layers right down to the skin working upwards. Repeat the procedure on the other side. Start at the head and work in the same manner as far as the belt. The hair may be brushed in both directions, so that the coat is groomed right through to the skin. With the poodle facing you, brush the hair on the chest downwards. Finally, brush the mane right over the back and head in a continuous sweep. Occasionally the mane may require tipping off to remove any straggly ends. On no account should it be heavily shaped as this spoils the general outline.

Topknot or Forelock

Remove the plastic or paper protection from the topknot by cutting the elastic band, and comb the topknot out thoroughly. Part the hair across the top of the head from just in front of one ear to the opposite ear. Pull this hair back and gather it up into an elastic band (see page 219) which should not be twisted more than three or four times. The hair in front of the eyes requires to slightly eased out, so that it does not drag the corners of the eyes up. Insert a finger carefully half way between the eyes and the band and ease the hair extremely gently, so that too much is not drawn out of place nor the hair broken by th elastic band in the process. Again, tip the ends of the topknot if this seems necessary, so that the line blends in with the mane. Then comb the topknot out to blend with the remaining hair on top of the head.

If there are any short hairs which are not gathered in by the elastic band, these can be made to stay in place by a slight application of a human hair gel or some similar preparation.

Ears

Finally remove the plastic or paper which is protecting the ear fringes, preferably by cutting the elastic band, and comb the fringes out carefully. No trimming should be required for the ear fringes.

Take a final, appraising look at the poodle, first from the front, then from both sides, from the back and also from above, to make quite certain that there is not a hair out of place.

Above all, do not forget to praise and admire the dog for his patience in behaving so well (even if he hasn't!). Obviously, it will take a great deal longer to work on a Standard Poodle than on a Toy Poodle; and therefore it is very necessary that the dog should be given frequent rests and a time to play and stretch himself between various procedures, particularly if be hecomes restless or fidgets. On the other hand, he must not be allowed to "get away with it", so that the rest period must only be given after a period of good behaviour, because otherwise he would soon associate bad behaviour with rest and play. This is particularly important with puppies.

VARIATIONS OF THE LION TRIM (or English Saddle Clip)
Kidney Patch

1. Instead of a clipped band between the pack and the mane, a small kidney patch is clipped away on the loin, midway between the top of the back and the tuck up. It is important that the kidney patch should not be clipped too far back, because this would make the dog appear to be weak in his hind quarters. The kidney patch is really situated in the centre of where the belt would be, the back of which, instead of being in a straight line as with the belt, is

slightly curved. This kidney patch may be set easily by placing a glass of appropriate size in the correct position and using this as a pattern to cut round. This area should be carefully scissored to the required shape before attempting to clip. The hair on the pack should then be brushed over the kidney patch and any ends which cover the area.

THE CONTINENTAL CLIP

This consists of a large mane, a long topknot, and one bracelet on each leg. The foreleg is clipped short from the bracelet to the elbow. There is a pompon on the tail, and the hind legs above the hock bracelet and the quarters are clipped really short. A rosette may be left on either side of the loins. This is a most attractive clip on a well constructed, sound poodle, the emphasis is on soundness, particularly in the hind quarters, because nothing could be uglier than a dog clipped in this fashion with straight stifles.

The Continental Clip is exactly the same as the Lion Clip (English Saddle Trim) from the belt forwards, and the pompon of the tail. The differences between the Continental and the Lion Trims are that the bracelet on the hind leg is larger and extends above the hock. The hind quarters are clipped clean up to the mane with a no. 15 blade instead of a pack being left as in the Lion Trim. A rosette may be fashioned on either side of the loins if desired.

SUGGESTED ORDER OF TRIMMING

Tools and Equipment required

Steady, non-slippery table
Electric clippers Oster A 5 blade no. 15
7-inch french scissors with shank
46-toothed thinning shears
Wide-toothed comb
Spray
Grooming mirror
Electric hair dryer
Hindes pin brush
Nylon mane cover
Elastic bands
Ear papers or plastic

1. *Bracelet.* Set the position of the bracelet on the hind leg by scissoring a line above the hock (Toy Poodles ¾ of an inch), (Miniatures 1 inch) (Standards 1½-2 inches). This garter line slopes slightly forward at the same slant as for the Lion Trim hind bracelets.
2. *Tail and Loin.* Scissor a line from the top of the root of the tail down to the tuck up, on either side of the dog.

3. *Hind Leg Bracelet.* Using a no. 15 blade start from the hind leg bracelet and clip carefully up to the scissored line. The inside of the leg requires to be extra carefully clipped, and the genitals must be protected when this area is reached. Another vulnerable area is at the tuck up itself, where the skin may all too easily be nicked.

4. *Rosettes.* The rosettes are best set by using a glass or a jam jar or a pastry cutter as a pattern, to ensure that the rosettes are completely circular. The size of the rosettes is determined by the variety of poodle being clipped and also on its conformation. There are no hard and fast rules as to the exact positions of the rosettes, provided that they are similarly set on each side and at an equal distance on either side of the back bone. Toy Poodles would require rosettes from $1\frac{1}{2}$ to 2 inches in diameter and $1\frac{1}{2}$ inches in height, Miniature Poodles rosettes from $2\frac{1}{2}$ to 3 inches in diameter and $1\frac{1}{2}$ to 2 inches in height, and Standard Poodles from $3\frac{1}{2}$ to $4\frac{1}{2}$ inches in diameter and 2 to 3 inches in height.

5. Place the glass in the proposed position of the rosette and scissor the hair all round the edge of the glass. Repeat the procedure on the opposite side, making quite certain that the rosettes are sited identically.

6. Again, using a no. 15 blade, clip the remaining hair from the root of the tail round each rosette. A final clip should go against the growth of the hair to correspond with the clipping of the leg and the rest of the thigh.

7. Each rosette is fluffed out by combing and scissored round and then scissored over the top in all directions, leaving the rosettes about $1\frac{1}{2}$ inches high in Toy Poodles, $1\frac{1}{2}$-2 inches high in Miniatures and about 2-3 inches in Standards.

8. *Bracelets.* The bracelet on each hind leg is combed and fluffed out and then scissored and shaped in proportion to the bracelet on each foreleg.

VARIATIONS ON THE CONTINENTAL CLIP

A variation on the Continental Clip can be:

1. An extra bracelet made at the stifle joint.
2. An extra bracelet made at the stifle joint and a rosette shaped round the base of the tail.

There are miriads of slight variations which may be adopted by enthusiastic poodle fakers; which is not meant detrimentally in any way, because there is probably no subject more controversial than how a poodle should be clipped and scissored. Obviously no two poodles are clipped or trimmed in exactly the same manner. It is the overall effect of improving the dog that counts in the eye of the beholder.

DUTCH CLIP

This consists of a clipped belt which divides long Dutch trousers on the hind legs from a jacket with long pantaloons on the forelegs. The width of the belt depends on the length of back of the dog. Long-bodied dogs look much better with narrower belts and vice versa. The tail is trimmed with a pompon and the head has a scissored topknot. The ears may be trimmed in numerous ways, with tassels cut square or round, but they are frequently left with their natural fringes.

The Dutch Clip is not permitted in the show ring, but it is permitted in obedience classes. The Dutch Clip is popular with pet owners who require a more chic and exotic looking poodle than their neighbours. Pet owners often demand a Dutch Trim or one of its numerous variations. This can be quite an attractive trim when the dog is kept tidy, but owing to the long trousers, it has its disadvanages: firstly from the point of view of the coat matting, and secondly because, when the legs get wet, the coat is difficult to dry, there being very little body heat in a dog's legs. With modern, powerful, electric dryers, however, the legs may be dried reasonably quickly. The Dutch Trim probably only looks well on a young, healthy, well conditioned poodle, as the least signs of obesity are naturally accentuated by this trim.

SUGGESTED METHOD OF CLIPPING

Tools and Equipment required

Steady non-slippery table	Grooming mirror
Oster A 5 electric clippers blades nos. 6, 7, 10 and 15	7–inch scissors with open-ended shank
Thinning shears, 46-toothed	Hindes pin brush
Wide-toothed comb	Slicker brush

1. The feet and tail are trimmed in an identical manner to the Lion Trim.

2. *Ears*. With the dog sitting, hold the ear carefully in the palm of the hand, and using a no. 10 blade, clip up the ear from about ½ an inch from the end of the ear, the exact starting point depending on the size of the dog. Leave enough hair on the ends of the ear to form a tassel. Clip up the ear as far as a line level with the corner of the eye, taking care, when trimming the edges of the ear, to use only the edge of the blade and clipping in the direction of the growth of the hair, because otherwise the ear may be nicked. The inside of the ear leathers are trimmed out, and great care must be taken with the folds of skin on the edges of the ear and around the ear orifice, as these areas are also liable to get nicked with the clippers.

3. *Cheeks*. Clip from the top of the clipped line of the ear to the corner of the eye and continue clipping down the sides of the muzzle to a line where the mouth begins.

4. With a no. 15 blade clip the top of the muzzle to a straight line between the eyes. Do not clip above the inside corner of the eyes.

5. *Necklace*. Scissor a semi-circle at the base of the neck to form a necklace.

6. *Backbone Clip*. With the dog standing and using a no. 10 blade or a no. 15 on a Standard Poodle, clip from the same line which extends from the eye across the ear, starting at the top of the neck, and clip a straight line right down the centre of the backbone. If the dog is well covered, this can be carried out in one operation; but if the bones of the spine protrude, tilt the blade to one side and work down to the end, then start again, tilting the blade on the opposite side and repeat, continuing straight down the body and up to the pompon on the tail. This line starts off by being the width of the clippers. The final width is purely a matter of preference, and depends, as always, on the conformation and size of the poodle being trimmed. It is never less than the width of the clippers, but too wide a strip should be avoided, because this definitely spoils the look of the dog. This strip may be clipped in the opposite direction starting at the base of the tail and clipping up to the neck. The same effect is obtained by using a no. 15 blade with the growth of the hair or a no. 10 blade working against the growth of the hair. It very much depends on the individual sensitivity of the poodle's

skin to clippers. If he can take a close cut, then the clip will last longer and the dog will look neater.

If there is any difficulty in clipping the spinal strip, use a ruler or a piece of cardboard cut to the desired width and place this on the dog's back and scissor a line down the edge of the ruler on either side.

7. *Throat.* Clip up the throat to the corners of the mouth, taking care not to clip the moustache, but if preferred, the clip line can clean out the entire lower jaw, taking care to tighten the skin at the fold of the mouth.

8. *Necklace.* Scissor a line from the side of the necklace in a slight curve to approximately just above the withers.

9. *Side of the Neck.* With a no. 10 blade clip from the clipper line on the top of the neck, going down the sides of the neck and joining up with the already clipped line of the throat. As the hair grows in different directions on the side of the neck, the clippers can finally be run straight down the neck towards the shoulders.

10. *Pantaloons.* Next shape the 'Dutch trousers' (or 'pantaloons') on the hind legs. A strip should be clipped starting about 1 to 2 inches in front of the hip bones. Scissor a slightly circular line from the clipped area on the rump going forward between 1 and 2 inches in front of the hip joint and curving gradually round and forward at the sides before continuing down to about 2 inches in front of the tuck up.

11. *Jacket.* The next scissored line is made at the back of the jacket behind the shoulder. The width of the belt is narrower at the sides than it is on top of the back and on the underside. The curve of the jacket should correspond with the curve of the top of the Dutch trousers but in the opposite direction.

12. *Belt.* Stand back from the dog and decide whether the width of the belt is correct for the proportions of the dog. It is quite a good idea to cut a piece of plastic or cloth to the correct shape and to pin it round the dog's body tightly to give the correct impression. It will soon be apparent which width of belt suits the dog.

13. Clip from the back down the sides of the body in the direction in which the hair grows, following the pattern set by the scissored line. Clip the belted area carefully until the sides are completed.

14. *Stomach.* Clip the stomach with a no. 10 or no. 15 blade.

The stomach is an extremely vulnerable area especially in bitches, because of the teats the stomach may be clipped with a no. 15 blade or it may be scissored with the aid of a comb drawn through the hair to protect the teats. If clippers are used, the clipping should start just in front of the testicles or vulva, taking extreme care round the teats. Clipping must always be done with the growth of the hair and NEVER against it. The clipped area of the stomach should extend right up to the belt line if there is one, or to the beginning of the mane. Well behaved dogs will stand quietly on their hind legs with their forelegs held or supported, but dogs who will not stand still while being clipped must be held and controlled by a second person in order to avoid accidents. This completes the clipping for the Royal Dutch Clip.

SCISSORING

15. *Moustache.* Comb the moustache downwards and scissor neatly into the desired shape, which may be round or square.
16. *Topknot.* Comb the topknot in an upward and forward direction and scissor it round or square, according to whether a round or square moustache has been made.
17. *Ear Tassels.* The ear tassels are combed out and trimmed round or square to match the topknot and moustache. Any ear style is suitable for this trim.
18. *Dutch Trousers.* Comb out the Dutch trousers, fluffing out the coat all over. Starting at the ankle, brush the coat down and trim off the hair in a very slight curve.
19. Shape the leg by scissoring, cutting from the bottom upwards and ending each cut at the hip joint. Work all round the leg in this manner and scissor as far up as possible on the inside of the leg. The scissors should be held flat against the coat while scissoring and only a small quantity of hair should be removed at a time. The scissors must be kept upright to avoid digging the points into the coat at any time, as the symmetry of the pantaloons can quickly be ruined.
20. Lift one hind leg and cut the inside of the opposite leg right up as far as the eye can see. Repeat this with the other hind leg. Take a good look at both hind legs together to make certain that the size, shape and contours are equal.
21. Comb out the hair on the hips and hind quarters in an upward and forward direction over the clipped areas. Then scissor

the whole of the top contour of the pantaloons, continuing the pattern of the gentle curve from just below the root of the tail, going over the rump and hip and continuing down to finish off the shape of the pantaloon.

22. Repeat the procedure for shaping the other pantaloon making certain that both pantaloons are equal.

23. *Jacket*. The hair should be combed upwards and outwards, particularly over the clipped areas. The pattern must then be scissored in the same manner as for the pantaloons. Start by scissoring a slight curve, commencing at the bottom of the belt and working all the way round as far as the necklace.

24. Comb the hair upwards on the necklace over the clipped area and scissor off neatly.

25. With the poodle still facing forwards, comb the hair down between the forelegs and trim the hair at the same length as the rest of the jacket. Continue to shape the jacket right round the front of the chest taking in both shoulders.

26. With the poodle standing, take a good look at the jacket pattern at all angles and make any corrections necessary.

27. *Forelegs*. The forelegs are then shaped, starting with the sides, after the hair has previously been combed out well. Comb the ends over the ankles and scissor neatly in a slight curve.

POODLE CLIPS

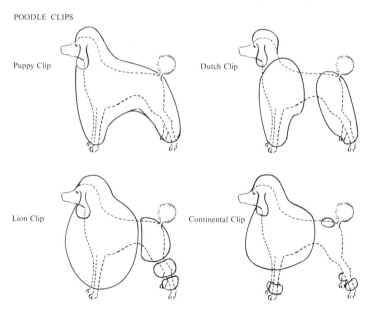

Puppy Clip

Dutch Clip

Lion Clip

Continental Clip

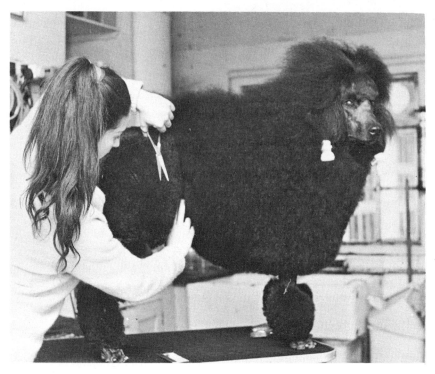

56. The trimming is skilfully performed by scissoring the coat to the correct length.

Photo: Anne Cumbers

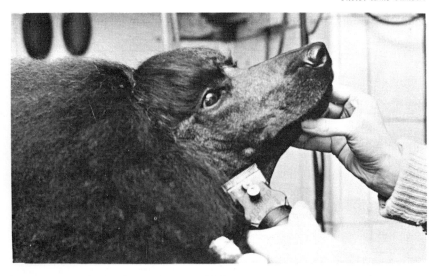

57. The face being clipped. This is generally done next after the feet.

Photo: Anne Cumbers

POODLE CLIPS

There are a great number of fancy poodle clips which are used in various countries. In a book of this size it is, unfortunately, not possible to give instructions for all the clips. There are, however, some which are described. The more important clips include the Puppy Clip and the Show Clip, or Lion Clip, the Continental Clip and the Dutch Clip.

Clipping and Scissoring

Clipping and scissoring a poodle is not difficult. It is, however, an art and some people are undoubtedly better at it than others. It is really a question as to whether you enjoy the job or not. If you do and you are a perfectionist, then preparing a poodle for a show can be a great pleasure. If you are not, then I would suggest you choose another breed which does not need clipping or scissoring, unless the dog can be taken regularly to a dog parlour.

Equipment Required

Any good electric clippers with correct blades may be used. I propose to describe the Oster A 5. The following equipment is recommended: An Oster A 5, or a similar make with detachable blades that clip on and off, for the Puppy Clip, and for the Show Clip blade no. 10; a good, well balanced pair of barber's scissors, ones with pointed ends, and a second pair with rounded ends; blades about seven inches long are generally preferred although shorter blades may be more useful for the Toy Poodle; a good slicker brush and a cushioned, rubber-based brush with long pliable pins is probably the best; for Standard and Miniature Poodles, combs with heavy round teeth about two inches long are best; and for the Toy Poodle, a comb with graded teeth is useful. Some poodles, if they are not well trained, may require a grooming post or grooming sling, but these are apt to be dangerous if a poodle is left even for a second or two on its own. A large grooming mirror is strongly recommended for hanging behind the grooming table, to reflect the far side of the dog being groomed.

It is better to bath the poodle before clipping, since this preserves the blades and the hair is easier to clip. In actual fact, few people do bath their dogs before clipping, but, whether the dog is bathed or not, it is absolutely imperative that the coat should be brushed right down to the skin before clipping and any bad knots or mats should be dispersed or teased out with the finger and thumb.

Procedure

It is important that the trimming and clipping procedure be performed in the same order, the exception being with young or nervous dogs. Some Poodles dislike having their faces done, and some dislike having their feet done. Whichever the dog dislikes least, do this area first.

Order of Work for a Neglected Coat

If the poodle has not had his coat attended to regularly every six weeks, and his coat is in a bad state, it is quite a good idea to rough clip the dog first. This should include the feet, the face and the tail, and perhaps the removal of some of the dog's coat before bathing, as this is time saving when it comes to drying the dog.

Vulnerable Area Requiring Special Care

Some dogs will be found to have more sensitive skin than others, and these dogs should never be clipped with a fine blade. The blades should be disinfected and cleaned well before use. These sensitive-skinned dogs are extremely likely to suffer from what is called 'clipper rash' in dog parlance. Clipper rash is initially caused by a dog being allergic to clippers. Secondary skin trouble may then occur with sepsis which can spread extremely rapidly and is often difficult to cure.

Great care must always be taken when clipping the genital areas and this should always be done with the growth of the coat. In the case of bitches, extreme care must be taken near the teats, and it is often better to scissor this area using a comb to protect the vulnerable prominent teats. In some poodle parlours for the sake of speed, kennelmaids do in fact use clippers on this area, and tragic cases have been known where teats have been completely cut off. It is worth remembering that electric clippers, although easy to use, can be dangerous in inexperienced hands and great pain and distress can be caused to the dog, not only from clipper, but also from nicking the skin on the lips, the edges of the ears or the vulva and the scrotum.

Other areas which may also be nicked are the webbing between the toes, the feet, and particularly the bony area of the knuckles and also the tongue. Although the hair between the pads should always be scissored, clippers are frequently used as a time-saving device and, unless great care is taken, the pads may be nicked, particularly with dogs who do not have enough road exercise to keep their pads hard. Many breeds do, in fact, suffer from soft, thin pads, and this is generally caused by a recessive gene.

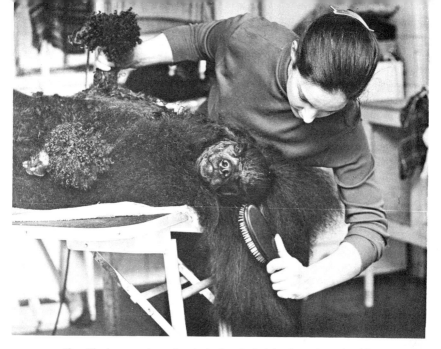

58. The long coat requires to be brushed right through to the skin.

Photo: Anne Cumbers

59. This large dog with his massive coat requires two powerful dryers for him to be dried quickly.

Photo: Anne Cumbers

60. Nails must be kept short. There is a close affinity between this champion and his mistress, as can be seen in their expressions.

Photo: Anne Cumbers

Clipping the Feet
Hind Feet. The feet are best clipped with the dog sitting squarely in front of the trimmer. It is generally found to be easier to start with the hind feet first, although this is entirely a matter of preference. The blades used for the feet are required to be fine and a no. 15 or 30 blade is excellent. The clippers should be held flat against the skin, and clipping should be commenced near the nails working upwards towards the leg. The hair must be removed between the toes, although clipping this area too closely can cause soreness, and this must be guarded against, because otherwise the dog will only make matters worse by licking and chewing his feet.

In order to work between the toes, the first finger should be inserted between the large pad and the toes, the thumb being on top of the foot or vice versa. By using slight pressure on the foot, the webbed toes will automatically be spread apart and this will enable the edge of the clipper head to be worked up between the toes first on one side and then on the other. Repeat the procedure for the other hind foot.

The back of each foot is clipped with the dog in a standing position; the foot may be bent backwards as with a horse and clipped up the back of the leg, according to the pattern. The outside of the foot is clipped next, stopping, of course, just before the beginning of the toes, unless otherwise indicated by the pattern. The hair is next clipped between the pads if clippers are being used, not forgetting to spread the toes again. Many people, however, prefer to cut the hair from between the pads with scissors.

Forefeet. Place the dog in a sitting position again and ,starting with the left foot, extend it firmly but gently, and without pulling it too far forward, as the dog will ast adversely to this and will probably try and get up. Proceed to clip from the bottom of the nails working to the top of the foot again, according to the pattern. Clean out the hair between the toes as with the hind feet, taking care not to cut the hair too close, particularly on poodles with ultra-sensitive skins. This generally applies to the lighter coloured poodles, especially the whites and those which lack pigment, although there is no hard and fast rule about this.

Spreading the webbed toes is exactly the same as for the hind feet, and is done by placing a finger between the large pad and the smaller toe pads

61. A Wire Fox Terrier in show trim.

Photo: Sally Anne Thompson

62. A Bedlington is an excellent town or country dog but requires clipping, trimming and scissoring.

Photo: Sally Anne Thompson

The under side of the foot is still clipped with the dog in the sitting position, but it is clipped nearly as far as the extra pad which is found about an inch above the back of the foot. When all four feet have been clipped, give a last minute check that there are no straggly hairs left, particularly around the base of the nails, and see that all four feet are clipped to the same height up the leg. It may be found to be easier to remove any stray hairs quickly with scissors rather than use the clippers again.

ENGLISH SADDLE CLIP, OR LION CLIP

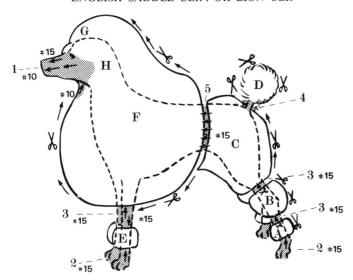

Clipping: (1) Face; (2) Feet; (3) Legs; (4) Tail; (5) Belt; Blade No. 10; Blade No. 15.

Scissoring: (A) Lower Hind Bracelet; (B) Top Bracelet; (C) Pack; (D) Pompon; (E) Front Bracelet; (F) Mane; (G) Top Knot; (H) Ears.

Difficult Dogs

Occasionally, it may be necessary to have assistance when clipping a young puppy or an exceptionally nervous dog, particularly if the dog has never been clipped before. It is a great help if an assistant would steady the dog from behind, but in most cases it is better for the trimmer to handle the actual limb which is to be clipped.

Most poodle clippers prefer to work on their dogs without unnecessary aids, such as grooming controls where dogs are either suspended or attached. These are particularly dangerous if the dog has to be left alone for a few seconds, and, as I have previously

I

63. An Irish Water Spaniel, showing his ringlets.

Photo: Anne Cumbers

mentioned, it is sadly not unknown for a dog to be strangled while an assistant answers the telephone. Being tethered may also be a terrifying experience for a young puppy, particularly if it has never been leash trained previously.

Clipping the Tail

Clipping the tail of the poodle is not difficult. Stand the dog facing forward so that the tail can be held firmly in the left hand. It is a matter of personal preference as to which area of the tail is clipped first. It must be remembered, however, that the tail is a very vulnerable area for clipper rash to appear; and if the dog is frightened or hurt during the clipping procedures, it may affect the carriage of his tail, which could be a serious problem if the dog is to be exhibited at a show the following day. The following is a suggested order of work:

1. *Tail.* Hold the tail firmly in the left hand pulling it slightly so that it fits the angle of the clippers. Proceed to clip from the beginning of the pompon up to the root of the tail, clipping first up the centre and then up both sides.
2. Holding the tail upright and slightly forward, taking great care on no account to stretch the skin, because this is apt to lead to clipper rash, clip carefully on the underside from the root of the tail to the base of the pompon. In poodles that are known to have ultra-sensitive skin, and are therefore more susceptible to clipper burns, this area of the tail should be clipped in the opposite direction, in other words, with the growth of the hair; or this may be done equally well with scissors, or even very fine thinning shears can be used instead.
3. *Pompon.* It is most important to remember that the base of the pompon should be equal all round; otherwise the finished pompon will not be symmetrical and the whole balance of the poodle will be spoilt.
4. *Anus.* The anal opening should be clipped round with great care, because this is a vulnerable and sensitive area. With some poodles, it may well be better to use curved surgical scissors or 46-toothed thinning shears.

Clipping the Face

It is a matter of personal preference as to whether the face is clipped with the trimmer standing behind the dog, in front of the

64.   A pet poodle saying good-bye to his mistress.

Photo: Anne Cumbers

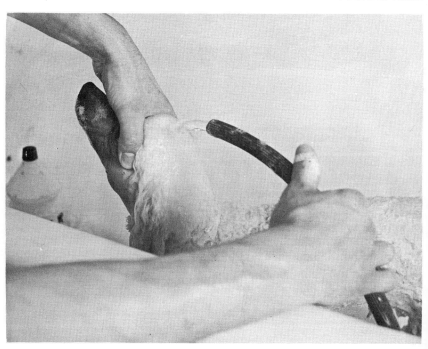

65.   Into the bath and demonstrating how the head is held up with the finger and thumb across the eyes, to prevent the soap from getting into the eyes while rinsing.

Photo: Anne Cumbers

CONTINENTAL CLIP

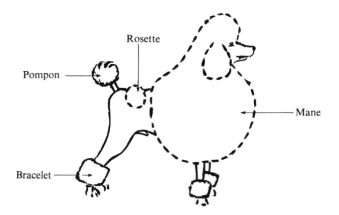

Rosette

Pompon

Mane

Bracelet

POODLE TRIMMING

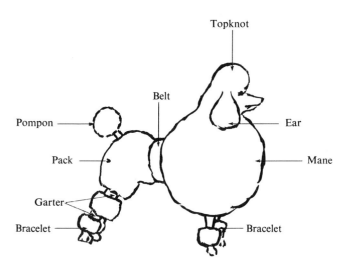

Topknot

Belt

Pompon

Ear

Pack

Mane

Garter

Bracelet

Bracelet

POINTS OF A POODLE CLIP

dog, or at the side of the dog. The finished result is exactly the same. A suitable order of work is:

1. *Face.* Turn back the ear, and with the edge of the clipping blade, clip a straight line from the ear to the outside corner of the eye, and continue down the muzzle holding the blade flat against the face. This line is also the line for what will be one side of the topknot. Make quite certain that this line goes exactly to the corner of the eye, as this is extremely important. If the line is taken above the eye, too much hair will be removed from the topknot, and this cannot be put back; and, if the line is taken below the corner of the eye, there will be too much hair in the topknot, and this would spoil the symmetry. This is the lesser of the two evils, because this of course, can be quickly rectified by accurately cutting the hair to the corner of the eye.

2. *Eye Protection.* It is a matter of preference how the eye should be protected, but it is nonetheless extremely important that some protection should be given when clipping the hair in this area. The eye may be covered with the thumb and first finger extended across the stop, or the hand may be held the other way round so that the thumb keeps the skin taut, but not stretched, at the outside corner of the eye. The lower lid requires to be extended upwards and backwards towards the top of the head. This automatically closes the eye, and the hair immediately below can then be clipped with impunity. If there is any doubt lest the dog may not co-operate and sit quietly while this clipping procedure is being carried out, then for heaven's sake get someone to hold the dog!

3. On no account must any hair be removed from above the poodles' eyes either with scissors or clippers.

4. Clipping should be continued forward along the cheek and the side of the face.

5. *Mouth.* It is important to take great care while clipping the area near the mouth, that the skin is held taut. This is best done with the dog's head bent slightly upwards so that the skin is taut, remembering always to clip against the growth of the hair. Proceed to clip the side of the lip with the edge of the clippers only; otherwise the lips may be nicked or caught by them.

6. *Jaws.* The jaws must be held firmly together with the thumb underneath and the first finger on top just below the stop, so

that the hair on the lips and around the front of the muzzle may be removed smoothly. The firm holding of the jaws also prevents the dog from licking his lips, because even the smallest nick on the tongue will cause profuse bleeding. Many dogs object to having their muzzle enclosed in the trimmer's hand, and they should be humoured.

7. *Inverted V.* Holding the muzzle firmly in one hand, an inverted V must be made running between the eyes in the Lion Trim, but the hair is clipped straight across in all modern clips. The V made when putting a dog into Lion Trim must be made with the clippers facing towards the muzzle, with the apex of the V being formed by the top outer edge of the clipper.

In some cases the same result may be achieved by using the clipper head the other way round so that it is used against the growth of the hair, although this is not a method to be recommended.

8. The position of this V depends entirely on the shape of the poodle's head and, according to where it is placed, it can correct a head for an obvious fault. The V should never be cut too deep and the apex of the the V should be level with the top of the eye. If the impression required is that the head should be lengthened, then the apex of the V should be made slightly higher than the top of the eyes. This gives the impression that there is a greater stop than, in fact, there actually is.

9. *Muzzle.* The hair on the top of the muzzle must now be clipped from the V to the nose.

10. Lift the head up and, depending on the pattern, clip the hair from the adam's apple to the end of the lower side of the muzzle.

11. This general clipping procedure is the same for the Lamb or Utility Clip, the Puppy Clip and the English Show Trim, as well as the English Saddle or Lion Trim. It is also basically correct for a number of the more exotic and rarer trims. Since there are numerous varieties of trim, however, it must be remembered before embarking on any of the lesser known patterns, that it is important to ascertain how far the basic clip is applicable before starting.

PUG

The Pug is yet another breed which originated in China. The standard requires that the coat should be fine, smooth, soft, short and glossy, neither hard nor woolly. There are no grooming problems. The coat should be brushed daily with a good bristle brush. This should be followed with finger massage to keep the skin supple. A little mink oil sprayed sparingly on to a soft brush for a final gloss over the coat gives a good sheen, particularly if the coat is then polished with a chamois leather or a piece of silk. The ears should be cleaned out with a piece of cotton wool moistened in alcohol, and the ears should be dusted with ear powder. The eyes should be gently wiped over with something like weak tea. Wrinkles must be wiped clean and kept dry by the application of Johnson's baby powder. Teeth should be rubbed over with cotton wool moistened in hydrogen peroxide and milk, or cleaned with human toothpaste. Nails are required to be kept very short. They should be cut frequently, because the more often that they are cut the shorter they can be kept, since every time that the nail is cut the quick recedes a little up the nail. Pugs should be bathed the day before a show. Nails look well if they have been polished. Human nail polish powder is excellent for this, and even a slight smear of vaseline on the nails and nose before entering the ring makes the dog look extra smart.

PYRENEAN MOUNTAIN DOG

This is one of the largest breeds of dog and it was used for centuries as a protector of the shepherd and his flock. The standard requires a fine, white undercoat and a long, flat, coarser outer coat. The hair must be straight or slightly undulating.

The coat, surprisingly, does not take a great deal of brushing and grooming. The coat should be brushed vigorously once a week at least, followed by a good finger massage all over the body. The coat can be kept clean and white by using either starch or Johnson's baby powder. A good spirit dressing shampoo, rubbed well into the coat with a flannel, keeps the coat clean and sparkling, especially if it is used regularly once a week.

SUGGESTED METHOD OF GROOMING

Tools and Equipment required

L. Hinds wire brush no. 6002   Spirit shampoo
Nylon brush   Starch

Wide-toothed comb	Johnson's baby powder
Scissors	Ear powder
Artery forceps	White hair rinse
Tooth scaler	Electric trunk hair dryer

Method
1. Brush the coat up, starting at the top of the neck, and work down layer by layer to the root of the tail.
2. Work from the extremities in the same manner up to the spine, in 3-inch strips on the body.
3. Repeat the process for the other side.
4. Brush the breechings and leg feathering.
5. Part the tail down the centre and brush in layers, going right down to the skin.
6. Brush thoroughly under each hind leg.
7. Brush the coat from the chin to the forelegs.
8. Make the dog extend each foreleg in turn and brush the extended one and the inside of the other.
9. Brush the ruff thoroughly.
10. Brush the ears both inside and outside.
11. Brush the head gently and carefully.

Cleaning the Coat
1. Take a flannel and dip it into a spirit shampoo.
2. Rub the coat over in the same order as for brushing, working the spirit in well.
3. Brush the coat down in the way it grows.
4. Comb out the leg feathering, the belly, coat and the tail.
5. Wipe the eyes round with Diamondeye lotion.
6. Place a spot of vaseline on the end of the nose.
7. Scale and clean the teeth if necessary.
8. Put ear powder in the ears once a week.

Trimming
1. Trim hair from between the pads if necessary.
2. Trim hair round the feet if below ground level.
3. Trim mats away from double dew-claws on the hind legs.
4. Trim the hair round anus if necessary.

Bathing
Pyreneans may be bathed in any good shampoo. The coat requires a thorough rinsing. A final rinse with one of the excellent

I*

rinses made for white coats certainly helps to make the coat look whiter than white.

Drying

There is nothing better to dry a large dog than one of the excellent trunk hair dryers. These are also more than useful for ordinary grooming set at 'cold'. The strong blowing action separates the coat while brushing, but care must be taken not to allow the cold air to blow on to the stomach.

These dryers are also most useful for drying wet legs after a walk.

RETRIEVERS, FLAT-COATED AND GOLDEN

Flat-Coated Retriever

This is a bright, active, medium-szied gun dog. The standard requires the coat to be dense, as flat as possible and of fine quality and texture.

Golden Retriever

This is a powerful, strong, popular gun dog. The standard requires the coat to be dense with a good water-resisting undercoat, covered with a flat or wavy top coat. There should be good feathering on the legs, tail, breechings and on the underline.

The coat requires stripping on both these breeds in areas where it becomes too thick and heavy and therefore spoils the outline of the dog. Stripping should, however, be kept to a minimum, and scissoring is only required for tidying up and tipping. Hair should be cut from between the pads but not removed from between the toes.

Fine thinning shears can be used to great advantage on the coat and in many ways their use is preferable to stripping. The shears, however, must be kept lying flat and close to the skin whilst scissoring with them, thus removing the undercoat and only leaving the longer hair on the top. If this is required to be shortened, then the shears may be used on top of the coat. Thinning shears are useful on the head and on the ears, and also on the sides of the cheek.

SUGGESTED METHOD OF GROOMING

Tools and Equipment required

Hard brush   Artery forceps for ear cleaning

Soft brush

Wide-toothed comb

Fine-toothed comb

Stripping knife

Thinning shears, 46-teeth

Nail clippers or file

Ear powder

Whitening to aid stripping

Mink oil

Velvet polishing glove

Hound glove

7-inch scissors.

Method

1. Brush the coat thoroughly, removing any mats and tangles.
2. Comb out any dead hair.
3. Finger massage all over the body, starting to work from the stern forward and lifting the body coat as you work.
4. Comb the hair in the direction in which it lies.
5. Brush the leg feathering and the tail.
6. Comb all the feathering through from the skin.
7. Wipe the eyes round.
8. Powder the ears and clean if necessary.
9. Cut or file the nails as necessary.
10. Remove hair from between the pads by scissoring.
11. Spray the brush lightly with mink oil and brush the coat with the soft brush.
12. Polish the coat with a velvet pad or use the hands.
13. Clean or scale the teeth when necessary.

Stripping

Strip the hair wherever necessary, but the dog must look natural. Stripping should be done during moulting only. Fine-toothed shears are kinder and are just as efficient at other times.

Bathing

Retrievers may require bathing from time to time and many look better for a bathe the day before a show.

Working Dogs

Feathering and fringes may be trimmed down, in order to avoid burrs causing mats and tangles on the coat. Burrs, brambles, and other extraneous matter should be removed immediately after a walk or a day's shooting, because, if they are left in, the coat will mat, felt and tangle. This in turn may lead to infestations of parasites. The coat should be dusted from time to time with anti-flea powder.

RHODESIAN RIDGEBACK

As the name implies, this breed comes from Rhodesia. It is somewhat similar to a Labrador Retriever but it has a Foxhound gait.
The interesting peculiarity of the breed is the curious ridge of hair
which grows up the back in the opposite direction to that of the
rest of the coat.

Grooming is simple. It requires a daily brushing with a medium-
stiff brush and a polish with a hound glove, silk handkerchief or
velvet pad. A good hand strapping once a week will keep the skin
supple. Pressure points should be watched. The ears, teeth and feet
require the usual canine care. Nails may be polished for shows.

ROTTWEILLER

This large dog does not require a great deal of grooming. The coat
is thick with a good undercoat, and the top coat is short. A good
grooming with a hound glove, followed by finger massage and a
final rub over with a chamois leather, will bring the coat up in an
excellent sheen. As with all heavy breeds, pressure points require
to be watched. Ears should be cleaned and powdered once a week.
Teeth should be cleaned and scaled when necessary. The nails
should be kept short by cutting and filing and may be vaselined
or polished for shows. The inner lining of the lips requires to be
kept clean, as food sometimes accumulates in the fold of the lips.

ST. BERNARD

This is one of the largest breeds of dog. There are two distinct coats
the rough and the smooth. Neither is particularly difficult to groom.
The smooth variety is the original, the rough having been produced
by crossing with a Newfoundland. The standard requires the rough
variety to have a dense, flat coat, with a ruff round the neck and
good feathering on the breechings and on the tail

The smooth variety should have a close, hound-like coat, with only
slight feathering on the breechings and tail.

Tools and Equipment required

Hindes wire brush

Soft brush

Wide-tooth comb

Scissors

Tooth scaler

Spirit shampoo

Starch

Johnson's baby powder

Ear powder

White hair rinse

Electric trunk dryer

Method

Grooming the smooth variety is quite straight-forward. The rough variety may be groomed in a similar manner to a Pyrenean Mountain Dog. Nails may be vaselined or polished for shows. Pressure points must be watched and massaged regularly.

SALUKI

This gazelle hound originated in the Middle East. It is somewhat similar in build to the greyhound. There are two varieties: the Smooth and the Feathered. Grooming is simple, as the standard requires a smooth, soft, silky-textured coat, with slight feathering on the legs and breechings, and longer feathering on the ears and tail. There may be a slight, woolly feathering on the shoulders and thighs. Grooming should be done once or twice a week with a rubber-mounted bristle brush, and finger massage once a week.

General care should be taken of pressure points. A hound glove is useful for polishing, and also silk or velvet. A little trimming of the feathering may be required, and hair should be removed from between the pads. There is an erroneous belief that all hair in the pads should be left, as it is there to protect the pads from sand. But all long-coated breeds or ones with feathering grow hair between the pads, and the Salukis hair in this position should be trimmed away like in other breeds.

SAMOYED

This breed was originally used as a shepherd for reindeer near and within the Arctic circle. The name comes from a district bearing this name in the far north. The breed is really one of the Spitz group and has a coat typical of the group. The standard requires a thick, soft, short, dense undercoat with a harsh top coat growing through it and forming an outer coat. The coat should stand away from the body and must be free from any form of curl.

The coat requires daily grooming and with a dog of the size of a Samoyed it should take a good quarter of an hour a day. A powerful electric trunk hair dryer is useful for blowing the coat whilst grooming, and one is almost essential for drying the coat after bathing.

SUGGESTED METHOD OF PREPARATION

There is practically no trimming required. Only the hair between the pads should be removed when necessary. Tipping the coat for show purposes, particularly the feathering on the legs and the hair on the feet, gives a more groomed effect.

Tools and Equipment required

Brush with long bristles	Shampoo
Wide-tooth comb	White hair rinse
7-inch scissors	Johnson's baby powder or
Coat dressing	starch
Spirit shampoo	Mink oil
	Electric trunk hair dryer

Method

Brushing the coat is similar to that for any other long-coated breed of the same type as the Pomeranian, the coat being brushed upwards. A definite routine should be adhered to. The dog must learn to extend his forelegs, so that the hair can be well brushed under the elbows. It is an advantage if he will lie on his side.

Combing

Only the fringes on the legs and behind the ears are combed. The comb is especially useful for cleaning the brush whilst working, as the hair accumulates quite rapidly in the bristles.

Bathing

This should be done about five days before a show. The coat requires rinsing thoroughly and should have a final rinse with one of the many excellent rinses made specially for white-coated dogs.

The coat requires a great deal of drying and this is really best done with one of the strong electric trunk hair dryers.

Spirit Cleaning

A good spirit shampoo rubbed into and over the coat with a flannel once a week will keep the coat clean, well kept and white. Starch or Johnson's baby powder are also useful coat cleaners.

Nails will require filing or clipping regularly about once a month. They may be vaselined and polished for shows.

Teeth should be kept clean and scaled when necessary.

Ears should be dusted weekly with ear powder.

It may be necessary to dust the coat with flea powder occasionally.

SCHNAUZER

This is one of the most charming breeds and comes in two sizes: the Giant or Standard and the Miniature. The breed is of German origin and should really be classed as a terrier. The standard requires a hard, wiry coat, which should be just short enough to make the dog look smart. The coat should be clean on the neck, shoulders, ears and skull. There should, however, be plenty of good, hard hair on the forelegs. There should also be a good undercoat, which is really considered essential.

The coat requires stripping, particularly on the ears, cheeks and skull. Clippers are used on the head. The eyebrows require shaping as do the beard and whiskers. The hair should be trimmed between the pads, and the hair on the feet should be scissored round just covering the nails. The latter should be short. Hair growing in the ear canal should be removed with artery forceps, but only a few hairs should be removed at one session.

SUGGESTED METHOD OF PREPARING A SCHNAUZER

The detailed suggested method of preparing a Wire-Haired Fox Terrier could be followed for the preparation of a Schnauzer, except for the head and beard. The coat on the Schnauzer is required to be considerably longer than that on the Wire-Haired Fox Terrier, but the general principles remain the same, other than chalking and bathing.

Tools and Equipment required

Hard bristle brush	Electric clippers Oster A5
Steel comb with wide teeth	Blade no. 10
Razor comb	7-inch scissors

66.   A Schnauzer head study, showing his magnificent beard.

Stripping knife

Dolling-up pad

Nail clippers

Hound glove

Artery forceps

Coat dressing

Steady table

Large grooming mirror

Preparation of the Head

If the head is found to be difficult to pluck then it is far kinder to use electric clippers.

SUGGESTED ORDER OF WORK

1. Comb the hair forward from the top of the skull, including the eyebrows and the beard.
2. Clip from the V at the stop between the eyebrows to the inner corner of the ear. Clip straight up the skull to the occiput.
3. Clip a line from the outer corner of the eyebrow to the outer corner of the ear.
4. Clip from the outer corner of the eyebrow down to the corner of the mouth.
5. Clip from these lines working towards the angle of the jaw bone.
6. Clip from the adam's apple to a line running between the two corners of the mouth.
7. The ears may be plucked or clipped. If the ears are to be clipped, work from the base towards the tips with the growth of the hair.
8. The outer leather hair is also clipped, in the direction of the growth of the hair, from the boundary of the ear to the tip.
9. For the sake of hygiene the hair in front of the penis may be clipped too, or scissored.

Eyebrows

These are shaped in a similar manner to those of the Scottish Terrier. The ends are generally cut in one clean cut. Many Scottish Terrier owners prefer the edges to be jagged. It is purely a matter of preference.

Scissoring

This final trimming is extremely important, particularly the shaping of the eyebrows and the beard. Careful scissoring will give the correct expression and proportions to the entire dog.

1. Comb the eyebrows down straight over the muzzle, including the beard. Holding the points of the scissors open, so that they

correspond with the width of the inner corner of the eyes, insert the points through the eyebrow at the stop and trim the surplus hair from between the eyes, making certain that the scissors are kept parallel to the top of the muzzle whilst scissoring. The points, of course, must be facing forward.

2. With the dog facing forward trim the outer edges of the eyebrows, so that they correspond with the side of the head and are level with it.

3. Comb the eyebrows forward again and cut the eyebrows in one diagonal cut from the outer corner to the centre corner, so that the shape of the eyebrows is now two right angled triangles. The inner line of these triangles should be parallel and perpendicular. Great care must be taken when trimming the eyebrows to avoid serious accidents in the event of the dog moving suddenly or unexpectedly. Unless the dog is well trained and thoroughly used to this trimming procedure, it is wise to have assistance.

4. *Stop*. Scissor an inverted V between the eyebrows. This should extend from the centre of the stop to the inner corner of the eyes.

Ears

1. Scissor round the ear leather carefully on both sides. This is particularly necessary when the ears have been plucked.

2. If the ears have been clipped, as soon as the hair begins to grow, thinning shears may be used to remove the undercoat coming through. This improves the colour on the ears and makes the hair lie close and flat to the ear, giving the impression that the ears were plucked and not clipped. It is nearly always kinder to use clippers than to use the plucking method, except when the coat has 'blown'.

3. Repeat the procedure for the other ear.

Beard

1. Comb the beard forward and cut the hair in a straight line from the corner of the mouth to the outer corner of the eyebrow. It is important, when cutting this line, that all the hair should be grasped in the hand which is holding the muzzle, because otherwise some of the precious beard may be cut off by mistake.

2. Comb the beard forward once again and square off to the desired shape.

Scissoring

The hair growing between the pads should be scissored, and the feet may be trimmed round, so that the hair is just off the ground.

Coat Cleaning

Schnauzers do not require bathing unless really dirty, because this tends to soften the coat. Daily grooming keeps the coat clean and in good condition, and Fuller's earth or one of the excellent spirit shampoos may be used with good effect.

The ears are best powdered and left awhile, before trying to remove any hair from the ear canal. The powder makes the hair brittle and easier to remove.

SCOTTISH TERRIER

The Scottish Terrier is one of the most attractive of the terrier breeds. He is a sturdy, thick-set, low-to-ground, alert and agile dog. The Scottish Terrier has two coats; the undercoat is short, dense and soft, whilst the outer coat requires to be dense, harsh and wiry. These two coats are weather resisting. The colour is usually black, wheaten or brindle of any colour. The coat of the Scottish Terrier requires considerable care and maintenance, which includes clipping stripping and trimming.

HOW TO LEARN THE ART OF PREPARING A SCOTTISH TERRIER

Practical experience under the supervision of an expert is the surest and best way of learning to deal with the Scottish Terrier coat correctly. The Scottish Terrier requires his first trimming of head and tail when he is about ten weeks old, although puppies should have any loose fluff on the top of the coat removed by hand between the ages of eight and ten weeks. The puppy coat requires to be stripped out either by hand or with a stripping knife when they are about five to six months old. This should include the back of the neck, body and tail. If there is any excess fluffy hair on the legs, it is advisable to remove this at the same time. The coat on the side of the body takes longer to grow than the coat on the back and neck.

With regard to clipping the Scottish Terrier, it is purely a matter of personal opinion as to how soon a dog should have his first clip, because with most breeds, the earlier you start any grooming procedure, the quicker the dog will learn to accept the discipline required. Many people prefer to use hand clippers, and since the area of clipping is small, these work well, but for those people who prefer to use electric clippers the earlier the dog gets used to the noise and vibration of these the better.

Stripping consists of stripping out the top harsh coat with finger and thumb or a stripping knife may be used if preferred.

Clipping the Scottish Terrier for a show is done in four stages. But when practising on a puppy, the whole clipping procedure could be done in one session. For show purposes, the top of the head is clipped two weeks before a show. The front and throat are clipped one week before the show, whilst, the ears are clipped between five and seven days before it, and the sides of the head are clipped two days before hand. The main body coat should be stripped out eight to twelve weeks before a show.

The method chosen to keep a Scottish Terrier in perfect trim, depends very much on the individual dog and the growth of coat. He probably requires clipping every two to four weeks, but since there is so little clipping to be done, this takes only a few minutes. The coat would probably otherwise not require attention, other than normal grooming, more frequently than every two to three months. Technically speaking, the coat should only be plucked or stripped when it has 'blown', otherwise it is cruel. Normally dogs moult twice a year, in the autumn and in the winter, but if dogs are kept in artificial surroundings with electric light, then they are apt to moult all the year round because of the extra light. This particularly applies to house dogs, in which case the coat may stripped without hurting the dog at any convenient time. A full description of stripping, plucking and carding will be found under the preparations for a Fox Terrier on page 162.

SUGGESTED ORDER OF WORK FOR STRIPPING, CLIPPING AND TRIMMING

It is an excellent idea to keep to a definite routine. The dog learns the routine and accepts the procedure, and he obeys the orders which are given by the person grooming.

A definite routine is also necessary, in order that important procedures may not be omitted. All tools must be collected together ready for use, the dog should be made to stand on a steady table with a non-slippery surface, and in some cases he may possibly require to be tethered, in which case, he should never be left for a second, in order to avoid a serious accident. A large grooming mirror is essential, as also is a good light. The latter is particularly necessary when preparing a black Scottish Terrier. There should be a container to take the removed hair, which prevents it not only from blowing about, but from getting into the dog's long coat, which would cause it to mat and tangle. The hair may also get between the pads, where it would mat with the long hair which grows there.

SUGGESTED METHOD OF PREPARING A SHOW SCOTTISH TERRIER

Tools and Equipment required

Oster A 5 electric clipper, with blade no. 10.
Hand clippers (if preferred)
Bristle brush
Steel comb, wide-tooth
Razor comb
Dolling-up pad
Stripping knife
7-inch scissors

Nail file
Nail clippers
Artery forceps
Hound glove
Ear powder
Steady table
Large mirror
Good light
Thinning shears, 46-teeth

ORDER OF PREPARATION FOR A SHOW

***STAGE I**—Stripping*
12 to 8 weeks before show

Body Coat and Tail are stripped out

***STAGE II**—Clipping*
2 weeks before show
1 week before show

5 to 7 days before show
2 days before show

Head is clipped
Front and Throat are clipped, nails are cut.
Ears are clipped
Sides of Head are clipped

***STAGE III**—Scissoring*
2 days before show

(*a*) *Feet* are shaped by scissoring
(*b*) *Eyebrows and Beard* are trimmed
(*c*) *Tail* is scissored

STAGE IV
A Scottish Terrier should not be bathed before a show, but the coat may be cleaned if necessary with a coat dressing.

GENERAL RULES FOR STRIPPING AND CLIPPING

Stripping

1. Stand the dog on a firm non-slippery table.
2. Have a grooming mirror behind the table.
3. Provide good light.
4. Stand behind the dog and start stripping from the top of the neck downwards over the body.
5. Stand in front of the dog when doing ears and face.
6. When working on the leg furnishings, hold the leg up which is not being worked on. This should make the dog stand still and keep him balanced. The same applies to both fore and hind *l*egs.
7. As each stage of the coat is worked, it is extremely important to take great care in blending the coat from one area to another. This is particularly important from the clipped line to the plucked area.

Stripping the Neck and Body

The coat is stripped after the dog has been in full coat and when the new coat is coming in. In terrier parlance this is known as the time when the coat has 'blown'. Stripping should take place within a week or two. Directions and suggestions for stripping a coat are given earlier under Wire-Haired Fox Terrier Stripping. Stripping the Scottish Terrier is somewhat similar, but the coat is stripped in slight curves down to the middle thigh side of ribs and shoulder. The rest of the coat remains long and is thinned if required. The coat should be stripped between eight and twelve weeks before a show, depending very much on the coat of the individual dog and also the time of year.

Clipping

8. *Skull.* It is a matter of personal opinion as to whether the hair on the skull should be clipped with the growth of the hair or against it. The same effect will be achieved using a finer blade with the growth of the hair, or with a coarser blade against the growth of the hair.

    First, comb the hair forward over the face from just above the eyebrows. Clip the skull, working from the eyebrows towards the occiput stopping about an inch from the occiput.

9. *Cheek.* Clip from the outer base of the skull in a straight line to the outer edge of the eyebrow and work down to the corners of the mouth where the beard commences.

10. *Front and Throat.* Clip up the throat to the corners of the

mouth to where the beard starts, forming a V at the bottom of the throat. Join the clipped area of the cheek between the outer base of the ear and the corner of the eyebrow. The hair grows in different directions below the ear and it should be clipped accordingly.

11. *Inside the Ears.* Clip the inside of the ears with a no. 10, or with a no. 15 blade if a closer finish is required. Clip from the centre working towards the outer edges, working away from the head as you clip. The edges of the ears must not be clipped, and the hair should be clipped with the growth of the hair.

12. *Outside the Ears.* The ears are clipped with the growth of the hair working towards the tips, leaving a short fringe of hair at the boundary of the ears to blend in with the hair on top of the head and neck. Work from the centre towards the edges, leaving the edges of the ears unclipped. If a coarser blade is used, the ears may be clipped from the tip to the boundary where the fringe is left. If it is more convenient to clip the ears more than two days before a show, a fine blade may be used against the growth of hair. Clipping with a fine blade with the growth of hair produces a sheen on the ears.

Scissoring

The final trimming is extremely important, particularly the shaping of the eyebrows, tufts and beard. Careful scissoring will give the correct expression and proportions to the entire dog.

1. *Eyebrows.* Comb the eyebrows straight down over the muzzle, which should include the beard. Holding the points of the scissors open, so that they correspond with the width of the inner corner of the dog's eyes, insert the points through the eyebrows at the stop and trim the surplus hair from between the eyes, making certain that the scissors are kept parallel to the top of the muzzle whilst working, with the points facing forward.

2. With the dog facing forward, trim the outer edges of the eyebrows, so that they correspond with the side of the head and are level with it.

3. Comb the eyebrows forward again and cut the eyebrows in one diagonal cut from the outer corner to the centre corner, so that the shape of the eyebrows is now two right-angled triangles. The inner lines of these triangles should be parallel

and perpendicular. Some owners prefer to make the edge of the eyebrows jagged. Great care must be taken when trimming the eyebrows to avoid any accident should the dog move unexpectedly. Unless the dog is well trained, it is wise to have assistance.

4. *Stop.* Scissor an inverted V between the eyebrows. This should extend from the centre of the stop to the inner corners of the eyes.

5. *Ears.* Scissor the hair about halfway down on the inside ear leather, so that it is the same length as the two tufts of hair which would previously have been left on the skull between the ears. Scissor down the outside of the ear carefully, fold the ears in half and cut the protruding hair in a straight line level with the edge of the ear leathers.

6. Repeat the procedure for the other ear.

7. Shorten the hair tufts to the desired length in front of and between the ears.

8. *Beard.* Brush the beard forward and scissor a straight line from the outer corner of the eyebrow to the corner of the mouth. Scissor the ends neatly in a diagonal straight line from the bottom of the beard to the corner of the mouth. Trim off the ends of the swept-down beard in a straight line, emphasizing the full beard so that it corresponds proportionally to the overhanging eyebrows and the tufted hair at the ears.

9. *Hind Quarters.* Trim the hair off as short as possible below the tail. The coat must be thinned out on the thigh, forming a slight or gentle curve which then gently blends into the long body coat. This curve corresponds with the thinned or stripped coat on the shoulders. The hair below the tail must be graduated into the long, thicker hair of the hind legs, so that the coat lies flat.

10. *Tail.* The tail requires to be thick at the root and to taper to a point at the tip. The carriage should be upright with a slight bend. Trim the hair close on the underside of the tail, starting about the middle and working towards the tip. Scissor off any untidy straggly hairs.

11. *Forelegs.* Thin the hair and shorten it at the elbows. Brush the leg hair down and thin out any tufts or straggly hair. The hair between the forelegs should be long and thick, like that on the hind legs.

12. *Body Coat.* This must be blended carefully from the short top

coat to the long coat of the flank and belly. The coat of the latter may be tipped if the ends are thin and straggly.

13. *Feet.* Brush or comb the hair in all directions. Lift each foot in turn backwards and remove the hair growing between the pads. Brush the hair down and, with the dog standing squarely on all four legs, trim the hair round the feet, so that it is just off the ground. Trim the legs from the hocks down, leaving the hair as thick as possible below the hocks and on top of the toes.

14. *Nails.* These should be kept short either by regular filing or by clipping with a guillotine nail clipper.

15. *Teeth.* These should be cleaned and scaled from time to time, if necessary.

16. *Ears.* These must be kept free of hair and ear powder should be used regularly.

SEALYHAM TERRIER

The Sealyham is one of the short-legged terriers, and does not shed its coat, which is generally white. It was originally used for digging out badgers. The standard requires the coat to be long, hard and wiry. The skull is slightly domed and is wide between the ears. The jaws are powerful and long and the muzzle is square. This is accentuated by the foreface hair and beard. The ears are rounded at the tip. The profile is not flat and there is a definite stop, which is accentuated by the long eyebrows and foreface hair and the closely plucked or clipped area of the skull and the short hair on the ears.

In the U.S.A. many Sealyhams are clipped on the head both for show and for pet purposes, but in Britain the Sealyham is not usually clipped on the head so extensively.

Show dogs should be stripped from an early age. Most breeders prefer to start ripping out the soft undercoat when the puppy is about ten weeks old. The head is generally scissored at this age, so that the shape can be seen. The ears are scissored both on the inside and closely round the edge of the ear leathers. The underside of the tail is also scissored to about a quarter of an inch in length, and the anal area should be kept short for the sake of hygiene. The feet are the only other scissored areas. The hair between the pads may be cut out, but the hair should not be cut from between the toes.

The hair is combed forwards and downwards at the back and side, and the overhanging hair is trimmed round neatly. Fine thinning shears are most useful for thinning the tree-trunk front legs, and also if the beard in older dogs becomes too thick. The head must look long not narrow. As a rough guide the hair should be about a quarter of an inch long on the head, ears, throat and on the shoulders, and also under the ears, which may be thinned out with thinning shears.

There should not be too much furnishings on the hind quarters, and the hair on the back is stripped to about two inches in length. The different length of coat must be so carefully graduated, that there is no real defining line from one length to another. There should be an apron over the brisket and the underline should be trimmed evenly, so that there is sufficient daylight underneath. A triangluar piece of hair is left on the neck. The apex, which is at the occiput, should be about a quarter of an inch at the top. The base of the triangle would be between two and three inches in length. The coat is graduated from the triangle into the shorter coat on the shoulders and the side of the neck.

The eyebrows are left undivided and should fall over the eyes in a triangle mingling with the beard. The eyes should just be able to be seen through the hair. The eyebrows should be trimmed close to the outer corner of the eye and stripped towards the nose with the hair getting longer towards the centre.

Show dogs are stripped regularly from the age of ten weeks, the soft coat being ripped out and the coat constantly carded and combed. In this way a dog's coat never gets out of hand nor becomes matted.

It is an excellent idea to remove as much coat as possible from a bitch when she is halfway through a pregnancy. The coat should be raked well after whelping. The new coat takes approximately ten weeks to grow in, but a bitch with a good, rough coat will be ready for a show in eight weeks from then on. If the coat is just topped every two or three weeks, the coat will be in show condition for ever.

Sealyhams are one of the breeds which grow hair in the ear canal. The ears must be powdered and later not more than a few hairs only should be pulled out at any one session. The powder dries the hair and makes it brittle, so that it becomes away easily.

Sealyhams which have their head clipped are clipped from the top of the eyebrows to the occiput, from the top of each ear to the corner of the eye, and from the eye down to the corner of the mouth. The throat may also be clipped from the adam's apple up to the corner of the mouth, and the areas between this and under the ear are joined up. Careful blending of the coat with thinning shears between the clipped areas and the plucked areas is necessary.

The nails and teeth must also be cut and cleaned regularly.

SUGGESTED METHOD OF PREPARING A SEALYHAM

It takes about eight weeks to prepare a Sealyham in full show coat. The coat is plucked, scissored, thinned and clipped in various stages, owing to the different length of hair required and also because of the difference of the rate of growth of the hair on different parts of the body.

Tools and Equipment required

Oster A 5 electric clippers, with blade no. 10
7-inch scissors
46-toothed thinning shears
Bristle brush
Wide-toothed comb

Grooming table
Grooming mirror
Artery forceps
Ear powder
Chalk

SUGGESTED ORDER OF WORK

STAGE I—*Eight Weeks before the Show*
Body Coat. This may be stripped right down with the finger and thumb. There is no reason why the neck and shoulders should not be stripped at the same time, making the dog look neater, although the neck and shoulders will require plucking closely again later. Continue topping every week, keeping the head and neck down to ¼ inch in length.

STAGE II—*Two Weeks before the Show*
Neck and Shoulders. The coat should be plucked closely down the neck.

STAGE III—*Ten Days before the Show*
The whole dog should be generally tidied up, including trimming or filing the nails.

STAGE IV—*Two Days before the Show*
Work on the legs.

STAGE V—*The Day before the Show*
Put the dog in the sink and wash his feet, face and beard. When

the coat is still damp, chalk the coat well and later comb it out thoroughly.

If the coat on the legs is not profuse enough, this may be helped by a little vaseline used on the furnishings so as to hold the chalk.

STAGE VI—The Day of the Show

Chalk the dog but be sure that all the chalk is well brushed out before he goes into the ring.

SHETLAND SHEEPDOG

This charming little dog, surprisingly, has nothing to do with Shetland. It is similar to a Rough Collie, only much smaller. The standard requires a soft, close undercoat, resembling fur. The outer coat should be straight and of harsh texture. There should be an abundant mane, and good feathering on the forelegs. The breechings too must be well feathered, but the legs from the hocks down should be covered in smooth hair. The muzzle is also required to be smooth.

The coat requires a certain amount of care, which includes stripping carefully. The dog, however, should always look natural. A few lessons from an expert will pay dividends, because stripping a Shetland Sheepdog correctly is not easily explained.

SUGGESTED METHOD OF PREPARING A SHETLAND SHEEPDOG

Tools and Equipment required

Long-bristle brush	Stripping knife
Wide-tooth comb	Cut-throat razor
7-inch scissors	Johnson's baby powder
Thinning shears, 46-teeth	Chalk
Mink oil	Coat dressing
Fuller's earth	Shampoo

Method

It normally takes anything from six to four weeks to prepare a Shetland Sheep Dog for a show, depending on the time of year and

67. A Rough Collie.

Photo: Sally Anne Thompson

the condition of the coat when starting. Grooming thoroughly on alternate days is usually sufficient throughout the year, but daily grooming should start two weeks prior to a show.

STAGE I—*Four Weeks before the Show*
1. Strip the coat carefully, removing it in the direction in which it grows naturally. Start at the skull, then do the sides of the cheeks.
2. Remove the tufts of hair near the dew-claws.
3. Work carefully round the tips of the ears and straighten the ear fringes.
4. Shorten the hair from the hocks downwards.
5. Trim the hair between the pads on all four feet.
6. Cut the nails with guillotine clippers and file the ends.
7. Scissor round the feet, so that they are oval in shape. This may be done from underneath, by lifting the foot up like a horse's hoof; or, with the dog standing, lift up the opposite foot to the one being trimmed, so that the dog has to keep the latter on the ground to balance himself.
8. Powder the ears and clean them if necessary.

STAGE II—*Two Weeks before the Show*
1. Change from grooming on alternate days to grooming every day.

STAGE III—*Four Days before the Show*
1. Part the coat in regular strips and apply a dry shampoo. This stage may be omitted if preferred. It is not suitable for tricolours, as it makes their coat look dusty.

STAGE IV—*Two Days before the Show*
1. Brush the coat vigorously.
2. Apply a coat dressing by pouring a little liquid into a dish and dipping the brush into the dressing.
3. Brush the dressing into the coat, going right down to the roots.
4. While the coat is still damp, apply chalk to the white areas.
5. Finally, check that all stripping and trimming is in order, that the nails have been filed short enough, and that the ears are clean and well tipped. If the ears are not sufficiently tipped, roll the ears when damp.

STAGE V—Day of the Show

Half an hour before going into the ring, brush the dog through with coat dressing and re-chalk the white areas. Brush the chalk out thoroughly before entering the ring. Tricolours should have their coat brushed through with a damp brush.

SHIH TZU

'Shih Tzu' means 'lion dog'. He is a charming little dog from Tibet, which is steadily gaining in popularity. The standard requires a good undercoat, covered by a long, straight, dense top coat. The tail should be heavily plumed. The ears are so heavily coated, that the hair on them mingles with the coat on the neck. It is interesting that the standard actually states that the Shih Tzu should be shock headed with the hair falling over the eyes. For many years now the Shih Tzu has always been exhibited with the hair drawn up from the stop and joined with the topknot between the ears, usually with an elastic band. The hair in the band is then divided in half, and half is draped on either side of the head. It is much better for the dog to have the hair drawn up from its eyes, so that it can breathe and see properly. The standard also requires a good beard and whiskers. The Shih Tzu has partings from the inner corner of each ear to the outer corner of the eye and a parting across the top of the head between the ears. A long parting goes from the top of the skull straight down the centre of the back to the root of the tail.

Unfortunately, the Shih Tzu is one of the many breeds which grow hair in the ear canal, and this must be removed regularly, but a few hairs only at any one session. The only scissoring that is required is the removal of the hair between the pads.

SUGGESTED METHOD OF GROOMING

Tools and Equipment required

Medium-stiff bristle brush
Mason Pearson or Hindes
  pin brush
Electric trunk hair dryer
Wide-tooth comb
Medium-tooth comb

Johnson's baby powder
Coat dressing
Ear powder
Eye lotion
Cotton wool

Nail clippers   Tooth scaler
Artery forceps   Elastic bands, small
Scissors   Hair protecting plastic or paper

General Cleaning
1. Wipe the eyes, using a clean cotton wool swab for each eye. Dab boracic powder on eye stain beneath the eyes.
2. Dry out the stop, wipe clean, and use either Johnson's baby powder or a little boracic powder.
3. Examine the ears, clean out with alcohol on a cotton wool swab, drop in some ear powder and leave it in for a short while.
4. Later pluck out a few hairs with artery forceps.
5. Clean the teeth with cotton wool moistened in hydrogen peroxide and milk, or use human tooth paste.
6. Cut or file the nails monthly.
7. Cut hair from between the pads, if necessary. The feet may be trimmed round, to keep them clean and dry.
8. Clean round the anal area if necessary.
9. Coat dressing or spirit shampoo may be rubbed into the coat for cleaning. Johnson's baby powder works well and a little flea powder could be added at the same time if necessary.

Grooming procedure with Brush and Comb
Brushing
The dog should be taught from early puppyhood to lie on a table to be groomed, or to lie in your lap.
1. With the dog lying on his back, start by brushing the hair layer by layer under the chin, holding the hair in one hand and flicking a layer forward with each stroke of the brush. Be sure to brush each layer right down to the skin. Work down from the chin to the hind legs.
2. With the dog lying on his side, start at the bottom of the foreleg and work up the body strip by strip to the neck.
3. Work from the bottom of the rib cage in the same manner to the spine.
4. Work from the hind leg up to the root of the tail.
5. Brush out the breechings.
6. Turn the dog over on to his other side and repeat the process.
7. Remember to clean the brush out with the comb as you work.
8. Brush out the tail feathering carefully.

9. With the dog facing you, brush out the ear feathering, making certain that there are no mats behind the ears.
10. Brush the hair back carefully on the head.

Combing
1. With the dog sitting, make a parting from the inner corner of the ear to the outer corner of the eye on both sides.
2. Make a parting across the top of the skull between the ears.
3. Draw the hair up into a point, comb it through, and place on an elastic band. Make certain that it is not too tight and that it does not draw up the corner of the eyes. Divide the topknot in half.
4. With the dog standing, make a long, straight parting from the skull, parting the coat between the ears and down the spine to the root of the tail. The skin may be very slightly stretched sideways, to help get the parting perfectly straight. There is quite an art in doing this.
5. Comb the coat out very carefully towards the ground, taking great care not to break the hair.
6. Make a parting down the centre of the tail and comb the feathering right through. Hold the hair near the roots, to prevent breaking it or pulling it out.
7. Comb the hair feathering carefully on the ears.
8. Comb the moustaches and whiskers downwards and slightly forwards, taking care not to break them. If they are dirty, they should be washed before grooming starts.
9. The leg feathering may be combed through carefully.

Show Dogs
Initially, a good coat is hereditary, and no amount of aids will create a coat if the basic requirements are not there. On the other hand, a perfect coat can be ruined in next to no time by neglect or careless grooming.

Cleaning aids are numerous, from good shampoos, dry shampoos and spirit shampoos to ordinary baby powder or Fuller's earth. Much depends on the colour of the individual dog.

Long hair has to be kept clean and cared for, if it is to be preserved. The best way to do this is to wrap the ends in paper or strips of polythene and to secure them with elastic bands, the hair being divided into 2 or 3 inch strips. Ear feathering, moustaches and beard may all be wrapped up. The wrappings should be undone

K

and the hair groomed out carefully on alternate days. If the hair is oiled and left in wrappers too long, it will felt up and be impossible to deal with.

The method of putting on elastic bands and hair wrappers will be found under Maltese. In fact, the grooming procedures are very similar. See diagrams on page 26.

Bathing

Shih Tzus should be bathed before a show. A trunk electric hair dryer is useful for drying dogs and also, when set at 'cold', to use on the coat grooming. Do not, however, allow the cold air to blow on to the stomach.

The pet Shih Tzu may be trimmed so that he permanently re-sembles a Shih Tzu puppy. Squared off ear fringes and moustaches can be most attractive, provided that the hair is trimmed with the scissor and comb method, so that the whole coat is about 1 to 1½ inches long—except for the tail which looks better if it remains its normal length. The hair on the skull does not require to be tied back, though it must be kept sufficiently short not to go into the eyes and cause severe eye irritation.

SKYE TERRIER

The Skye Terrier takes its name from the Island of Skye, which is off the north-west coast of Scotland and is where the breed originated. The Skye Terrier is one of the short-legged terriers. The standard requires a short, close, soft and woolly undercoat, but the outer coat must be long, hard, straight and flat: it must be free from waves or curls. The hair on the head is shorter and softer than the body coat, and it is drawn forward veiling the skull and eyes. The hair on the ears is combed forward and hangs over the erect ears, so that it falls down the skull and cheeks, mingling with the forelock and the rest of the face hair. This ear hair could probably be best described as a veiled fringe. It should not be so profuse as to hide the shape of the ears. The tail is long and gracefully feathered to conform with the rest of the coat.

As with any really long-coated dog, the Skye Terrier requires constant grooming to prevent the coat from forming mats and tangles. For show purposes, if the dog is allowed a normal amount of exercise, the coat should be protected with hair paper and elastic bands, to prevent the ends from becoming split or broken. The Skye Terrier should not be bathed unless it is really necessary. Regular brushing with a good bristle brush will keep the dog free from dirt and grease. Too much combing will destroy the under-coat. The comb, however, is useful for parting the hair from the nose to the root of the tail, and it is also useful for cleaning the brush and keeping it free of hair.

The grooming technique is very similar to that of the Yorkshire Terrier or the Maltese (see page 288), except for the ear fringes and forelock.

SPANIELS

There are seven varieties of Spaniel classified under Gun Dogs. These include the Clumber, Cocker, Field, Irish Water, English Springer, Welsh Springer, Sussex and the American Cocker. There is also the Cavalier King Charles Spaniel and the King Charles Spaniel both of which are classified under the Toy breeds. There is one other spaniel which is the Tibetan Spaniel. This is not a spaniel in the true sense, in that it is a breed somewhat similar to the Pekingese and originally it came from Tibet.

The American Cocker Spaniel is scissored and clipped extensively, whilst the Irish Water Spaniel requires little work on his coat other than an occasional teasing out of the curls and general tidying up. The rest of the spaniels require plucking and stripping, and some scissoring of the legs and feet. Some of the spaniels require more work on them than others, as do some individual dogs within each variety. The American Cocker Spaniel probably requires the most attention and this variety of spaniel will therefore be taken as a model.

Show Preparation
Preparing a spaniel for exhibition is hard work and takes time, and it requires to be done over a number of weeks. Coats vary in texture and rate of growth. The coat should only be plucked or stripped after or during the time that the dog is moulting and when the new coat is coming in. When it is, the coat is stripped, but at other times this can cause considerable discomfort to the dog. The fashion and custom has always been to strip dogs by hand. It is still considered essential to do this for all show dogs. Six weeks is generally considered an average time for preparing a dog for exhibition, spending about one hour each week stripping the coat.

68. The final grooming of an Old English Sheepdog requires the coat on the back to be brushed up in the shape of a pear.

Photo: Anne Cumbers

69. A perfectly trimmed Scottish Terrier.

Photo: Sally Anne Thompson

SUGGESTED METHOD OF PREPARING A COCKER SPANIEL

Tools and Equipment required

Medium-length bristle brush   7-inch scissors
Wide-tooth steel comb   Ear powder
Razor comb   Thinning shears
Nail clippers   Hound glove
Nail file   Large mirror
Whitening   Good light
Stripping knife   Steady table
Artery forceps   Nit comb

70.   Two resigned English Cockers on a show bench.

Photo: Anne Cumbers

STAGE I—*Six Weeks before the Show*
Body Coat
  1. As soon as the body coat has 'blown', strip the hair, using
     the finger and thumb or a stripping knife.
  2. The skull, neck and shoulders may be done now.

STAGE II—Four Weeks before the Show
1. Strip the skull, neck and shoulders, and blend into the body coat.
2. Rake the coat out once or twice a week.
3. Clip the nails.
4. Work on the ears, particularly underneath them.
5. Thin out the feathering where it bunches or is too think.
6. A fine nit comb is excellent for getting out the fine loose hair, particularly on the ears.

STAGE III—Two Weeks before the Show
1. Go over the head, ears, body and neck, and work round the tail area.
2. Thin the ear feathering and fringes, if necessary.
3. The front of the forelegs should be well thinned out, leaving neat feathering behind. This may be scissored evenly, just tipping the edges.
4. The tail and hind quarters feathering will need trimming.
5. Remove the hair from the hocks, trimming down very close.
6. *Feet.* Trim hair from between pads, brush the hair up between the toes, hold the toes together and trim the hair evenly. Scissor round the feet evenly.

STAGE IV—Day before the Show
1. Bath the dog.
2. Do all the final trimming.
Note. Plucking the hair on the head is often painful and cruel. It is far better to use fine-tooth thinning shears, keeping the blades flat to the skin, and working all the time under the long hair on the top. In fact, an excellent result can be achieved by using the thinning shears, going against the growth of the hair all over the dog. This is quicker and undoubtedly much kinder, as far as the dog is concerned. The majority of show people, however, still prefer to use the old-fashioned methods, but it is well worth experimenting with modern techniques.

Many breeders would be surprised to find that, even if a spaniel were clipped with electric clippers a month or so before a show on the area where the coat is required to be shortest, using an Oster A5 with a no. 10 blade, it would probably be extremely difficult to tell how the dog's coat had been trimmed originally, provided that the coat were kept thinned out just sufficiently to remove the under hair, so allowing the top hair to grow in the required direction. Even the top body coat could be clipped, provided that sufficient time were allowed for it to grow in again; but here again care is required to prevent the coat from growing upwards. This can still be prevented by the use of thinning shears. Such a method is well worth a try, particularly on pet spaniels.

CLUMBER, SPANIEL

This is a square, heavy and very massive spaniel. The standard requires that the coat should be abundant, close, silky and straight. The legs should be well feathered. Show preparations are similar to those described under Spaniels.

COCKER SPANIEL

This is the little spaniel often referred to as the merry Cocker Spaniel. The standard requires that the coat should be flat and silky in texture. There should be no wave or curl and the feathering should not be too profuse. Show preparations are as described under Spaniel.

ENGLISH SPRINGER SPANIEL

This is the oldest of the British sporting gun dogs. The standard requires that the coat should be close, straight, and weather-resisting. There could be good feathering on the legs and tail. Show preparation is similar to that given under Spaniel.

FIELD SPANIEL

This is a spaniel built for activity and endurance. The standard requires that the coat should be flat or slightly wavy but never curled. It should be dense enough to resist the weather but it must not be too short. The texture should be silky and there should be abundant feathering. Show preparations are similar to those given under Spaniel.

SUSSEX SPANIEL

This is rather a massive and muscular spaniel. The standard requires that the body coat should be abundant and flat, and that it should have no tendency to curl. The feathering should be moderate on the legs and stern. Show preparations are similar to those described in the general section under Spaniel.

STAFFORDSHIRE BULL TERRIER

This is a remarkably tough dog. The coat is smooth and short and lies close to the skin. There are no grooming problems. Use a soft bristle brush and a chamois leather for polishing the coat. Finger massage and extra hand strapping keep the skin and coat in good condition. Normal attention is required for the ears, nails and pressure points. Rotenone oil is useful against scurf. Nails may be vaselined or polished before a show.

TIBETAN SPANIEL

This is yet another breed which comes from Tibet. It slightly resembles a Pekingese, but the coat is not nearly so profuse. The grooming is easy. The coat should be brushed daily with a medium-stiff bristle brush and the feathering should be combed carefully. Ears should be cleaned by dipping a cotton wool swab in alcohol and wiping it round the interior of the ears. They should then be dusted with a good ear powder. Eyes require wiping round and nails must be kept short. Hair should be cut out from between the pads. There is little or no real trimming required, just general tidying up.

TIBETAN TERRIER

This small dog from Tibet resembles an old English Sheepdog, only in miniature. The coat is double with a fine wool undercoat, and the top coat is fine and profuse but must not be woolly or silky. The coat may be either straight or wavy.

Grooming is easy but, as with all long-coated breeds, it must be cared for daily. There is no stripping or clipping to be done. The hair, however, should be removed from between the pads by scissoring, and the anal area may require a little trimming for the sake of hygiene. A long-bristle brush on a rubber base is excellent and a wide-tooth comb is necessary for cleaning the brush and is useful for teasing out knots. Mats and felting of the coat should be prevented and the beard will require constant washing to keep it clean. Bathing is required before a show. Grooming procedures are similar to those for the Old English Sheepdog or any of the other long-coated breeds. Ears require regular cleaning and powdering, nails must be kept short, and teeth should be scaled and cleaned when necessary.

WEIMARANER

This is a most attractive breed. The coat should be short, smooth and sleek. There are no grooming problems. Use a medium-bristle brush and polish with a hound glove. Good weekly finger massage and strong hand strapping is recommended. Teeth, nails and ears require the normal care. Pressure points should be well massaged. Nails may be vaselined or polished before a show.

WELSH TERRIER

This is a grand little dog, but he is another terrier which requires a great deal of work to present him in show condition. The coat is required to be abundant, close, hard and wiry in texture, and there should be a good undercoat. The Welsh Terrier is more cobby and compact than the Fox Terrier, but he is similar to the Airedale Terrier only smaller. The coat is dealt with in exactly the same manner as that for the Wire-Haired Fox Terrier. The head, however, is trimmed in a slightly different manner. There is also no chalking.

The Welsh Terrier Head

The standard requires that the Welsh Terrier head should be more masculine than that of the Fox Terrier. In other words, it is a wider, heavier head all round, which also includes a heavier jaw.

Trimming the head is a matter of personal preference, the object

K *

71. This pet West Highland White Terrier is enjoying being massaged with the soap.

72. This dog takes his bathing philosophically.

73. He is having his nails trimmed. Dogs do not usually object to this if it is done regularly.

74. Pet dogs are clipped, because stripping and plucking require too much time.

Photo: Anne Cumbers

75. A powerful dryer quickly dries
his coat while it is being brushed.

Photo: Anne Cumbers

76. This pet dog has been trimmed and
clipped and is raring to show himself off
at home.

Photo: Anne Cumbers

being to strengthen the head. The hair above the eyebrows is combed forward into the foreface hair and beard; the eyebrows are trimmed in a triangle like that of the Fox Terrier, but slightly shorter; and more furnishing is left under the eyes, to give a slightly square padded appearance, which gives the effect of the jaw being more powerful than long. The hair is graduated in length on the muzzle, culminating in a squared off beard. The beard starts from the corner of the mouth. In some countries the skull is clipped as also are the ears, but this tends to remove the necessary colour, unless the under-coat is removed with fine thinning shears as it comes through.

WEST HIGHLAND WHITE

The West Highland White is a grand little terrier which requires little work to be done on his coat. The coat is pure white and the outer coat is straight and should be about two inches in length. The undercoat is soft and resembles fur. The whole coat should be dense. Stripping should be done twice a year when the coat has 'blown'. The hair under the neck and on the throat is thinned. The body coat is tidied up and the tail should be tapered. The legs also require a general tidying up. Pet dogs are frequently clipped and they can look extremely smart when prepared in this manner, as will be seen in the photographs.

WHIPPET

This is a smaller edition of the Greyhound. The coat is short, fine in texture and requires to be as close as possible. Grooming is simple with a short-bristle brush, and a finish with a hound glove or silk. A good finger massage weekly will keep the skin supple. Whippets should be bathed the day before a show if there is much white on the body. Nails should be vaselined or polished.

YORKSHIRE TERRIER

This is one of the smallest of the toy breeds and in spite of his long silky coat, he is a sporting little dog. The coat needs a great deal of constant attention for show purposes, it requires to be groomed daily, kept well oiled in almond oil and, to prevent the ends from breaking, the hair is kept in paper strips.

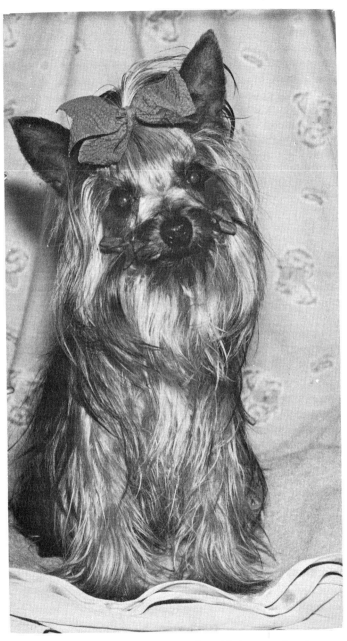

77. An appealing Yorkshire Terrier with bows on her topknot and even on her moustaches. This is a sporting little
dog and, for the pet owner who does not have time for the
full grooming procedures, the dog can look most attractive
with a one-inch trim all over.

Photo: Anne Cumbers

Tools and Equipment required

Brush with medium-length bristles and with a handle
Comb with medium-smooth-ended teeth and with a handle
Elastic bands or ribbon
Paper hair strip, or plastic strips
Otodex or Ear-Rite
Almond or mink oil

Boracic powder for eye stain or eye stain remover
Ear powder
Artery forceps
Blunt-ended surgical scissors
46-toothed thinning shears
Cotton for plaiting
Nail clippers

SUGGESTED METHOD OF GROOMING

1. With the dog standing, make a parting from the nose to the tail, stretching the skin slightly as the parting is made, so that it is absolutely straight.
2. *Eyes.* Comb out the hair beneath the eyes and place on boracic powder or stain remover, beneath the corner of the eyes.
3. *Ears.* Remove a few hairs from the ear canal with artery forceps having first powdered the ear canal with Ryotin or a similar ear powder. Clean the ears out with twists of cotton wool. If there is excess wax use Otodex drops.
   The ear leathers require to be plucked both inside and outside. This should preferably be done only when the dog is moulting, because then the hair comes away very easily, or the hair can be thinned out using the 46-toothed thinning shears. This is far less cruel and the hair can be taken down beautifully by this method.
4. *Chest.* With the dog lying on his back in your lap, or on a table, and with his hind legs towards you, start by brushing the hair, layer by layer, picking up a small portion in one hand, and brushing it down with a slight twist upwards, working slowly up the chest until the chin is reached.
5. Reverse the procedure, starting at the chin and working downwards, taking care to brush out the coat under the forelegs.
6. *Side of Dog.* With the dog lying with his back towards you, start working from the bottom upwards, holding the hair in one hand and brushing it downwards with a flick of the wrist upwards. Start with the foreleg, working up to the

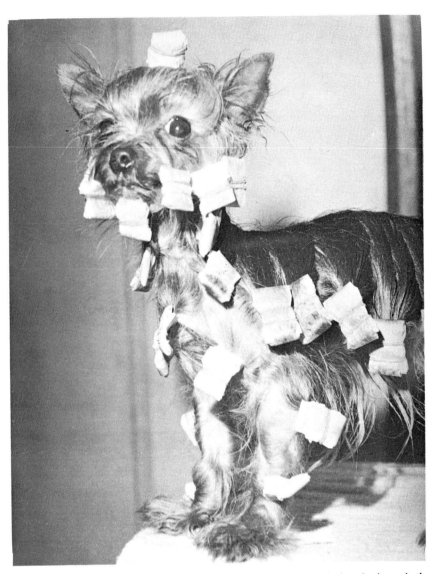

78. Preparing a Yorkshire Terrier for show. The ears are plucked and trimmed, the coat is parted down the centre of the back, the long hair is kept oiled with almond oil and it is carefully parted into equal strips, which are then folded into three and are secured with elastic bands.

Photo: Anne Cumbers

neck, and brush right down to the skin, progressing layer by layer.

7. *Ribs.* Take another strip of hair at the bottom and gradually brush up to the parting layer by layer, teasing out any knots as you work.

8. *Hind Leg to Back.* Holding the hair between the hock and the foot, brush out layer by layer, working up the leg and body once again until the parting is reached.

9. *Tail.* Brush the tail neatly.

10. Turn the dog on the other side and reverse the procedure, always starting to brush the coat out from the bottom, working slowly and gently all the way up the coat until the parting is reached.

11. *Muzzle.* Straighten the parting from the muzzle to the nose and, making a parting forming a V, brush or comb the moustaches downwards and forwards. Make another parting from the outside corner of the eye to the inside corner and the top of the ear, and another parting from the top of the ears right across the head.

12. *Topknot.* Comb the topknot upwards and secure with an elastic band or a small bow on the top of the head.

13. *Feet.* Check whether the hair requires trimming between the pads, and whether the nails require their monthly cutting.

14. Stand the dog on a level surface, and brush or comb the coat downwards, starting from the bottom and working upwards, and spray the coat if necessary with water or with a coat dressing.

15. *Show Dogs.* Show dogs require to be very carefully groomed, so that almost not a hair is lost in the process. To prevent the ends from breaking, the coat should be parted in strips from the centre parting downwards, each strip being two or three inches in width. The coat may be put into light oil such as mink oil or almond oil, which are excellent if the dog has been bathed frequently for exhbiition. Tissue paper or toilet paper or fine polythene should then be cut into oblong strips about four inches by three inches. The hair strip is placed length-wise in the centre and the curling paper is folded into three, one side covering the hair strip, and the other the paper strip. This is then folded from the bottom upwards, again into three, the bottom going a third of the way up and the fold at the bottom being folded forward

to the top, so that the strip of hair is also divided into three. The whole strip is secured firmly at the top with a small elastic band. The hair on the front of the chest can be divided into two strips and can then also be put into paper strips. A paper strip may be used too for the topknot, and one on each side for the moustaches, which helps to keep them unstained after eating. See diagrams on page 26.

The curlers should be removed on alternate days. If they are left longer, the silky-coated hair quickly felts.

Oiling the Coat. To promote the growth of the hair and to prevent the ends from splitting, the dog can be put down in oil. The majority of breeders use almond oil. The coat is moistened and combed through with oil, or the coat may be sprayed sparingly all over with fine oil whilst grooming. St Aubrey make a really excellent preparation called St Aubrey Royal Coatalin a revolutionary dog grooming preparation which is easy to apply either with a brush or with the fingers. Oiling prevents the coat from tangling to a certain extent, but for show purposes the long coat should be done up in paper or polythene strips.

Conclusion

Regarding breeds which are long-coated or which require any form of stripping, thinning or clipping, the object in the past has been to improve or to show up the lines and conformation of individual breeds to their best advantage. Show standards never give exact indications as to what may or may not be trimmed, so that fashions are created by strong members of club committees and are then handed down by word of mouth until they eventually become unwritten laws. New members of a breed club, particularly the younger members, may join with experience from some other breed and these naturally bring with them their fashions and interpretations.

Dogs these days are bred as much for show purposes as for pets, and it will be noticed over the years, and particularly since World War II, that many of the long-coated breeds have far longer and more profuse coats than previously. It is particularly interesting to look at old photographs of breeds like the Poodle, the Afghan, the Scottish Terrier, the Spaniels, the Sealyham and the Pomeranian. The dogs of these long-coated breeds before 1880 were not nearly so well coated as they are today.

Coats have to be bred for, fed for and cared for, but when exhibiting a long coated breed, coat seems to take priority with most judges. The old diehards, who prefer the more sporting shorter coats, particularly in breeds like the Sealyham, the Scottish Terrier and the American Cocker Spaniel, do not favour the modern tendency for coat growth to cover the legs and movement. It must be remembered, nevertheless, that a breed like the ubiquitous poodle was once a sporting dog too. Whatever breeders do to their dog's coats, it would take centuries to breed out the inherent instincts of the true sporting breeds: Scottish terriers, for instance, will long have their aggresive sporting tendencies, as will American Cocker Spaniels their good nose. But coats are here, and coats have come to stay, certainly for the show specimens. The question is, which are the best methods of looking after the various coats in the individual breeds and, when the dogs are kept as pets, whether the same techniques should be used or whether the dog would be happier with his coat barbered and trimmed.

Long-coated breeds which are groomed daily are easily maintained in good condition; but, when coats are neglected, and the dogs are then expected to undergo hours of painful grooming, involving the combing out of knots and tangles, which must be most unpleasant and in some cases even cruel for the dog, it would be better for him to be severely barbered in an exotic style which makes life happier for the dog and easier for his owner. Exceptions would be for breeds which are either groomed regularly or taken to dog parlours.

Methods have changed over the years to more modern techniques of grooming and dealing with coat problems. In this mechanized age mechanization has come to dogs too. The most important advancement is in the excellent electric clippers which are now on the market. They are simple to use and the coat can be clipped from one inch downwards. As with all modern gadgets, there are many breeders who abhor such modern aids and prefer to use the old methods of plucking and stripping by hand. Provided that stripping and plucking are done when the coat is 'blown', there is no doubt that the coat comes out easily; but even so, if the dog's skin is examined afterwards, it will be seen that it is often pink from irritation, and, if the coat is plucked at the wrong time, the skin becomes red and must be extremely sore for a short time.

Many people believe that if clippers are used over a coat, particularly on a breed with an undercoat, then the coat will never grow correctly again but will always tend to stand up instead of perhaps lying flat as it should. In actual fact, this is an 'old wives' tale', and the coat standing up as it grows can easily be prevented by the correct use of fine-toothed thinning shears. These must be sharp and they should have 46 teeth. The reason why the coat will grow standing up is because, after clipping, the two coats are the same length, and the top coat is pushed upwards by the soft undercoat. If clippers are used, then the soft undercoat must be removed with thinning shears as it comes through. The shears must be held flat against the skin. Provided that this undercoat is removed, the top coat will always grow and lie in the direction that is required.

I have experimented with this on a number of breeds, and I cannot help feeling that clippers and thinning shears are not only kinder to the dog, but also that this method is much quicker, time being precious to so many people in these days.

Glossary of Grooming Terms

Artery Forceps–Used for holding cotton wool for cleaning the ears.

Beard–Long hair under the chin.

Belt–The clipped line round the body of a Poodle.

Bib–Protection for the ruff, used when grooming an Old English Sheep Dog.

Blades–The cutting part or head of clippers, which come in various sizes.

Bloom–Fine condition of a coat.

Blown–A dead coat ready for stripping.

Bracelet–The long hair left on the legs of a Poodle.

Breechings–Long hair on the thighs.

Brushes–Tools for imparting a sheen to the coat.

Carding–Removing the excess undercoat with a comb or rake, leaving the hair in the comb to accumulate whilst working.

Chalk Block–Chalk in solid form for whitening a dog for a show.

Chalking–Applying chalk in powder form or by block to whiten the coat.

Clippers–Clipping instrument.

Clipping–Cutting the hair short with clippers.

Comb–Tool for passing through the coat.

Curry Comb–Strong implement for cleaning.

Curved Scissors–Scissors for cutting hair between the pads.

Dolling-up Pad–Pin brush on rubber cushion used on Terriers.

Dewplex Dresser–Stripping tool used on Terriers and certain other dogs.

Elastic Band–Narrow rubber band used for keeping the topknot out of the eyes of breeds like Yorkshire Terriers and Maltese.

Feathering–Long hair on the rear part of the legs, tail, ears and hind quarters.

Frill–Long hair on the chest.

File–Tool for shortening the nails.

Furnishings–Thick coat on the legs.

Garter–Clipped area on the legs of a Poodle between two bracelets.

Grooming Mirror–Large mirror to enable the far side of dog to be observed.

Grooming Table–Table on which to stand dogs for grooming.

Guillotine Clippers–Tool for cutting the nails.

Hair Wrappers–Polythene or paper strips used for protecting long hair.

Hound Glove–Bristles fitted to the palm of a fingerless glove.

Jacket–Tight body jacket of Terrier in full bloom; also the scissored front area of the Poodle Dutch Clip.

Mane–The long coat round the shoulders of a Poodle.

Nit Comb–Fine comb for removing nits; also used for removing undercoat.

Pack–The scissored area on the hind quarters of a Poodle in the Lion Trim.

Pantaloons–Trousers of the Poodle Dutch Clip.

Plucking–Removal of dead hair by the finger and thumb method.

Pocket Stripping Knife–Tool for stripping.

Pompon–Rounded tuft of hair left on the tail of a Poodle.

Put Down in Oil–Yorkshire Terrier coat oiled.

Raking–Combing out the undercoat.

Razor Comb–Tool for shortening hair.

Razor Stripper–Tool for stripping the coat.

Ridging–Method of cutting the coat by partings and drawing the comb upwards through the coat and cutting off the ends.

Ridges–Ugly uneven lines on the coat after scissoring or clipping.

Rolling–Rolling out the dead hair between the thumb and forefinger, so that it breaks off.

Ruff–Thick longer growth of hair around the neck.

Sacking–A towel for wrapping over the coat to dry it flat.

Scalers–Implements for removing tartar from the teeth.

Scissoring–Cutting hair with scissors.

Shears–Scissors with teeth.

Slicker Brush–Fine wire brush with hooked ends.

Spray–Liquid sprayed on to the coat.

Stripping–Removal of dead coat by hand or with a stripping knife.

Stripping Knife–Tool for removing dead coat.

Tassels–Triangular long hair left on the end of the ear leather in breeds like the Bedlington Terrier.

Thinning–Cutting away the undercoat with thinning shears.

Tipping–Cutting the ends of the coat, usually of the ruff and mane.

Topknot–Long hair on the skull.

Trimming–Scissoring the hair.

Trim–Various methods of shortening the coat, as, for example, the Lion Trim in a Poodle.

Trimming Knife–Tool for stripping the coat.

Trousers–Long leg hair; long coat on legs.
Trunk Dryer–Electric hair dryer with a long nozzle.
Underline–Belly coat.
Whiskers–Long hairs on the chin and muzzle.
Xtra Hand Control Stand–Grooming aid.

SELECT BIBLIOGRAPHY

GLYNN, SIR RICHARD, *Champion Dogs of the World*, George G. Harrap and Co. Ltd., 1967.

LAMPSON, SONIA, *The Observer's Book of Dogs*, Frederick Warne and Co. Ltd., 1967.

LAPAGE, GEOFFREY, *Veterinary Parasitology*, Oliber and Boyd, 1968.

LEHANE, BRENDAN, *The Complete Flea*, John Murray, 1969.

SHELDON, MARGARET, and LOCKWOOD, BARBARA, *Dogs and How to Groom Them*, Pelham Books, 1968.

STONE, BEN, and MIGLIORINI, MARIO, *Clipping and Grooming your Terrier*, Arco Publishing Company Inc., New York, 1968

STONE, PEARL, *Clipping and Grooming your Poodle*, Arco Publishing Company, Inc., New York, 1967.

WOODHOUSE, BARBARA, *The Book of Show Dogs*, Max Parrish, London, 1959.

APPENDIX

CLIPPER BLADE APPROXIMATE EQUIVALENT SIZES

(Kindly provided by Simpson's of Langley, Limited)

Oster	Aesculap	Select	Hand Clippers
No. 40	$\frac{1}{20}$ mm.	$\frac{1}{20}$ mm.	0000 (approx. $\frac{1}{20}$ mm.)
—	$\frac{1}{10}$ mm.	—	—
No. 30	$\frac{1}{4}$ mm.	—	000 (approx. $\frac{1}{4}$ mm.)
No. 15	$\frac{1}{2}$ mm.	$\frac{1}{2}$ mm.	—
—	1 mm.	—	00 (approx. 1 mm.)
No. 10	2 mm.	2 mm.	0 (approx. 2 mm.)
—	3 mm.	—	—
No. 7	—	—	No. 1 (3–4 mm.)
No. 5	5 mm.	No. 5	No. 2 (4–5 mm.)
No. 4	7 mm.	—	—

NOTE—Many druggists no longer sell boracic acid in powder form. In this case, it should be bought as crystals and powdered in a domestic electric grinder.

Index